Patternmaking for Jacket and Coat Design

BLOOMSBURY VISUAL ARTS
Bloomsbury Publishing Plc
50 Bedford Square, London, WC1B 3DP, UK
1385 Broadway, New York, NY 10018, USA
29 Earlsfort Terrace, Dublin 2, Ireland

BLOOMSBURY, BLOOMSBURY VISUAL ARTS and the Diana logo
are trademarks of Bloomsbury Publishing Plc

First published in Great Britain 2017
Reprinted 2019, 2021, 2022, 2023, 2024

Copyright © Bloomsbury Publishing Plc, 2017

Pamela Vanderlinde has asserted her right under the Copyright,
Designs and Patents Act, 1988, to be identified as Author of this work.

For legal purposes the Acknowledgements on p. 216 constitute
an extension of this copyright page.

Cover design: Louise Dugdale
Cover image © Scott Shigley

All rights reserved. No part of this publication may be reproduced or
transmitted in any form or by any means, electronic or mechanical,
including photocopying, recording, or any information storage or
retrieval system, without prior permission in writing from the publishers.

Bloomsbury Publishing Plc does not have any control over, or
responsibility for, any third-party websites referred to or in this book.
All internet addresses given in this book were correct at the time of
going to press. The author and publisher regret any inconvenience
caused if addresses have changed or sites have ceased to exist,
but can accept no responsibility for any such changes.

A catalogue record for this book is available from the British Library.

Library of Congress Cataloging-in-Publication Data
Names: Vanderlinde, Pamela, author.
Title: Patternmaking for jacket and coat design / Pamela Vanderlinde.
Description: London ; New York : Bloomsbury Visual Arts, 2017. |
Includes bibliographical references and index.
Identifiers: LCCN 2016009469 | ISBN 9781474235082 (pbk. : alk.
paper) | ISBN 9781474235099 (epdf : alk. paper)
Subjects: LCSH: Jackets--Pattern design. | Coats--Pattern design. |
Fashion design.
Classification: LCC TT535 .V36 2016 | DDC 646.4/5--dc23
LC record available at https://lccn.loc.gov/2016009469

ISBN: PB: 978-1-4742-3508-2
        ePDF: 978-1-4742-3509-9
        eBook: 978-1-4742-3572-3

Series: Required Reading Range

Typeset by Roger Fawcett-Tang
Printed and bound in Great Britain

To find out more about our authors and books visit
www.bloomsbury.com and sign up for our newsletters.

Patternmaking for Jacket and Coat Design

Pamela Vanderlinde

BLOOMSBURY VISUAL ARTS
LONDON · NEW YORK · OXFORD · NEW DELHI · SYDNEY

CONTENTS

PREFACE
6

INTRODUCTION
BLOCK DEVELOPMENT
8

10 Patternmaking fundamentals
12 Blocks manipulated
23 Seam allowances

CHAPTER ONE
THE BLAZER
24

26 The history of the blazer
28 Contemporary blazers
30 The pattern
36 Muslin or toile fitting
40 Production pattern
46 Technical flats and finished pattern pieces

CHAPTER TWO
THE TUXEDO
48

50 The history of the tuxedo
52 Contemporary tuxedos
54 The pattern
60 Muslin or toile fitting
64 Production pattern
68 Technical flats and finished pattern pieces

CHAPTER THREE
THE MILITARY JACKET
70

72 The history of the military jacket
74 Contemporary military jackets
76 The pattern
86 Muslin or toile fitting
90 Production pattern
94 Technical flats and finished pattern pieces

CHAPTER FOUR
THE MOTORCYCLE JACKET
96

- 98 The history of the motorcycle jacket
- 100 Contemporary motorcycle jackets
- 102 The pattern
- 110 Muslin or toile fitting
- 114 Production pattern
- 120 Technical flats and finished pattern pieces

CHAPTER FIVE
THE MAO JACKET
122

- 124 The history of the Mao
- 126 Contemporary Mao jackets
- 128 The pattern
- 136 Muslin or toile fitting
- 140 Production pattern
- 146 Technical flats and finished pattern pieces

CHAPTER SIX
THE BALMACAAN COAT
148

- 150 The history of the Balmacaan coat
- 152 Contemporary Balmacaans
- 154 The pattern
- 164 Muslin or toile fitting
- 170 Production pattern
- 176 Technical flats and finished pattern pieces

CHAPTER SEVEN
THE FROCK COAT
178

- 180 The history of the frock coat
- 182 Contemporary frocks
- 184 The pattern
- 196 Muslin or toile fitting
- 202 Production pattern
- 208 Technical flats and finished pattern pieces

APPENDIX
210

- 210 Glossary
- 211 Bibliography and recommended reading
- 212 Picture credits
- 213 Index
- 216 Acknowledgments

INTRODUCTION

PREFACE

As a designer, I have often wondered why a specific coat or jacket has been popular season after season. What is it in its history that has continued to inspire designers to use it as a form of inspiration? Whether these pieces are used as a direct reference or just implied, they seem to set the theme for entire collections. This got me thinking: why isn't there a patternmaking book out there that covers the historical relevance of jackets along with the instructions for making them?

Patternmaking for Jacket and Coat Design offers a dynamic and exciting approach to the patternmaking techniques for seven classic jacket and coat designs. Each chapter is devoted to a historically significant design, starting with the most iconic jacket, the blazer. The content of each chapter encapsulates the history and relevance of each design and gives examples of how it is used as inspiration by designers today.

For each project, detailed step-by-step instructions with corresponding illustrations guide the drafting of the complete pattern. Photographs of each jacket or coat are included at both the muslin or toile and final fitting stage along with technical flats to show the design details. The jackets/coats depicted in this book are meant to be used as inspiration only and are not historical replicas. This allows the student/designer the ability to branch out creatively and use these projects as reference in future designs.

But most importantly, my goal in writing this book was to combine my love of jackets and their history into a patternmaking text that would be approachable, easy to understand, and yes, a bit sexy.

| PREFACE | INTRODUCTION: BLOCK DEVELOPMENT | PATTERNMAKING FUNDAMENTALS | BLOCKS MANIPULATED | SEAM ALLOWANCES |

0.1
Photoshoot for the book of muslin or toile fitting.

"It is only the modern that ever becomes old-fashioned."

Oscar Wilde

INTRODUCTION

INTRODUCTION:
BLOCK DEVELOPMENT

Patterning concepts learned:
- **jacket block**
- **mannish block**
- **coat block**
- **1-piece sleeve**
- **2-piece contoured sleeve**

"Fashion is only the attempt to realize art in living forms and social intercourse."

Sir Francis Bacon

0.2
Illustration showing jacket terminology.

INTRODUCTION

PATTERNMAKING FUNDAMENTALS

There are three types of patternmaking used in the fashion industry: pattern drafting, draping, and flat patterning. The flat pattern method relies on the manipulation of blocks (also called slopers) to develop the pattern for any given design. Every patternmaker will have their own set of blocks with which they create these designs. These blocks will correlate with the sample size for their intended target market within the industry.

In this introduction you will find directions to modify the basic bodice, torso, and sleeve blocks that are necessary to pattern the jackets and coats outlined in the book. I have not included a sizing chart or instructions for drafting the basic block set because those blocks must directly correspond to the dress form. Having a good set of blocks is critical in flat patternmaking; without them it would be impossible to fit the garment accurately at all stages of the design process.

If you do not have a set of basic blocks, you will need to draft them according to the measurements of the form you are using. There are many patternmaking books that will aid you in the development of these blocks and some are mentioned in the bibliography section of this book.

Once you have developed the blocks illustrated here, you will not only have the patterns necessary to develop the seven projects outlined in the book, but you will also have the patternmaking tools and concepts needed to design your own unique creations.

TIP

- Patternmaking terminology is covered in the Glossary section of the book.

- A sizing chart for drafting the basic block set has not been included because blocks must directly correspond to the dress form. The Bibliography section of the book lists patternmaking books that will aid in the development of blocks.

- Both imperial and metric measurements are included in the instructions, so there is no need for a conversion chart.

Torso (black), jacket (green), mannish (red), and coat (blue) blocks overlapped

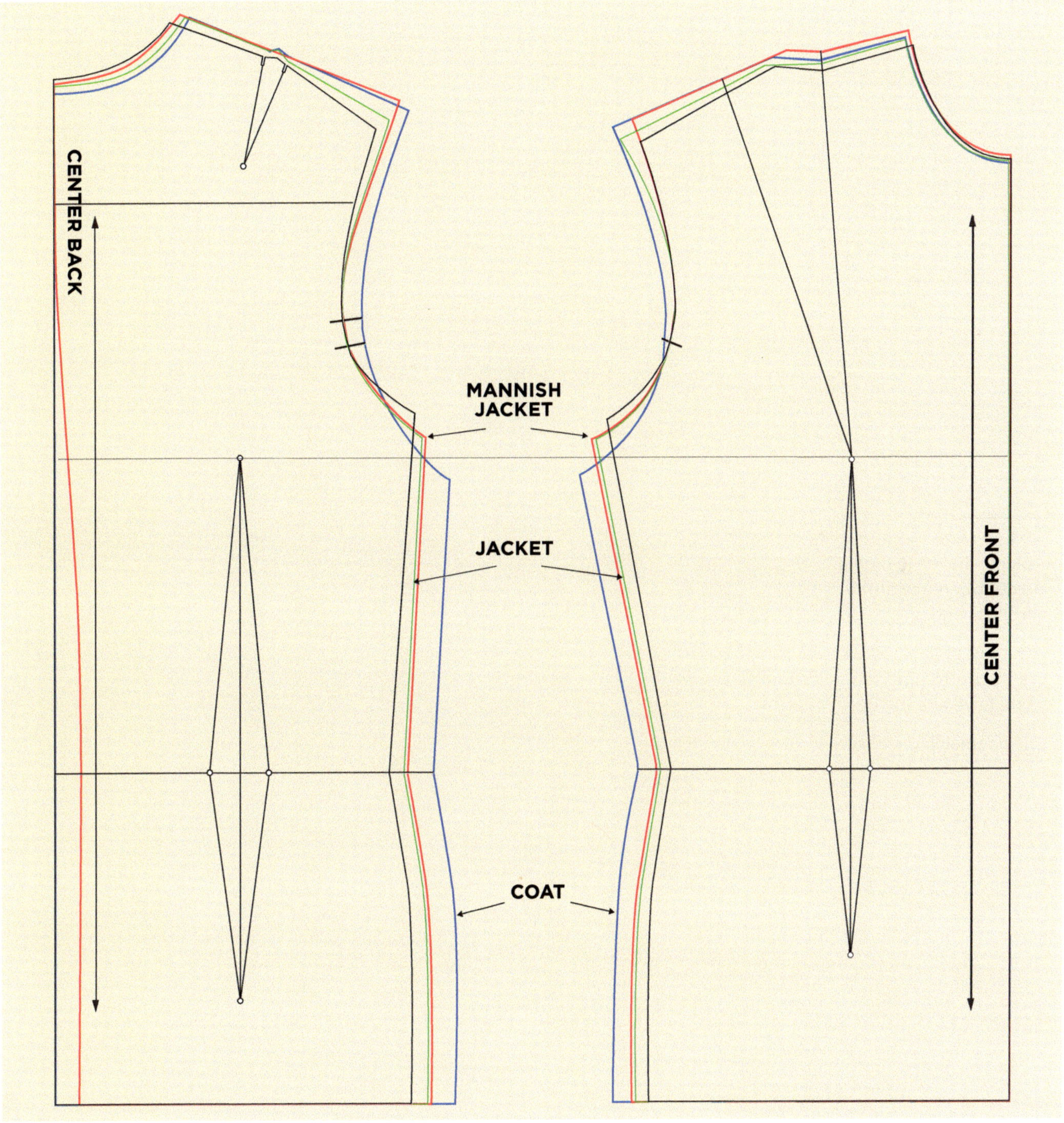

BLOCKS MANIPULATED

The basic set of blocks needs to be developed into the jacket, mannish, and coat block for the projects outlined in the book. With each block manipulated, you must also draft a new sleeve to correspond with the new armhole measurements. Always test-fit your blocks on the dress form to ensure you are happy with them before you start a new design.

Basic bodice, torso, and sleeve blocks

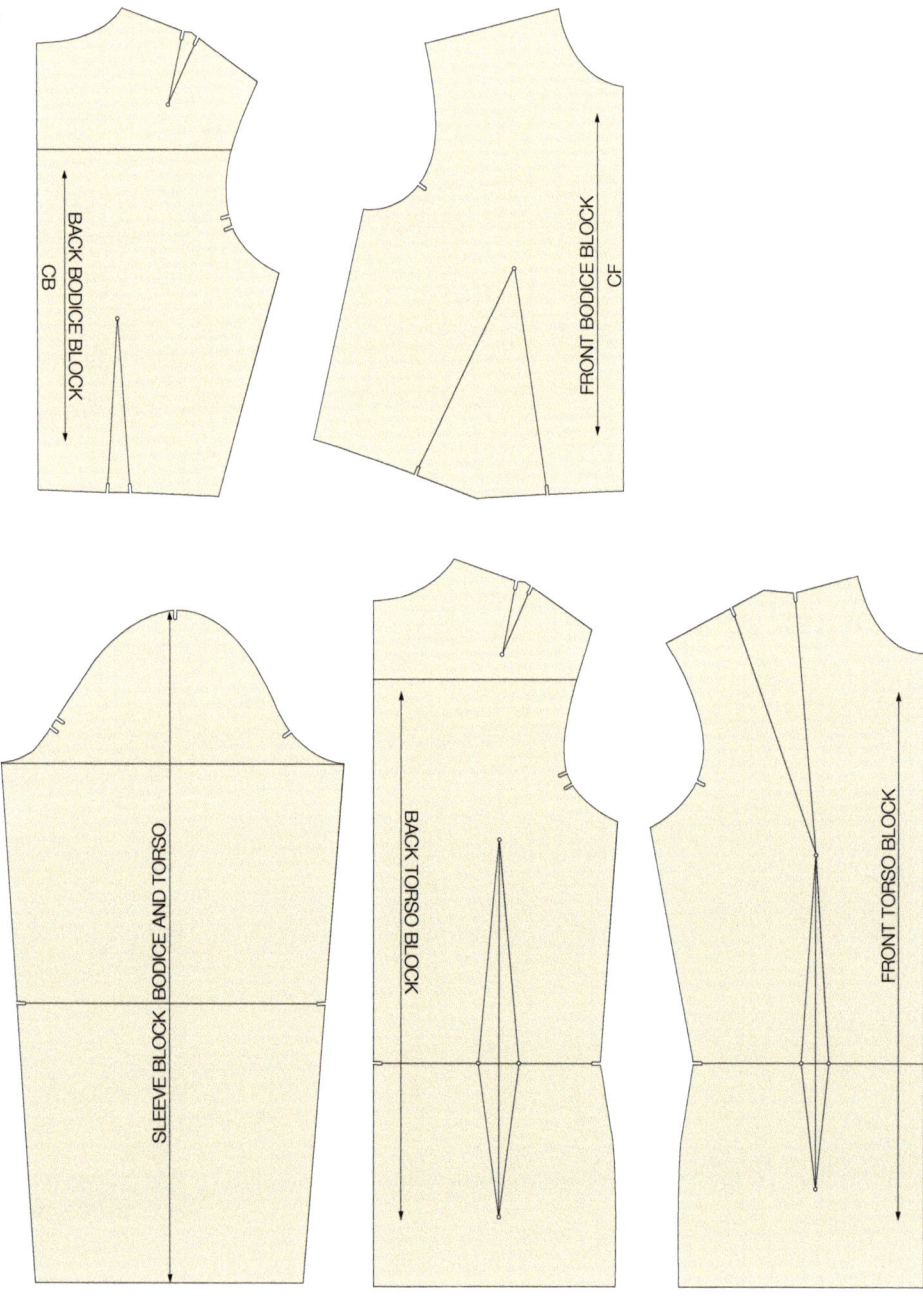

Jacket block

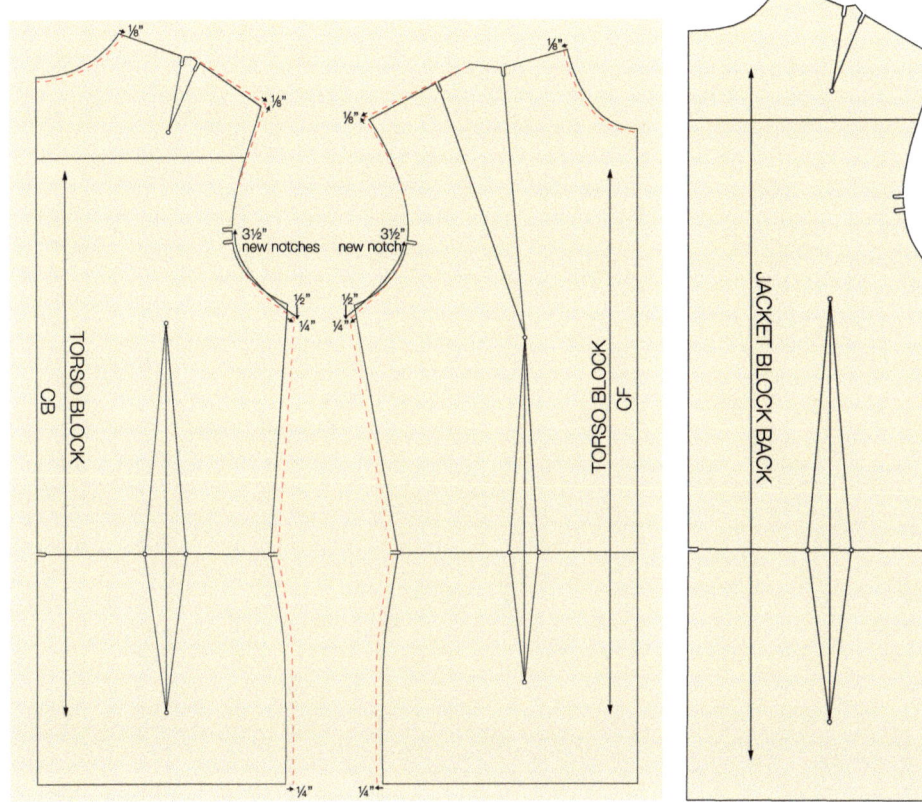
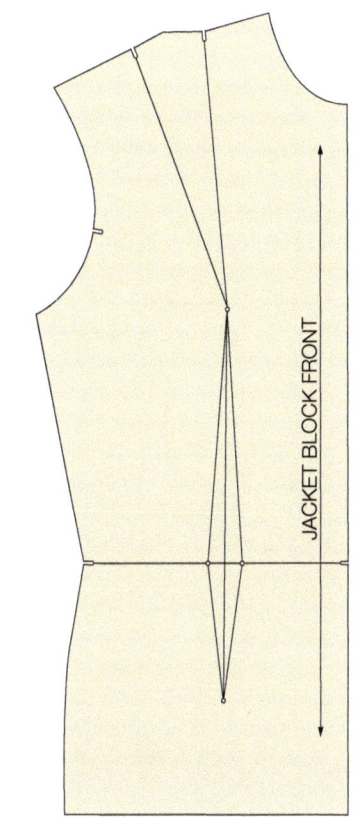

The basic torso block is developed into the jacket block, which is made larger so that it can be worn over a blouse or dress.

1. Trace the basic torso blocks.

2. Lower front and back necklines ⅛ inch (3mm).

3. Extend shoulder up and out ⅛ inch (3mm).

4. Drop armhole ½ inch (1.2cm).

5. Draw new side seams ¼ inch (6mm) out from original seam.

6. True up armhole curve with French curve making sure the back armhole measurement is ½ inch (1.2cm) larger than the front armhole measurement.

7. Measure and mark front and back notches 3 ½ inches (8.75cm) up from under-arm.

Mannish block

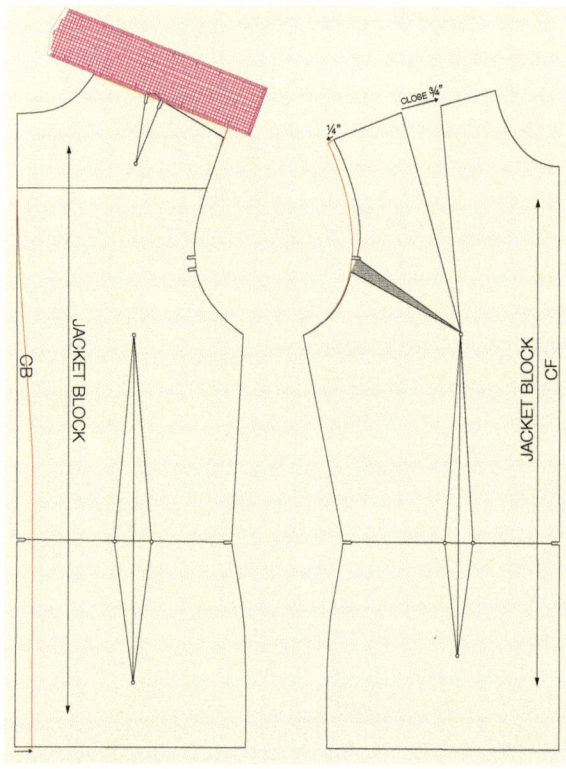

The jacket block is developed into the mannish block which gives a relaxed fit for a jacket while still retaining shape to the garment.

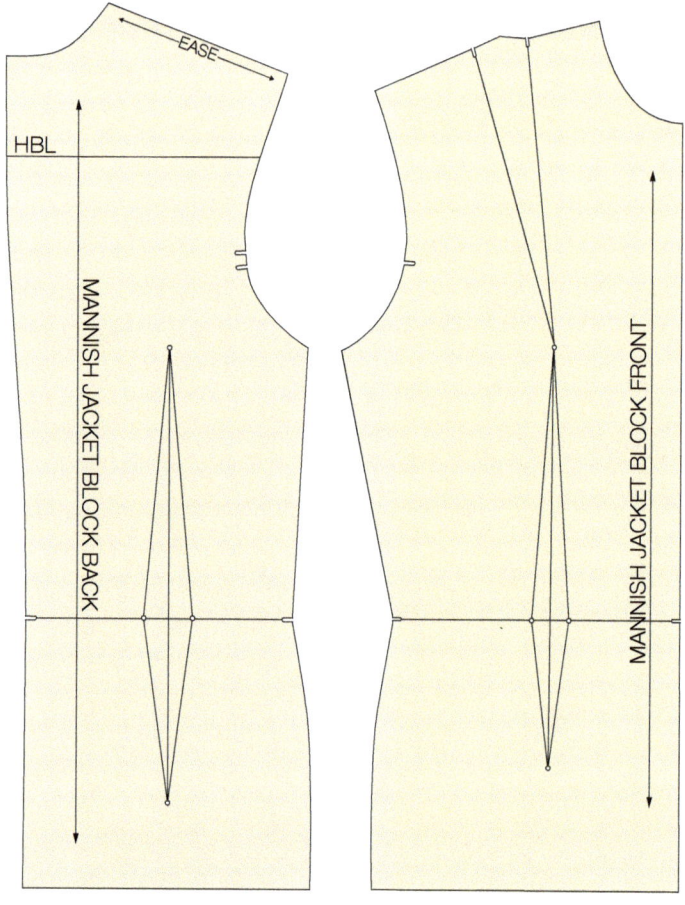

1. Trace the jacket block.
2. For the back block, you must first eliminate the shoulder dart.
3. Place ruler even with shoulder line at the neckline and draw a straight line.
4. Blend back armhole curve to new shoulder line.
5. Draw a parallel line ⅝ inch (1.5cm) in from the center back seam past the waistline and curve to HBL line.
6. For the front block transfer ¾ inch (1.75cm) to the armhole by using the slash and spread method.
7. Extend shoulder out ¼ inch (6mm).
8. True up front armhole curve with French curve making sure the back armhole measurement is ½ inch (1.2cm) larger than the front armhole measurement.

Coat block

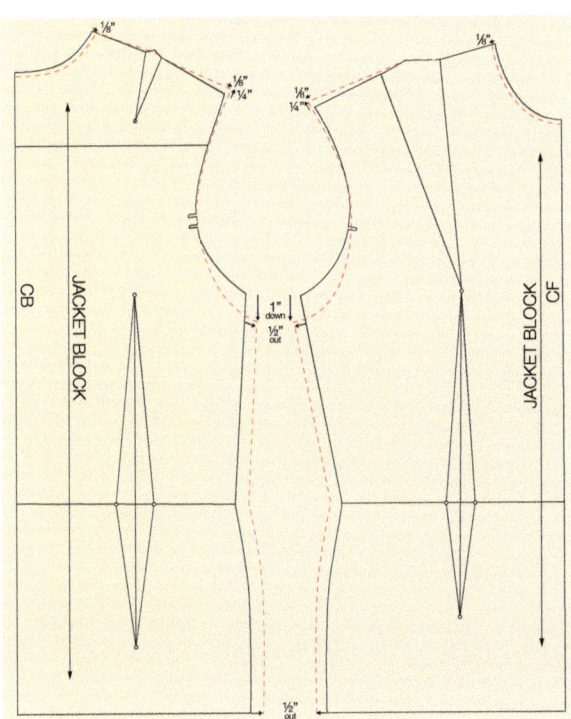

The jacket block is developed into the coat block, which allows the most ease of the blocks manipulated, and is intended for outerwear and oversized jackets.

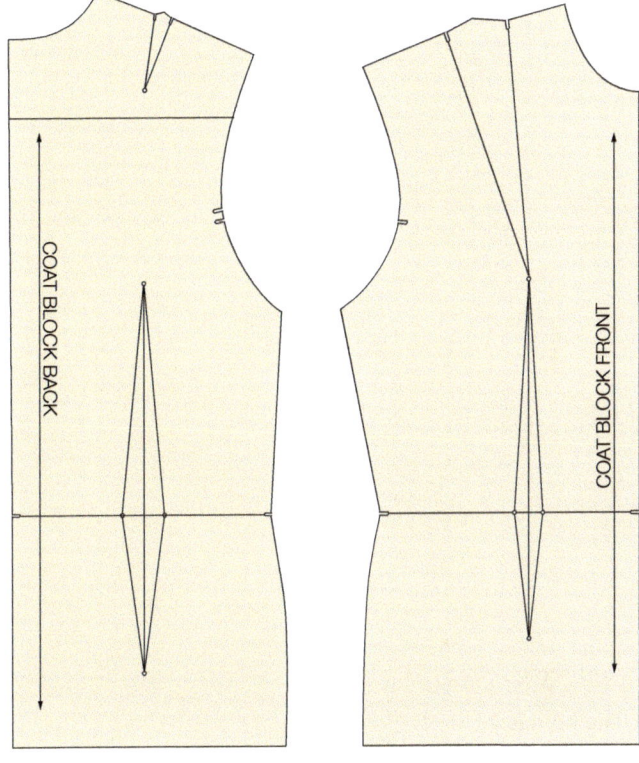

1. Trace the jacket block.
2. Lower front and back necklines ⅛ inch (3mm).
3. Extend shoulder up ¼ inch (6mm) and out ⅛ inch (3mm).
4. Drop armhole 1 inch (2.5cm).
5. Draw new side seams ½ inch (1.2cm) out from original seam.
6. True up armhole curve with French curve making sure the back armhole measurement is ½ inch (1.2cm) larger than the front armhole measurement.
7. Measure and mark front and back notches 4 inches (10cm) up from under-arm.

INTRODUCTION

1-piece sleeve

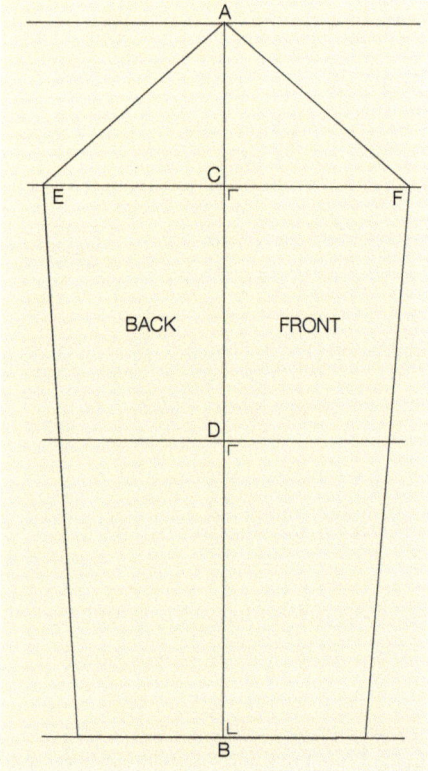

1. Measure the front armhole of the block you are using, record_____.

2. Measure the back armhole of the block you are using, record_____.

3. A to B = desired sleeve length to wrist.

4. A to C = cap height.

5. D = ½ of B to C plus ¾ inch (1.75cm).

6. A–E and A–F = front armhole (FAH) measurement plus back armhole (BAH) measurement divided by 2 + ⅛ inch (3mm).

7. Your design determines the wrist measurement—the average is 10 inches (25cm).

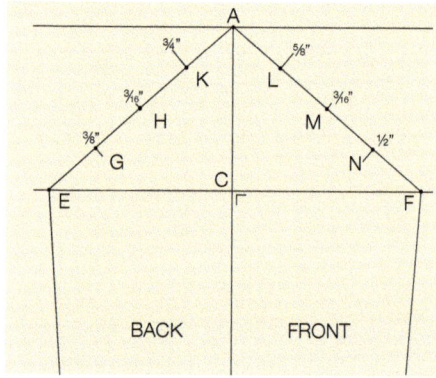

1. Fold paper into fourths from A to C and square lines as shown
   - G: in ⅜ inch (1cm)
   - H: out ³⁄₁₆ inch (4mm)
   - K: out ¾ inch (1.75cm)
   - L: out ⅝ inch (1.5cm)
   - M: out ³⁄₁₆ inch (4mm)
   - N: in ½ inch (1.2cm).

TIP The cap height for a standard set-in sleeve using a ½ inch (1.2cm) shoulder pad will equal ⅓ of your total armhole measurement.

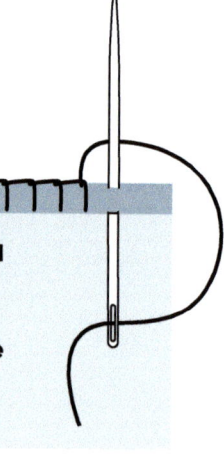

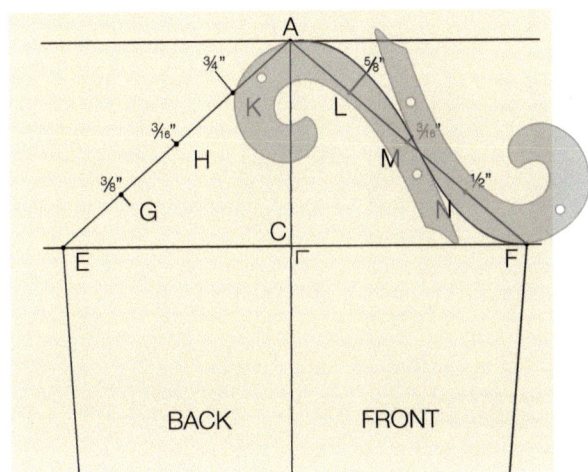 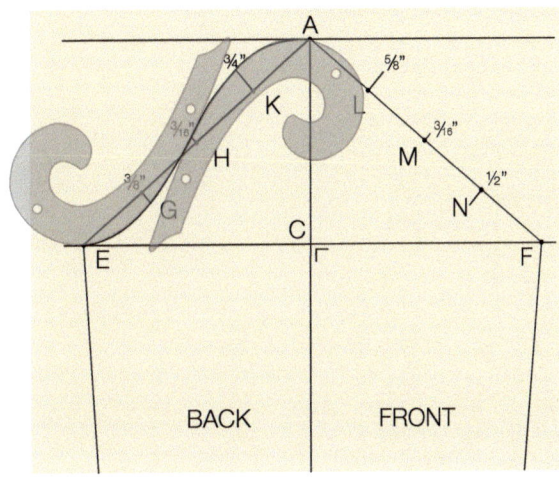

1. To draw the front sleeve cap place French curve touching points F, N, M and draw a line extending beyond M.

2. Flip the French curve and touch points A, L, M making sure both curves blend smoothly.

3. To draw the back sleeve cap place French curve touching points E, G, H and draw a line extending beyond H.

4. Flip the French curve and touch points A, K, H making sure both curves blend smoothly.

5. Measure the total armhole: ease should be at least 1 ¼ inches (3cm) but no more than 1 ½ inches (3.75cm) larger than the total armhole measurement of the block you are using.

6. Notch ¼ inch (6mm) away from center line toward the front for your shoulder notch.

7. Measure and mark front and back control notches so they correspond with the notches of the block you are using.

INTRODUCTION

2-piece contoured sleeve

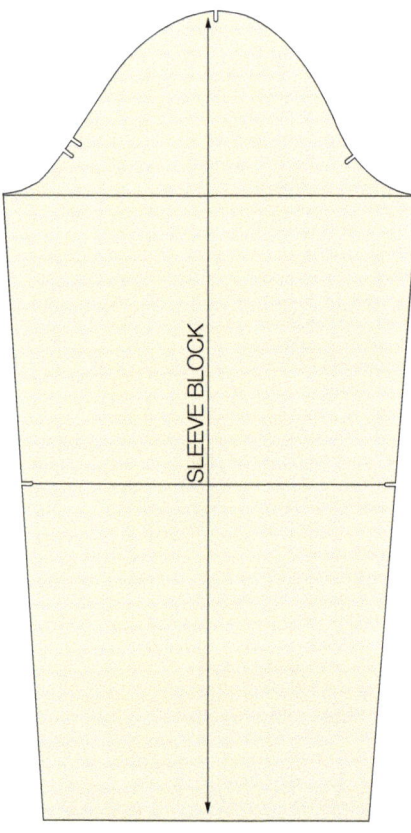

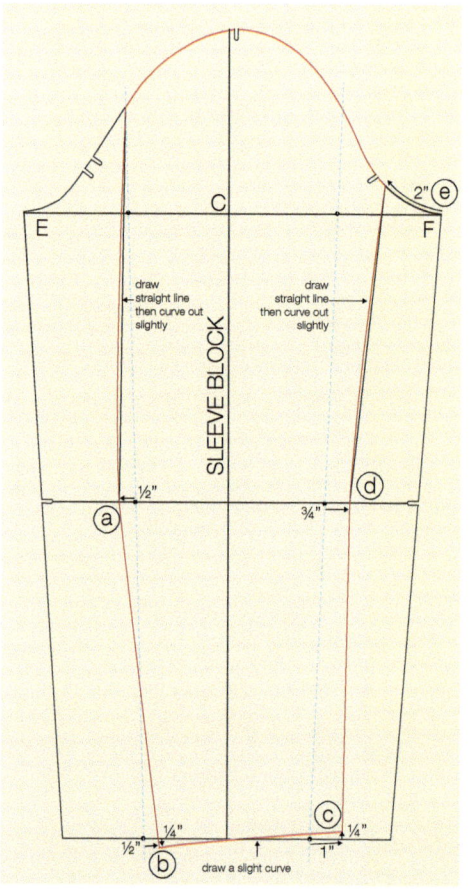

1. Draft the 1-piece sleeve according to armhole measurements of the pattern that you are using.
2. For the upper-sleeve, find and mark the midpoint of the bicep, elbow, and wrist and draw a line (dotted line).
3. Cross-mark:
   - Mark a ½ inch (1.2cm) out from midpoint
   - Mark b ½ inch (1.2cm) in and ¼ inch (6mm) down from midpoint
   - c = ½ of the wrist measurement plus 1 inch (2.5cm) and ¼ inch (6mm) up from midpoint
   - Mark d ¾ inch (1.75cm) out from midpoint
   - Mark e 2 inches (5cm) up from F.
4. Draw lines connecting the cross-marks as shown.
5. The upper-sleeve is outlined in red.

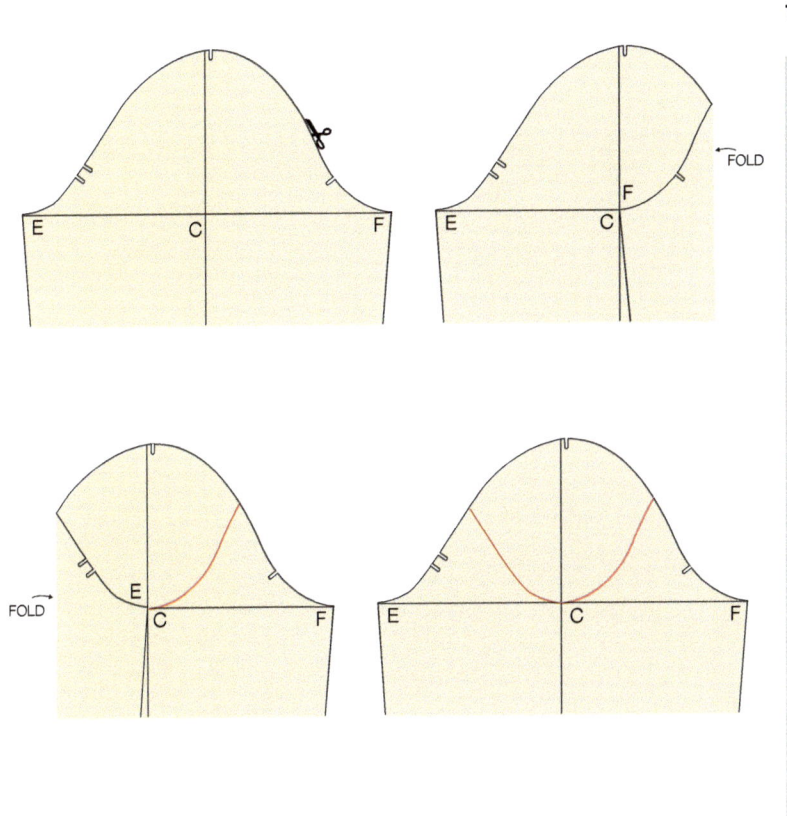

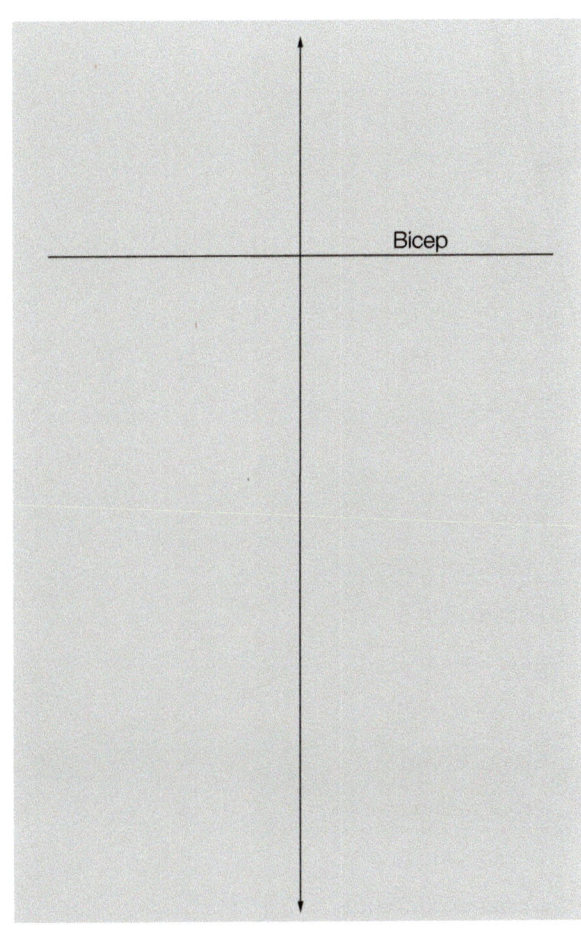

1. Cut out the sleeve cap.
2. Fold F to C and trace the front armhole (red curve).
3. Fold E to C and trace the back armhole (red curve).
4. Fold a piece of tracing paper in half lengthwise and draw a grainline on the fold.
5. Cross-mark for the bicep line.

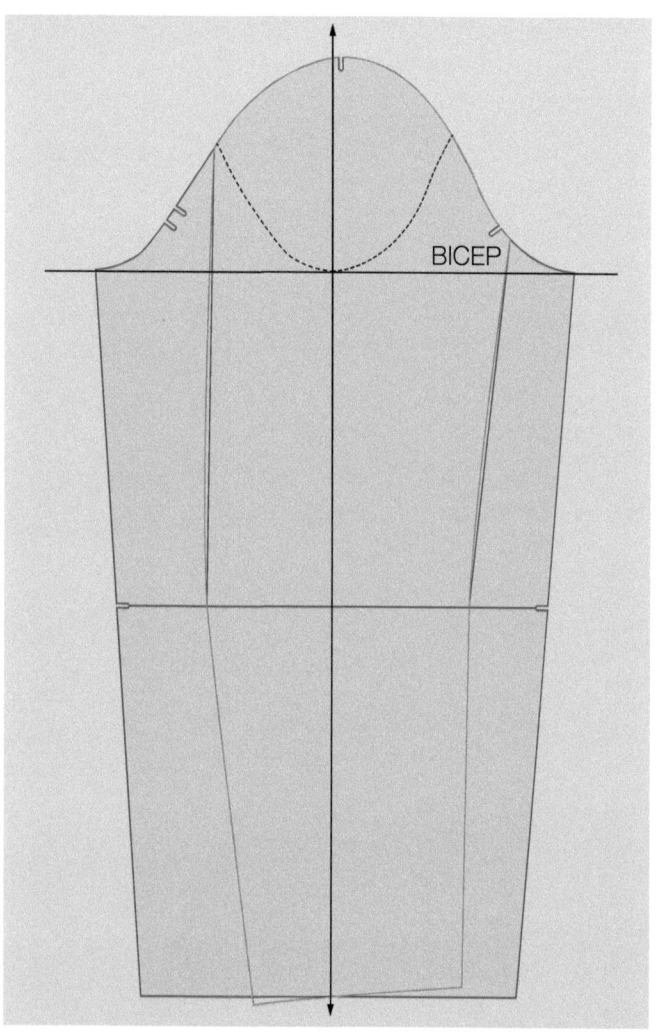 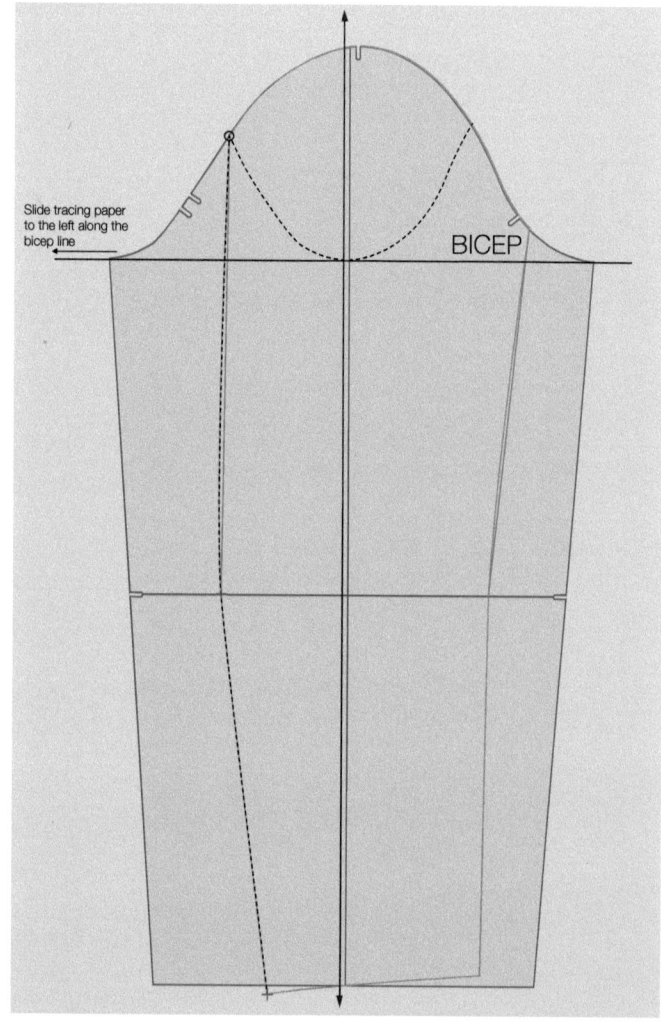

6. Place the tracing paper over your sleeve pattern, lining up the bicep and grainlines.

7. Trace the front and the back armhole curves onto the tracing paper (dotted lines).

8. Slide the tracing paper to the left until the traced armhole curve touches the back curve of the upper-sleeve.

9. Copy back curve to the wrist and cross-mark (red) at the elbow and the wrist.

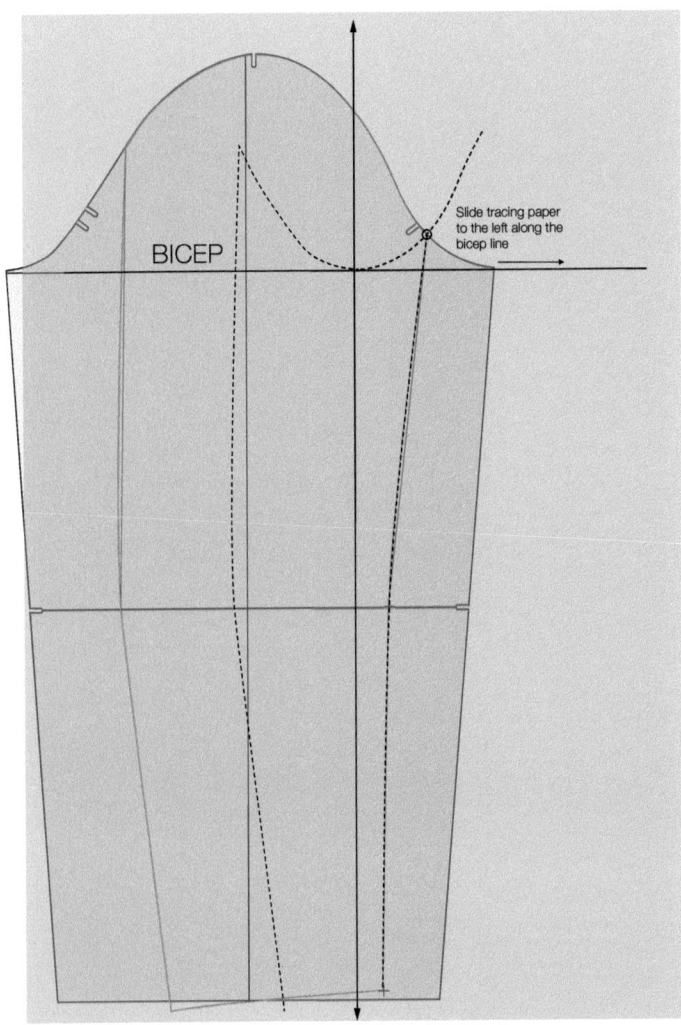
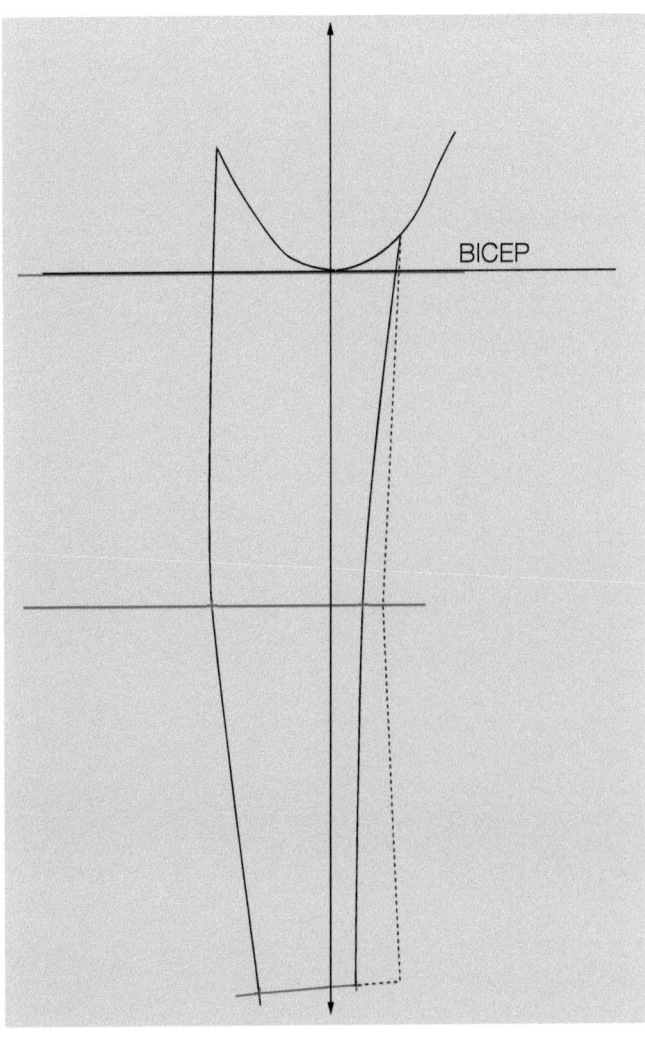

10. Repeat for the front armhole curve, sliding the tracing paper to the right along the bicep line until the armhole curve touches the front curve of the upper-sleeve.

11. Copy front curve to the wrist and cross-mark (red) at the elbow and the wrist.
Note: This will result in a much smaller shape than the back, which will be adjusted.

12. To adjust the wrist measurement, measure the distance between the cross-marks at the wrist.

13. Calculate the amount you need to add so the under-sleeve wrist plus the upper-sleeve wrist equals the total wrist measurement of the original sleeve block you used.

14. Balance at the elbow and blend to bicep curve.

15. Make sure to walk your pattern, adjusting the under-sleeve pattern if necessary.

INTRODUCTION

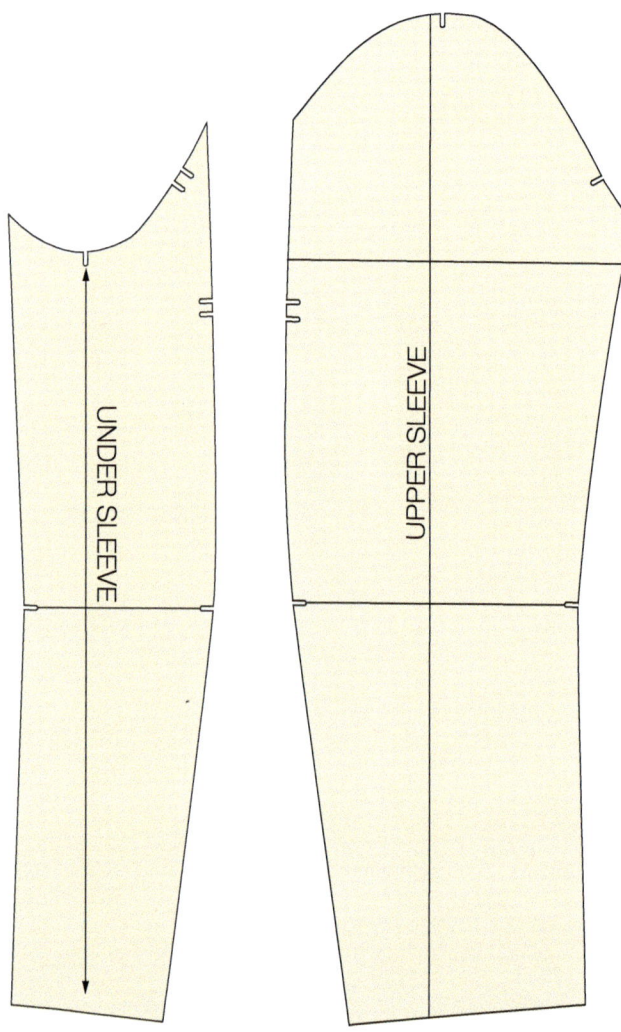

16. Flip tracing paper over and retrace under-sleeve pattern and notch.
17. Cut out the upper-sleeve pattern and notch.

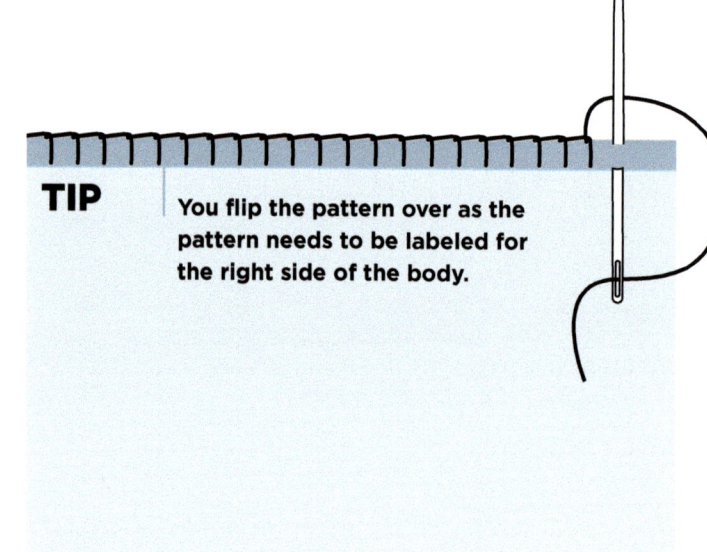

TIP You flip the pattern over as the pattern needs to be labeled for the right side of the body.

SEAM ALLOWANCES

The following information is a general guideline for seam allowances used for patternmaking in the professional garment industry.

¼ inch (6mm):

- All faced areas (enclosed seams)
- Sleeveless armholes
- Narrow spacing
- Extreme curves
- Necklines
- Down center front in a blouse/jacket/coat
- Collars, lapels.

½ inch (1.2cm):

- Armholes with sleeves
- Waistlines
- Style-lines
- Side seams
- Zipper seams (with the exception of separating and lapped zippers)
- Center front lines in skirts/trousers.

CHAPTER ONE:
THE BLAZER

CHAPTER ONE

THE BLAZER

Patterning concepts learned:
- **mannish block**
- **3-panel style-line**
- **semi-notched lapel**
- **2-piece contour sleeve**
- **single welt pocket**

1.1 Designed blazer front.

CHAPTER ONE:
THE BLAZER

THE HISTORY OF THE BLAZER

1.2 Participants of the Cambridge University Boat Race, 1905, well known for wearing blazers.

1.3 Yale football tackle Philip Tarasovic trying on a suit jacket at J. Press., New Haven, Connecticut, 1954.

The blazer is perhaps the most well-known jacket, with two equally fascinating stories behind its origin. One suggests the term *blazer* originated in 1825, with the jackets worn by the Lady Margaret Boat Club, the rowing club at Cambridge. The term *blazer* was given to the bright red cloth the jackets were made of and soon became the jacket of choice on campus for university students in the UK.

The double-breasted version has its roots in the uniforms of the British warship, the HMS Blazer, whose crew members began wearing a striped version of these jackets in 1837, the same year Queen Victoria visited the ship. It has been noted that the sailors were quite a scruffy bunch, and it is believed the captain had these jackets made in order to impress the Queen. She was indeed impressed and these *blazers* became the Royal Navy dress uniform.

Regardless of the origin of its name, the blazer has endured the test of time and continues to evolve.

In the late 1950s, the look known as *Ivy style* was popular on the campuses in the United States, where the blazer was adopted by Ivy League students as a must-have wardrobe essential. Clothiers Brooks Brothers and J. Press were the go-to places to shop for the style. The look came to represent the privileged lifestyle of the wealthy elite who attended one of the eight prestigious Ivy League universities and lived the life of the "gentleman".

"I don't wanna be the same as everybody else. That's why I'm a Mod, see?"

Jimmy from *Quadrophenia*

1.4 Mods in London, 1979, for whom blazers were all the rage.

1.5 Preps dressed in blazers, part of the "uniform" for the preppy style.

The *Ivy* look was so well regarded, other cultures sought to copy it. The photographic book, *Take Ivy*, first published in Japan in 1965, featured candid photographs taken on the campuses of Ivy League universities. The book developed a cult-like following with the students who hung out in Tokyo's Ginza shopping district, where the look became popular.

At the same time in London the youth movement known as the Modernists, or Mods for short, had a significant role in keeping this style of jacket popular. Mods were working-class teenagers who were obsessed with dressing up in smart suits and blazers and tooling around London on their Vespa scooters. They had an affinity for American soul music, hanging out at coffee houses, and going to modern jazz clubs. They even had their own Friday night TV program, *Ready Steady Go!*, which allowed the rest of Britain a peek into their world. Today, the movement continues to reinvent itself around the globe, with Mod-inspired music and clothing showing up on the streets and runways.

During the last part of the twentieth century, the navy blue blazer became the "uniform" for the *preppy style*. The preppy-style roots are embedded in the Ivy look, but with a sartorial twist. Whereas the Ivy look was a lifestyle, to be a prep one only needed to dress the part. *The Official Preppy Handbook*, published in 1979 by Lisa Birnbach, takes a humorous approach to the preppy style whereby she insists that every prep must own a blue blazer.

Today, whether in a classic or avant-garde version, the blazer is still considered to be the staple of most wardrobes.

CHAPTER ONE:
THE BLAZER

CONTEMPORARY BLAZERS

1.6
Moncler Gamme Bleu: Men's Spring 2015 Runway, Milan Menswear Fashion Week.

1.7
Vivienne Westwood Red Label: Runway, London Fashion Week AW14.

| THE HISTORY OF THE BLAZER | **CONTEMPORARY BLAZERS** | THE PATTERN | MUSLIN OR TOILE FITTING | PRODUCTION PATTERN | TECHNICAL FLATS AND FINISHED PATTERN PIECES |

1.8
Creatures Of The Wind: Runway, Mercedes-Benz Fashion Week Fall 2014.

1.9
Yohji Yamamoto: Runway, Paris Fashion Week Womenswear Fall/Winter 2014–2015.

**CHAPTER ONE:
THE BLAZER**

THE PATTERN

Start with mannish front, back, and sleeve blocks

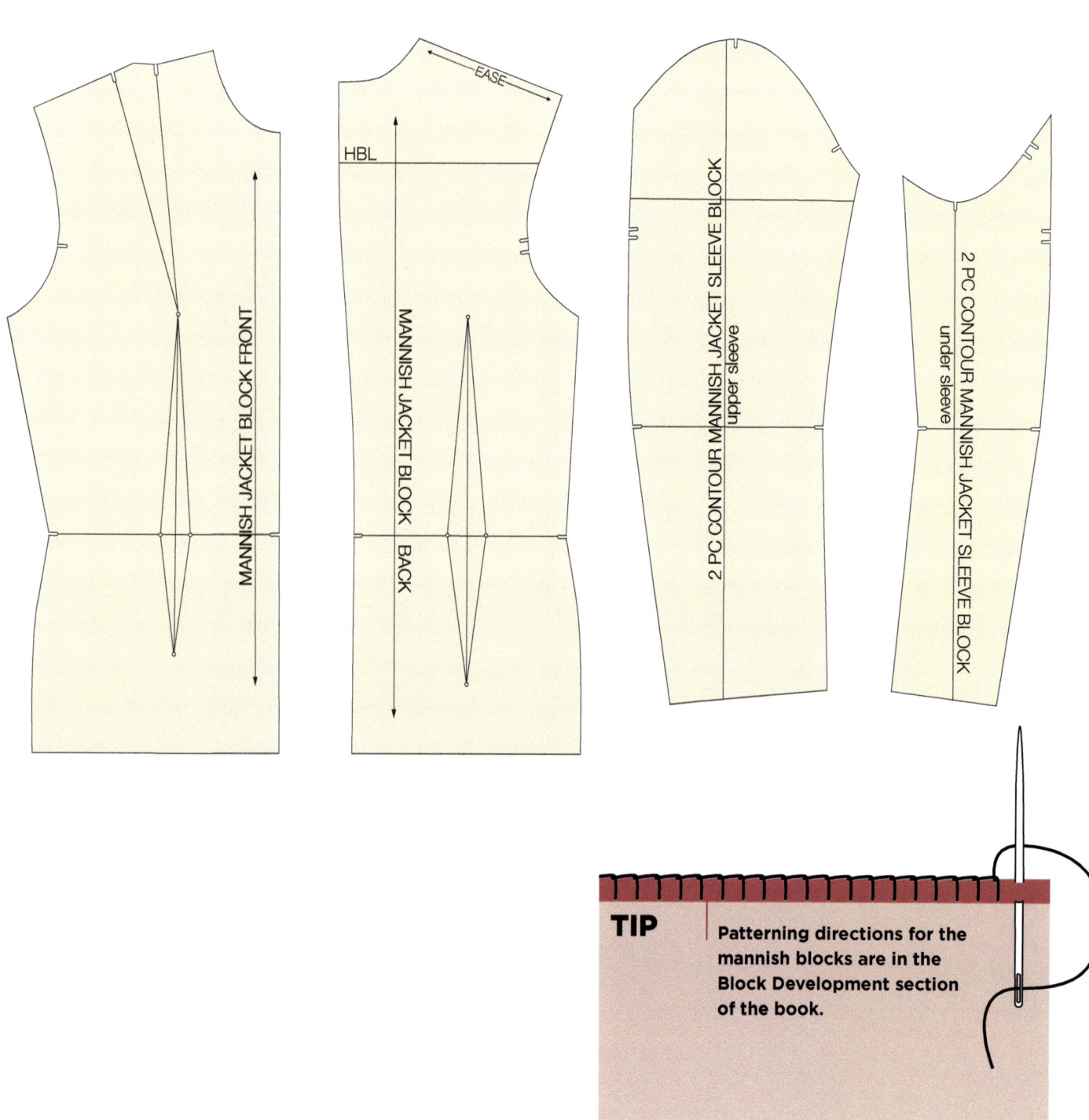

TIP | Patterning directions for the mannish blocks are in the Block Development section of the book.

3-panel style-line

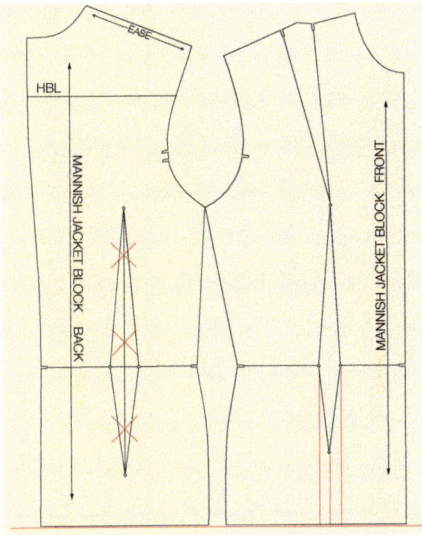 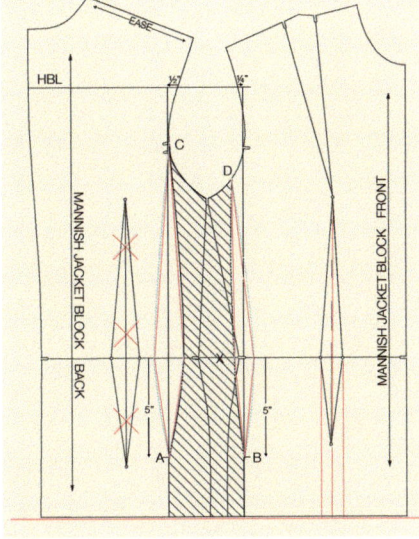 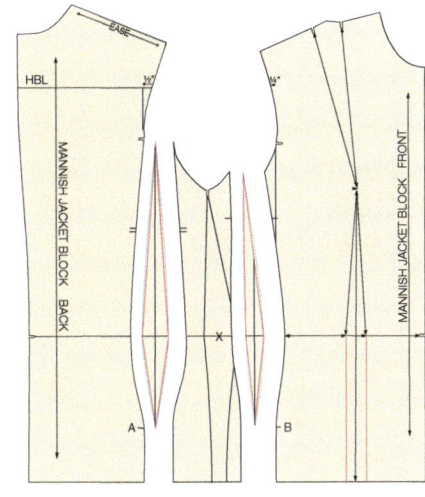

1. Draw a horizontal guideline (red line) on paper.

2. Place the mannish jacket block back pattern on the guideline and trace, omitting the back contour darts.

3. Place the mannish jacket block front pattern on the guideline with armholes touching.
   Note: If the armholes do not match, equalize and blend.

4. Mark the side seam notch.

5. Extend the front contour darts to the hemline, creating an open-ended dart.

6. Mark waist level X.

7. On the back pattern, mark ½ inch (1.2cm) in from armhole (AH) on the horizontal balance line (HBL) and square a guideline down to hem.

8. On each side of the guideline, mark out ¾ inch (1.75cm) at X.

9. Mark down 5 inches (12.5cm) on back guideline and label A.

10. Draw a straight line (red line) from A to X.

11. Draw a straight line (red line) from X to midpoint of side seam and HBL (C).
    Note: This will resemble a contour dart.

12. Curve lines slightly (see dotted lines).
    Note: It is easier to draw a straight line and then curve it.

13. On the front pattern, mark ¼ inch (6mm) in from AH, using the same guideline as for the back pattern.

14. Square a guideline down from hem.

15. Mark down 5 inches (12.5cm) on front guideline and label B.

16. On each side of the guideline, mark out ½ inch (1.2cm) at X.

17. Draw a straight line (red line) from B to X.

18. Draw a straight line (red line) from X to midpoint of side seam and front notch (D).

19. Curve lines slightly (see dotted lines).

20. The shaded area is your new side panel.

21. Cut out the 3-panel style-line.

22. Walk seams from waist up and waist down, equalizing and truing if necessary.

23. Mark front notch 2 ½ inches (6cm) and back notch 3 inches (7.5cm) down on new style-lines.
    Note: Make sure that you are happy with the fit of the 3-piece style-line before you continue drafting the pattern.

**CHAPTER ONE:
THE BLAZER**

Drafting the lapel

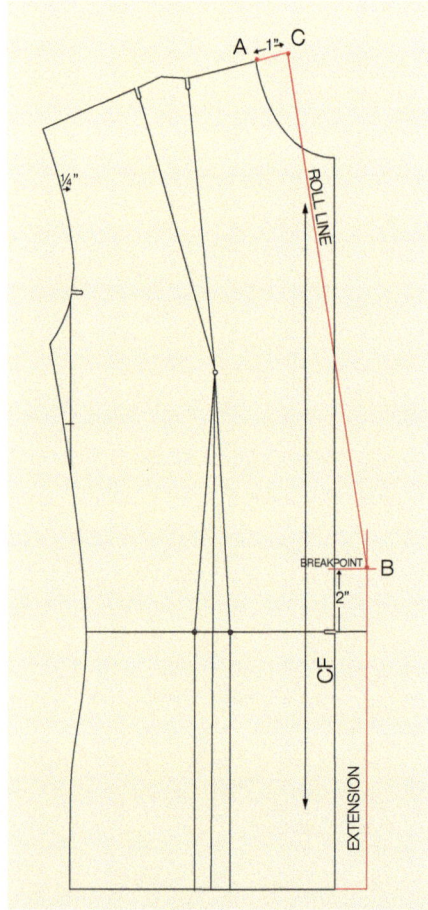
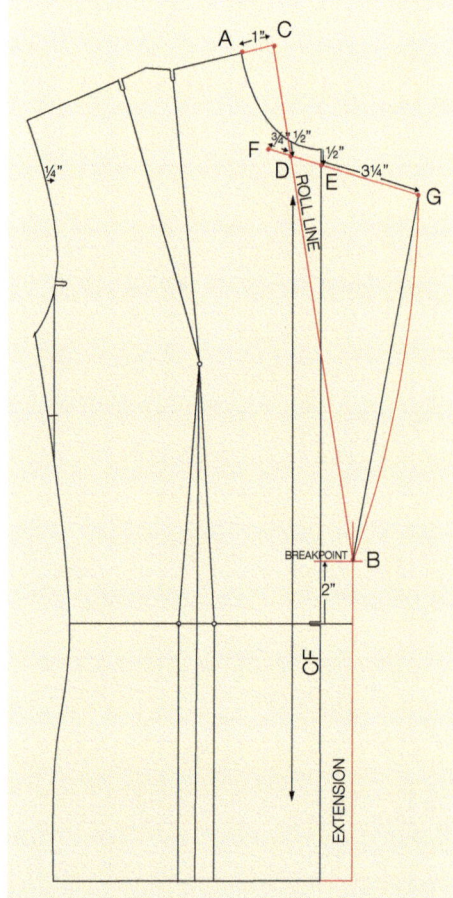

1. Trace the front pattern, leaving enough space for lapel and collar development.

2. Label high-point shoulder A.

3. Extend shoulder seam 1 inch (2.5cm) and label C.

4. Draw the button extension ¾–1 inch (1.75–2.5cm) parallel to the center front line (CF).
   Note: The size of the extension will equal the diameter of your button.

5. Mark the breakpoint B, 2 inches (5cm) up from waist and notch.

6. Draw a line from B to C (this is your roll-line).

7. Mark points D and E ½ inch (1.2cm) below neckline at roll-line and at CF.

8. Draw a straight line through D and E, extending the line ¾ inch (1.75cm) from D to F and 3 ¼ inches (8cm) from E to G.

9. Draw a straight line from breakpoint B to G and then curve slightly.
   Note: This is the shape of your lapel.

Collar development

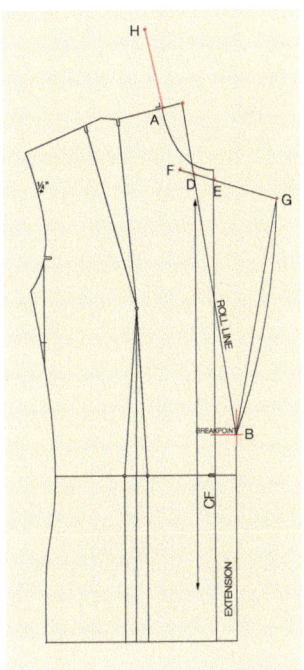
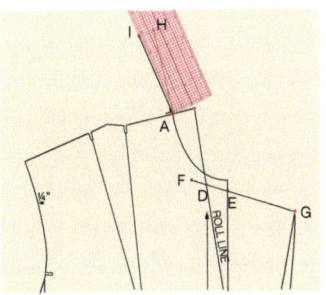
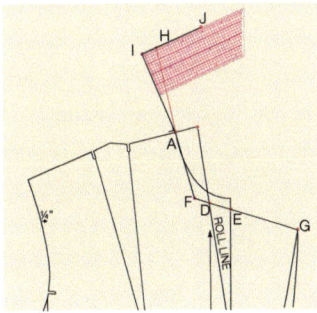
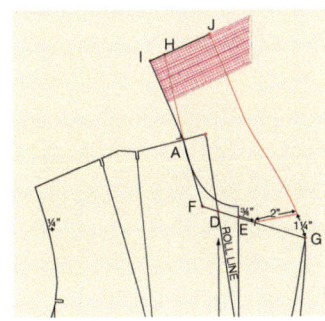
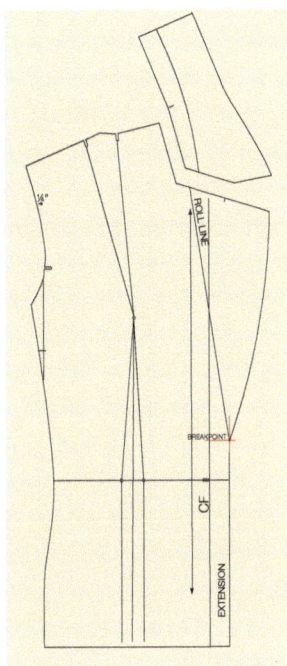

1. Measure back neckline + ⅛ inch (3mm), record _____.

2. Continuing on front pattern, using this measurement, square a line up from high-point shoulder A, label H.

3. Using the same back neck measurement, place ruler on A and draw a new line ¾ inch (1.75cm) to the left of H, label I.

4. Draw a line from A to F and blend to smooth.

5. Square a line 3 inches (7.5cm) from I and label J.
   Note: This will be the CB of the collar.

6. Starting at E, draw a 2 inch (5cm) line (red line), spaced 1 ¼ inches (3cm) from G.
   Note: This is the spacing of your "notch" between the collar and the lapel.

7. Square down from J to shoulder by drawing a line parallel to the A to I line.

8. Continue line to H to finish the collar development.

9. Cut out collar making sure to notch the shoulder seam A.

10. Mark roll-line on collar 1 inch (2.5cm) from CB and blend with the roll-line already marked.

Shoulder dart to neckline

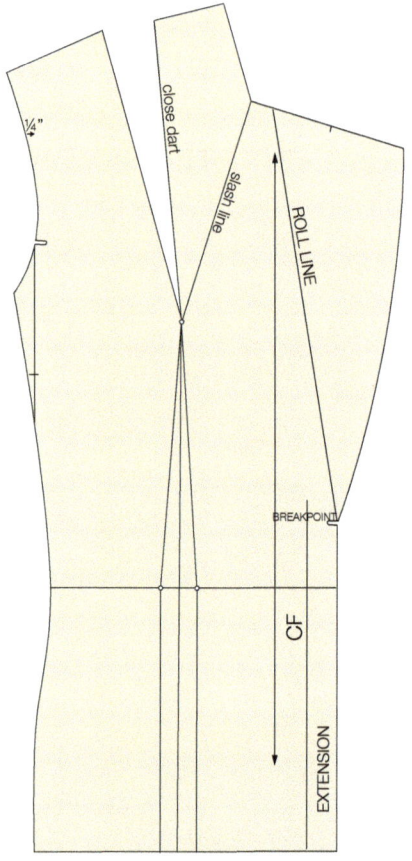
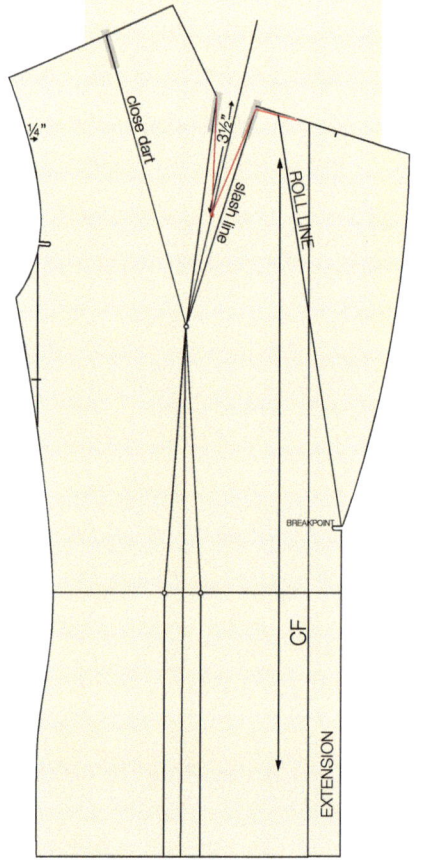

1. Trace front pattern and set aside.
   Note: This will be used to develop front facing and front lining patterns.

2. On original pattern, move shoulder dart to neckline using the slash and spread method.

3. Draw a slash line from neckline corner to bust point (apex).

4. Cut slash line to the edge of the bust point (apex).

5. Cut shoulder dart leg to the edge of the bust point (apex).

6. Close shoulder dart and tape shut.
   Note: Make sure to true the shoulder seam after closing dart if it is no longer a straight line.

7. Mark the midpoint of the dart opening and draw a straight line to the bust point (apex).

8. Redraw dart legs to measure 3 ½ inches (8.75cm).
   Note: This dart can be made longer if necessary; adjust at muslin fitting if there is too much ease, making sure the dart is hidden by the lapel.

Welt pocket placement

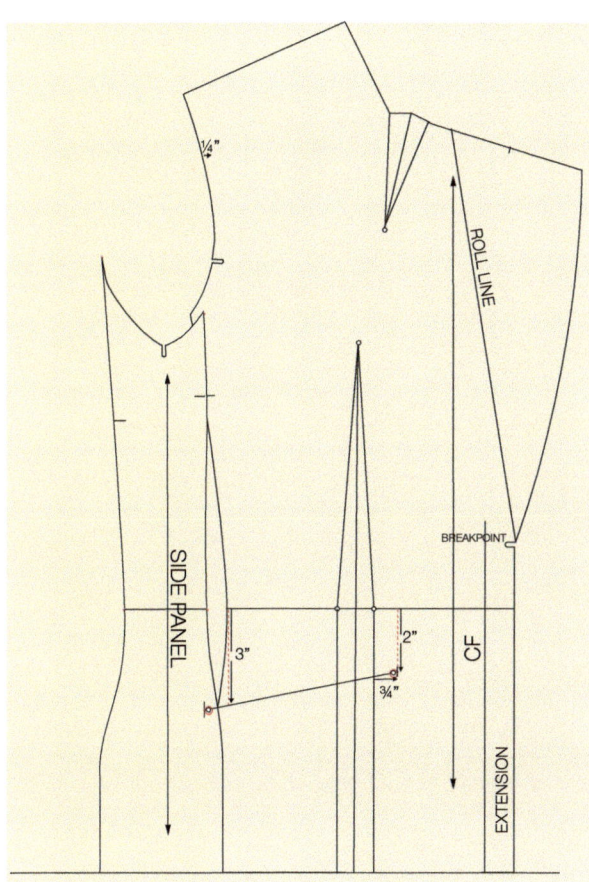

1. Draw a horizontal guideline on paper.
2. Place the front pattern on guideline.
3. Measure 2 inches (5cm) down from front dart at waistline and ¾ inch (1.75cm) towards CF and mark.
4. Measure 3 inches (7.5cm) down from side seam at waistline and mark.
5. Draw a line connecting the two points.
6. Place side panel on horizontal guideline with patterns touching where pocket line is drawn and extend the line into the side panel that equals 6 inches (15cm), making sure to subtract the dart opening measurement.
7. Circle and drill ⅛ inch (3mm) into the pocket.

**CHAPTER ONE:
THE BLAZER**

MUSLIN OR TOILE FITTING

- Before you draft the facing, pocket, and lining patterns, prepare a muslin for fit.
- Do not add seam allowance (SA) to pattern as you will most likely be adjusting the muslin for fit.
- Trace the mannish 2-piece sleeve block for the muslin.
- Draw the seam allowance (SA) directly onto the muslin after tracing the working pattern.
- Make any necessary fit corrections to pattern.
- Now you can move on to the facing, pocket, and lining patterns.

1.10 Overhead view of muslin.
1.11 Checking muslin for fit.
1.12 Pinning detail.

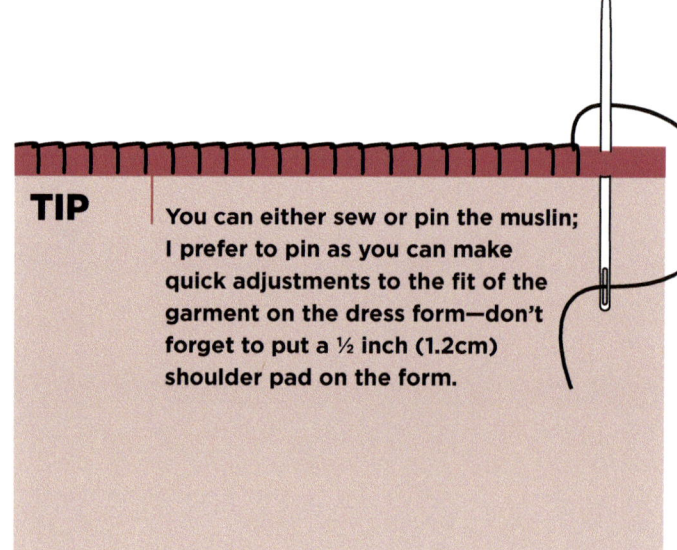

TIP You can either sew or pin the muslin; I prefer to pin as you can make quick adjustments to the fit of the garment on the dress form—don't forget to put a ½ inch (1.2cm) shoulder pad on the form.

Completing the upper- and under-collar

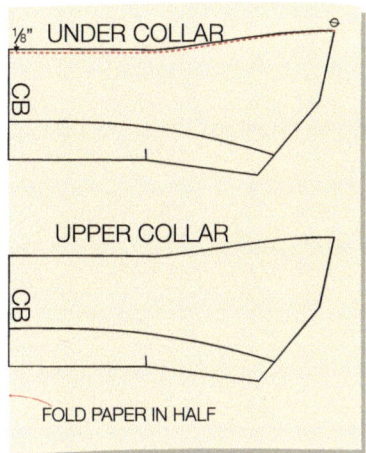

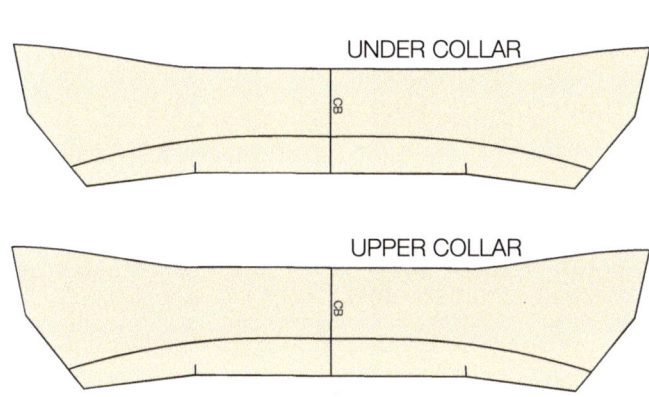

Front facing and front lining

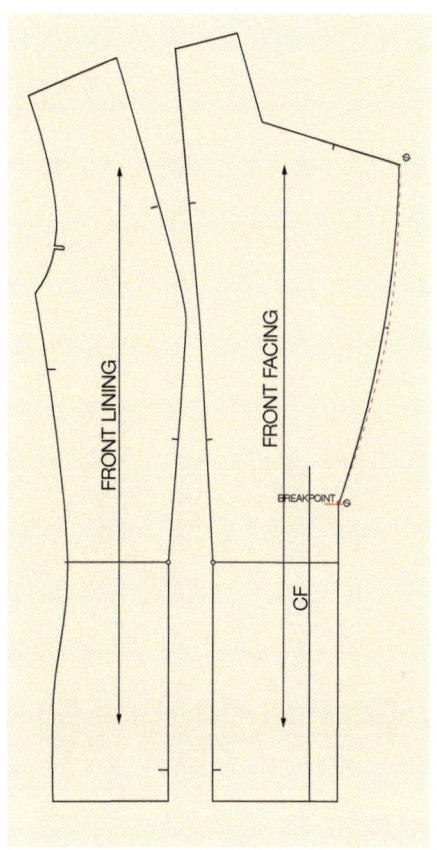

1. Fold paper in half and trace the collar twice; don't forget to mark your shoulder seam notch.
2. Mark the first pattern the upper-collar.
3. On the second pattern, draft under-collar by reducing the out-seam of the collar by ⅛ inch (3mm) at the CB and blending to zero at the collar point (red dotted line).
4. Mark grainlines parallel to CB.

1. Using saved front pattern piece, mark notches 2 inches (5cm) and 2 inches (5cm) below bust point (apex) and 1 inch (2.5cm) up from hem.
2. Add ⅛ inch (3mm) blending from breakpoint to edge of lapel (red dotted line).
3. Cut out the negative space of the darts, smoothing out bust point area.
4. Mark grainline on both patterns perpendicular to waistline.
5. Label the patterns front facing and front lining.

Side lining

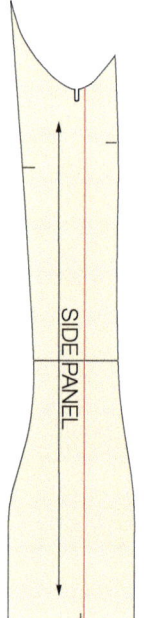
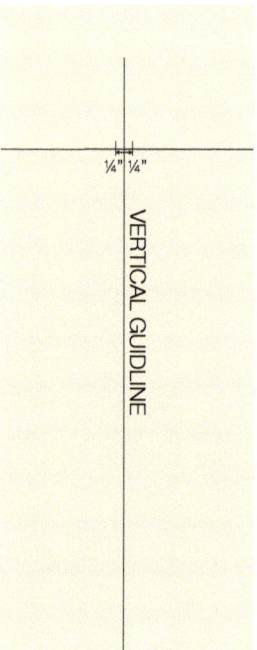
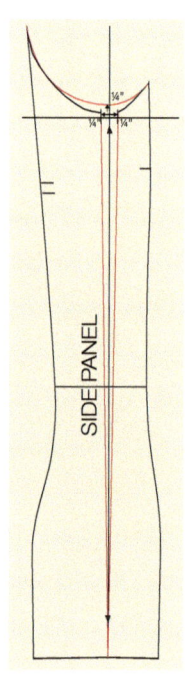

Back lining action pleat

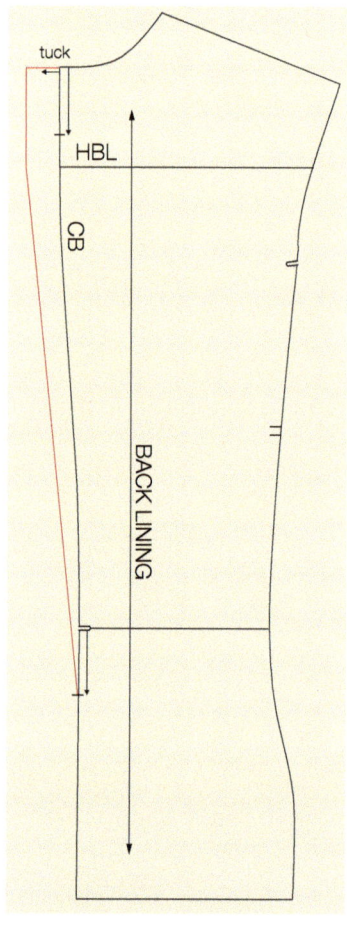

1. Trace side panel piece and cut out.
2. Square a slash line down from under-arm notch to hem and cut to—not through to—hem.
3. On paper, draw a vertical guideline; mark out ¼ inch (6mm) on either side of the guideline.
4. Place side panel on the guideline and spread open to meet the marks, tape down and trace pattern.
   Note: The guideline becomes your new grainline and under-arm notch.
5. At new under-arm notch, mark up ¼ inch (6mm) and blend to edges (red curved lines).

1. Trace back pattern.
2. Mark out 1 inch (2.5cm) from CB and square down to HBL.
3. Mark 2 inches (5cm) down from waist at CB and continue line to meet HBL.
4. At CB seam, mark 2 inches (5cm) down for tuck.

Under-sleeve lining

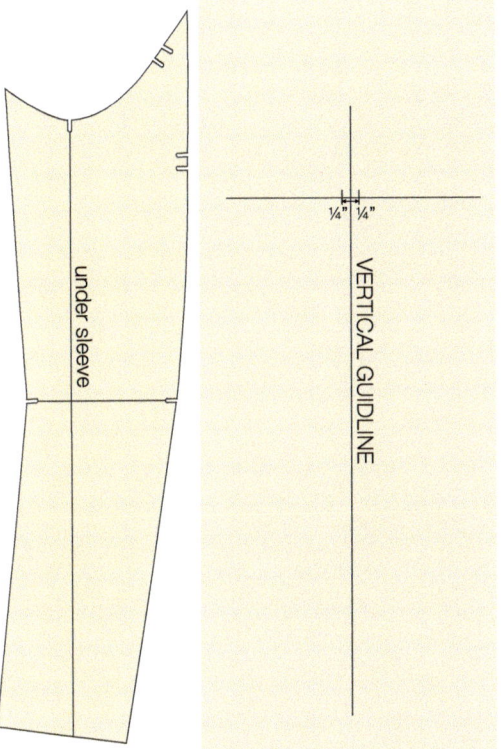
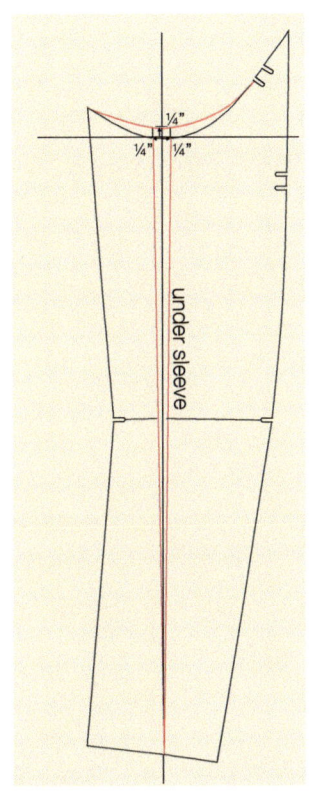

1. Trace upper-sleeve pattern and set aside.
2. Trace under-sleeve pattern and cut out.
3. Square a slash line down from under-arm notch to hem and cut to—not through to—hem.
4. On paper, draw a vertical guideline; mark out ¼ inch (6mm) on either side of the guideline.
5. Place side panel on the guideline and spread open to meet the marks, tape down and trace pattern.
   Note: The guideline becomes your new grainline and under-arm notch.
6. At new under-arm notch, mark up ¼ inch (6mm) and blend to edges (red curved lines).

PRODUCTION PATTERN

Seam allowances and hems

TIP
- Before adding SAs and hems, make sure to walk your patterns and make any necessary corrections if seams and/or control notches do not match.
- You will discard this "wedge" when cutting out the pattern.

Front pattern seam allowance and hem

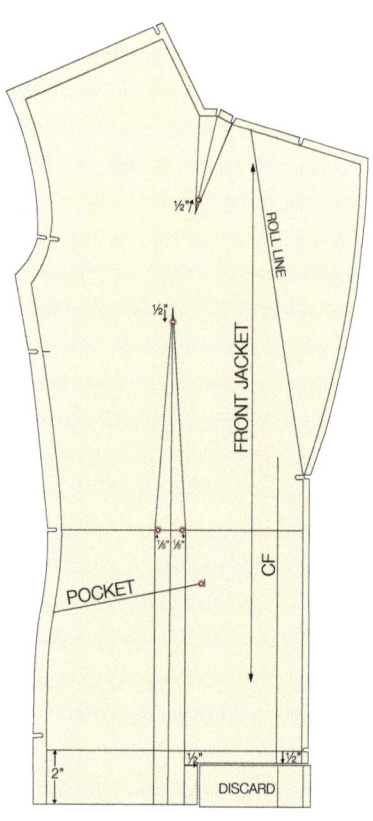

1. Trace front pattern.
2. Add ½ inch (1.2cm) SA to all seams with the exception of the front, neckline, and hem.
3. Add ¼ inch (6mm) SA to the front and neckline.
4. Mark hem 2 inches (5cm): this includes the ½ inch (1.2cm) SA.
5. Measure ½ inch (1.2cm) in from front dart and square down to hem.
6. Measure ½ inch (1.2cm) down from original hem and draw line to squared line.
7. Circle and drill vertical dart points ½ inch (1.2cm) into the dart and horizontal dart points ⅛ inch (3mm) into the dart.

| THE HISTORY OF THE BLAZER | CONTEMPORARY BLAZERS | THE PATTERN | MUSLIN OR TOILE FITTING | **PRODUCTION PATTERN** | TECHNICAL FLATS AND FINISHED PATTERN PIECES |

Back and side patterns seam allowance and hems

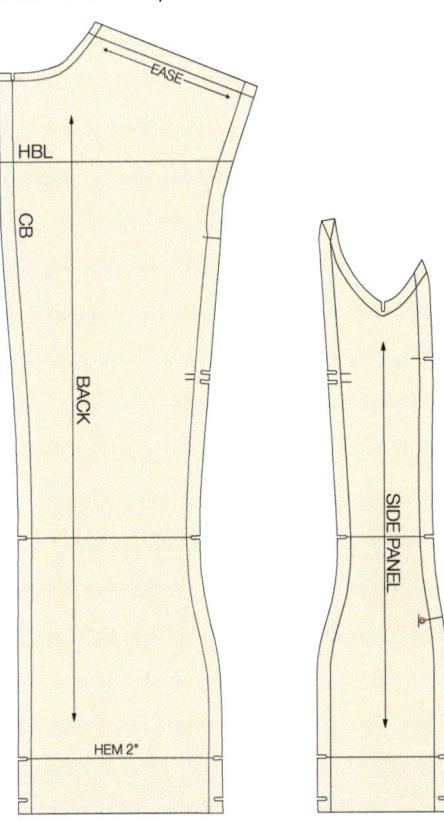

Front facing seam allowance and hem

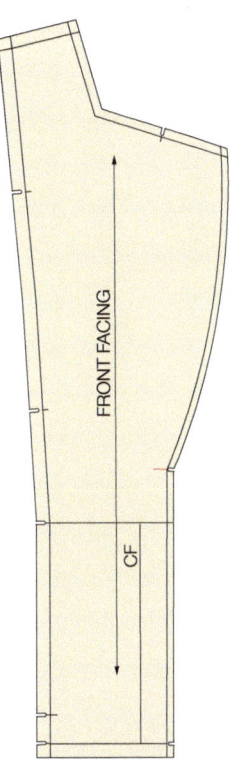

1. Add ½ inch (1.2cm) SA to all seams with the exception of the back neckline and hems.
2. Add ¼ inch (6mm) SA to back neckline.
3. Mark hems 2 inches (5cm); this includes the ½ inch (1.2cm) SA.

1. Add ¼ inch (6mm) SA to front neckline and down CF.
2. Add ½ inch (1.2cm) SA to all other seams.

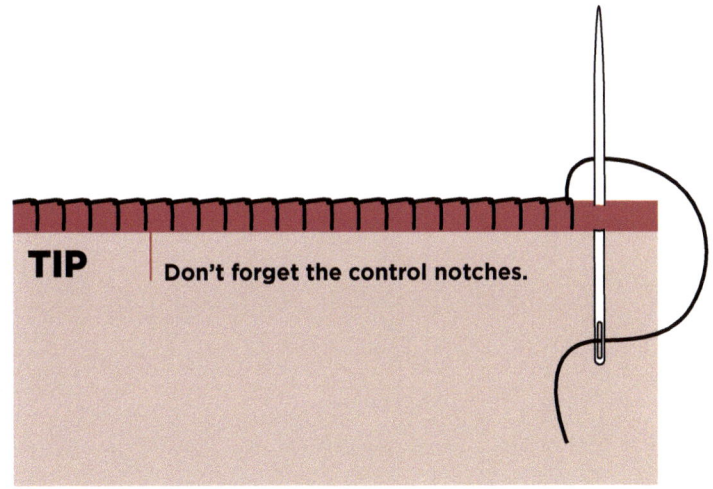

TIP | Don't forget the control notches.

**CHAPTER ONE:
THE BLAZER**

Sleeve patterns seam allowance and hems

1. Add ½ inch (1.2cm) SA to all seams with the exception of the hem.
2. Mark hems 2 inches (5cm).

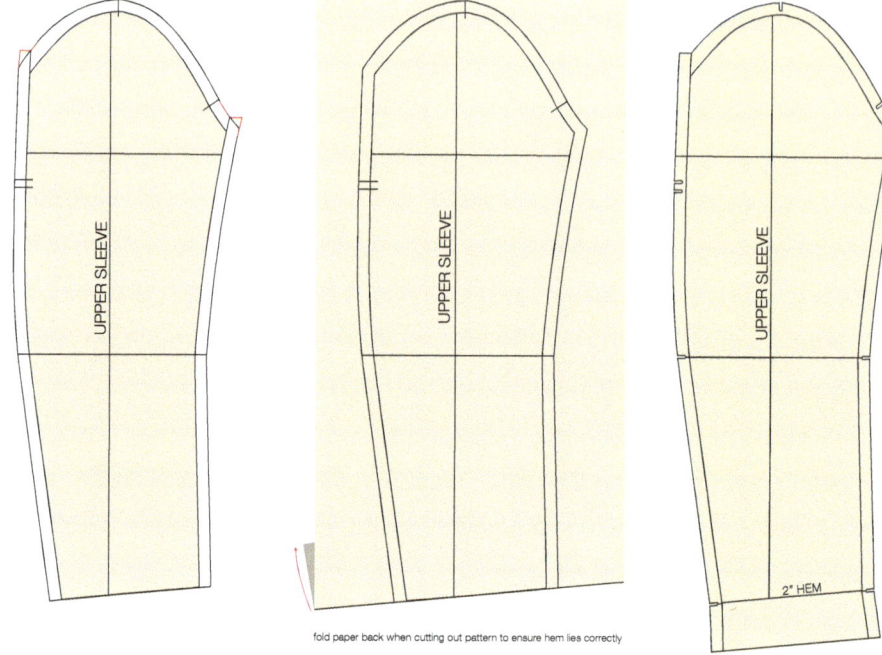

TIP Make sure to fold paper back at hemline when cutting out to ensure the hem lies correctly on garment.

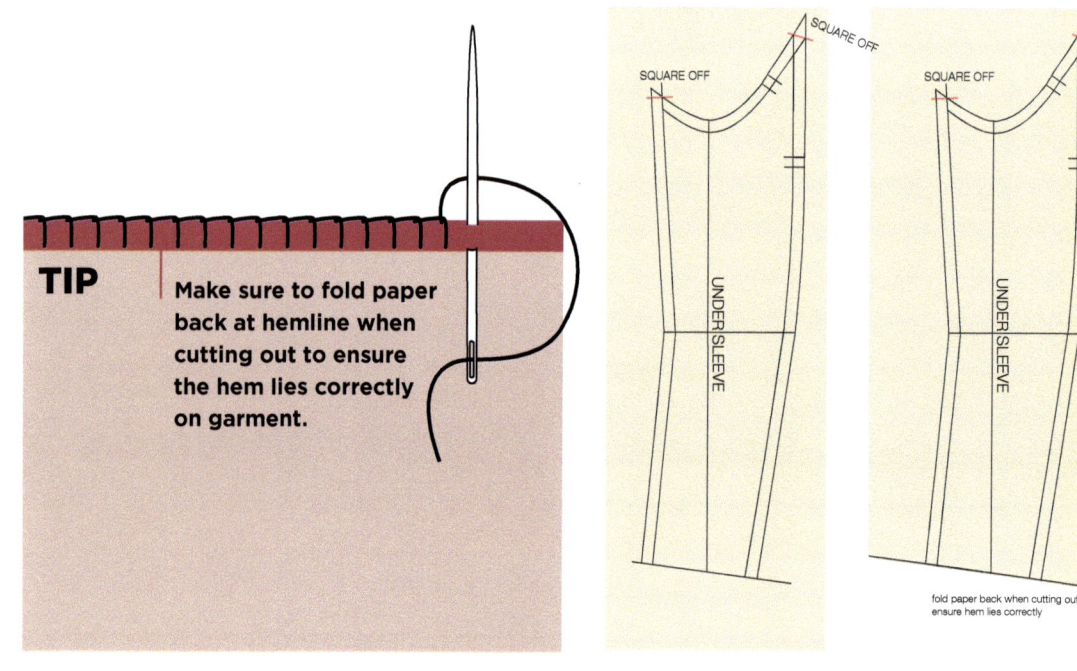

Upper-collar seam allowance

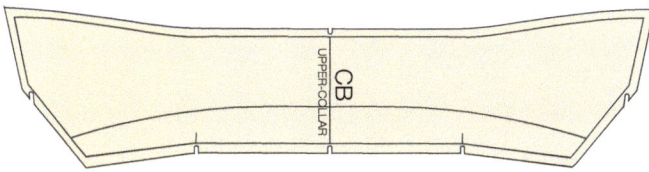

1. Add ¼ inch (6mm) SA to all seams for upper-collar.
2. Notch at CB, shoulder, and the SA.

Under-collar seam allowance

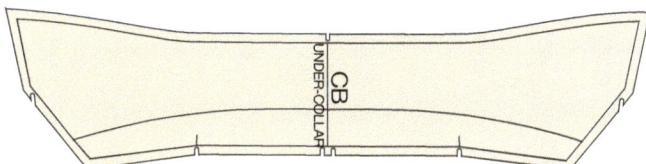

1. Add ¼ inch (6mm) SA to all seams for the under-collar.
2. Make a double-notch at back (one on each side of the CB).
3. Notch shoulder and the SA.

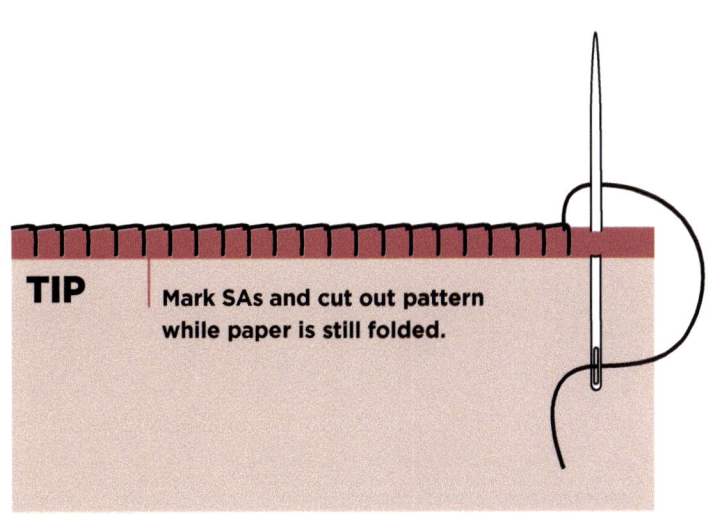

TIP | Mark SAs and cut out pattern while paper is still folded.

**CHAPTER ONE:
THE BLAZER**

Front, back, side, and sleeve linings seam allowance and hems

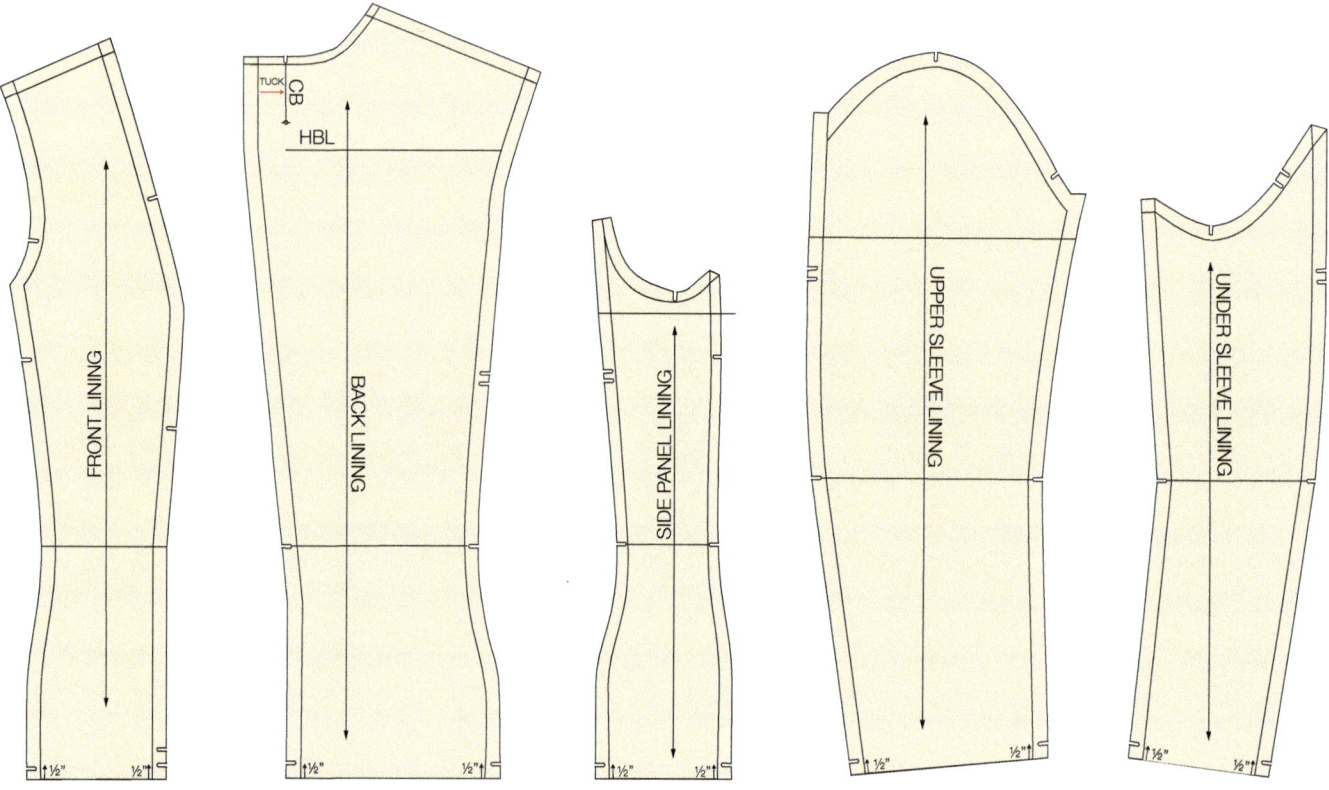

1. Add ½ inch (1.2cm) SA to all seams with the exception of the back neckline and hem.

2. Add ¼ inch (6mm) SA to the back neckline.

3. You do not add a SA to the hem as it is already "built in"; mark and notch up ½ inch (1.2cm).

Welt pocket

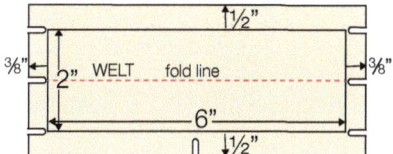

1. For a 1 inch (2.5cm) welt, square off a rectangle 6 inches (15cm) by 2 inches (5cm).
2. Mark dotted line (red dotted line) for fold-line at 1 inch (2.5cm) and notch.
3. Mark 3 inches (7.5cm) in on length of welt and notch.
4. Mark SA at ⅜ inch (1cm) and ½ inch (1.2cm) as shown.

Pocket lining

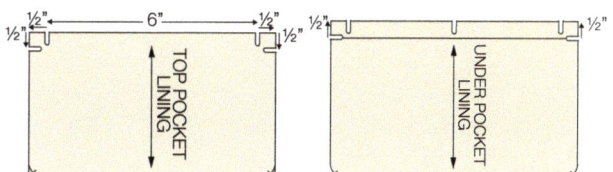

1. For top-pocket bag, measure the length of the welt (6 inches) + 1 inch for SA (17.5cm + 2.5cm).
2. Square down 4 inches (10cm) for the pocket depth.
3. Notch top-pocket bag as shown.
4. Curve pocket bag at corners and place a control notch on the curve.
5. For under-pocket bag, trace top-pocket bag and add ½ inch (1.2cm) to the length of the bag.
6. Notch under-pocket bag as shown.

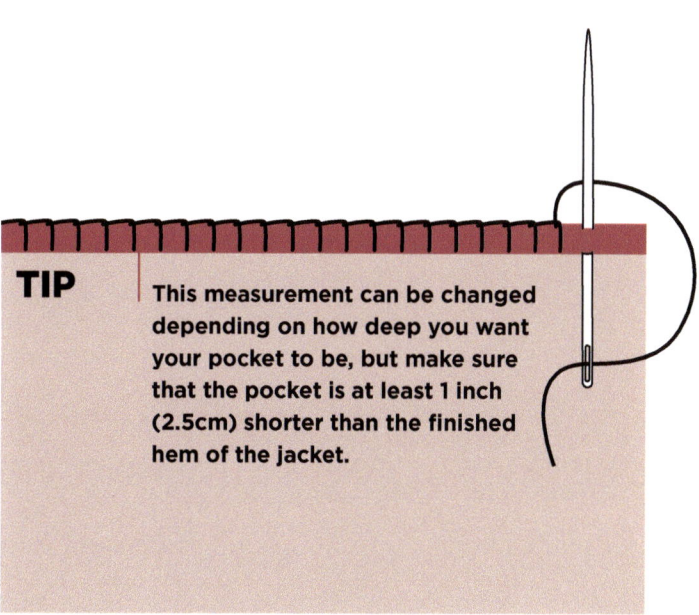

TIP This measurement can be changed depending on how deep you want your pocket to be, but make sure that the pocket is at least 1 inch (2.5cm) shorter than the finished hem of the jacket.

**CHAPTER ONE:
THE BLAZER**

TECHNICAL FLATS AND FINISHED PATTERN PIECES

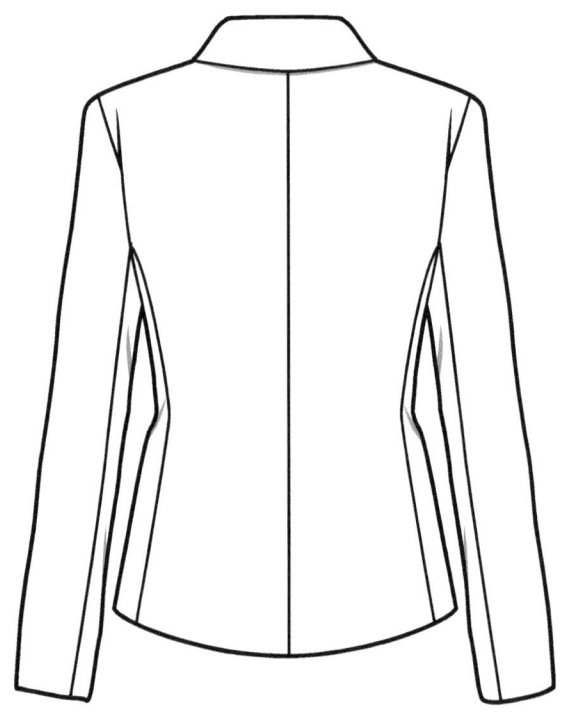

Self:

1. Front (cut 2).
2. Side (cut 2).
3. Back (cut 2).
4. Upper-sleeve (cut 2).
5. Under-sleeve (cut 2).
6. Upper-collar (cut 1).
7. Under-collar (cut 1).
8. Front facing (cut 2).
9. Welt (cut 2).

Lining:

1. Front (cut 2).
2. Side (cut 2).
3. Back (cut 2).
4. Upper-sleeve (cut 2).
5. Under-sleeve (cut 2).
6. Top-pocket bag (cut 2).
7. Under-pocket bag (cut 2).

> "Fashion only seems to make sense if it's rooted in some dimension of history or if it feels like a continuation of an idea."
>
> Douglas Coupland

| THE HISTORY OF THE BLAZER | CONTEMPORARY BLAZERS | THE PATTERN | MUSLIN OR TOILE FITTING | PRODUCTION PATTERN | **TECHNICAL FLATS AND FINISHED PATTERN PIECES** |

1.13
Collar/lapel detail.

CHAPTER TWO

THE TUXEDO

Patterning concepts learned:
- **shawl collar**
- **classic princess style-line**
- **2-piece contoured sleeve**
- **back vent**
- **welt pocket with flap**

2.1 Designed tuxedo front.

**CHAPTER TWO:
THE TUXEDO**

THE HISTORY OF THE TUXEDO

Legend has it that the Prince of Wales, known as Bertie to his friends, ordered a short evening coat with a shawl collar to be worn at the less-formal dinners he hosted at his country estate, Sandringham. Mind you, the usual mode of dress during the Victorian era was extremely conventional and dressing for dinner would have required full evening attire (also known as "full fig"), which included donning a jacket with tails.

Savile Row tailor, Henry Poole, obliged by cutting off the regulation tails and making the garment in a celestial blue color. This new evening coat caused quite a stir in 1865, when social norms and dress were rigidly prescribed by society. Had this new form of dress been attempted by anyone other than Bertie, who was known for his sense of style, this smart new ensemble might have gone unnoticed. Luckily for us, it wasn't and the dinner jacket was born.

But wait, you ask, why is the dinner jacket called a tuxedo? Now here's where the story gets interesting. Like all great stories, this one has many claims; the most recognized gives credit to American James Brown Potter, who crossed social paths with the royal a good twenty years after the jacket's initial debut. It seems Mr. Potter's better half was quite a beauty and while the couple was traveling abroad, the prince was so taken by the sight of Mrs. Potter that he invited the duo to visit him at Sandringham.

2.2
"Kick" tobacco trade card, 1892, featuring four men in tuxedos.

"Fashions fade, style is eternal."

Yves Saint Laurent

2.3
Marlene Dietrich in her Hollywood film debut *Morocco*, 1930, wearing the tuxedo which helped characterize her androgynous persona and attitude.

2.4
Publicity poster for Jamaican singer and actress Grace Jones' record *Nightclubbing* in France, 1981. Grace Jones' use of the tuxedo was central to her androgynous image, for which she is renowned.

2.5
Danielle Sauvajeon in Le Smoking, spring collection 1968. Le Smoking tuxedo suit for women, created by Yves Saint Laurent, garnered attention in both the world of fashion and popular culture.

Potter, at a loss as to what to wear in the country and wanting to make a good impression, solicited his London tailor for advice. As coincidence would have it, the man whose advice he sought was none other than Poole, Bertie's very own tailor. Poole suggested an informal dinner jacket for the visit, knowing it would be the perfect choice as he had been making the exact piece for the prince for the past two decades.

Potter returned to the United States with his tailless jacket in tow and began wearing it to events at the Tuxedo Park Club in New York and the rest is history.

From the 1930s onward, female artists, including Marlene Dietrich, Josephine Baker, and Grace Jones, have donned the tuxedo, to help characterize their androgynous personas and attitude.

The fashion flock took a bit longer to come on board. It wasn't until 1966 when, inspired by sculptor Niki de Saint Phalle's wearing of men's clothes, Yves Saint Laurent introduced "Le Smoking": his version of the tuxedo for women. It was such a huge success that the design house has shown a version of the tuxedo every year since its inception.

CHAPTER TWO:
THE TUXEDO

CONTEMPORARY TUXEDOS

2.6
Saint Laurent: Runway RTW,
Paris Fashion Week Fall 2014.

2.7
Ralph Lauren: Runway RTW,
New York Fashion Week Fall 2015.

| THE HISTORY OF THE TUXEDO | CONTEMPORARY TUXEDOS | THE PATTERN | MUSLIN OR TOILE FITTING | PRODUCTION PATTERN | TECHNICAL FLATS AND FINISHED PATTERN PIECES |

2.8
Jean Paul Gaultier: Runway, Paris Fashion Week Womenswear Spring/Summer 2015.

2.9
Alexander Wang: Runway, New York Fashion Week Fall 2015.

CHAPTER TWO:
THE TUXEDO

THE PATTERN

Start with jacket front, back, and 2-piece sleeve blocks

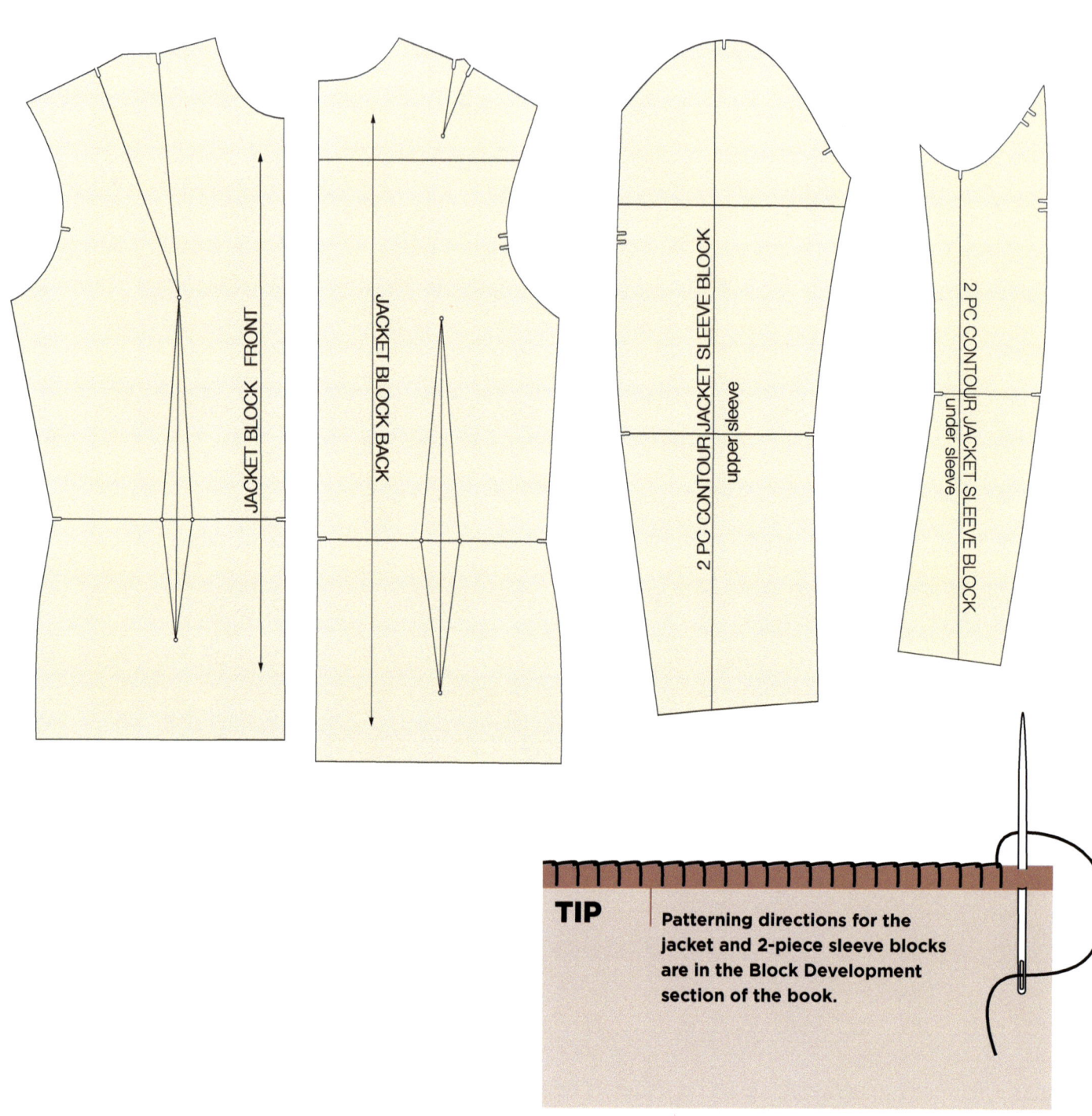

TIP Patterning directions for the jacket and 2-piece sleeve blocks are in the Block Development section of the book.

Shawl collar development

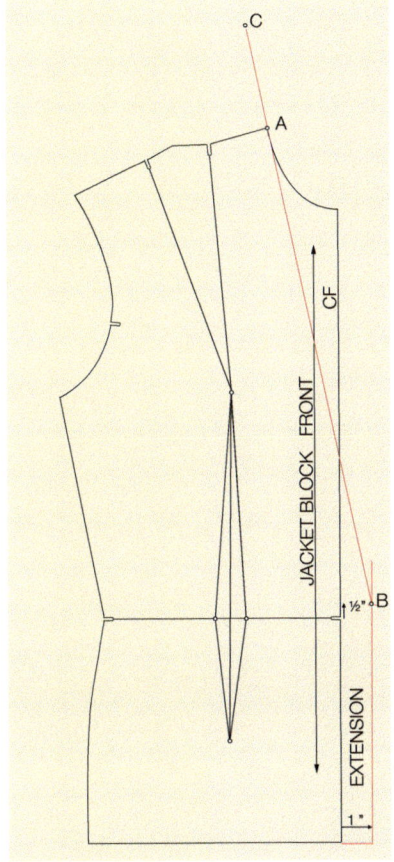
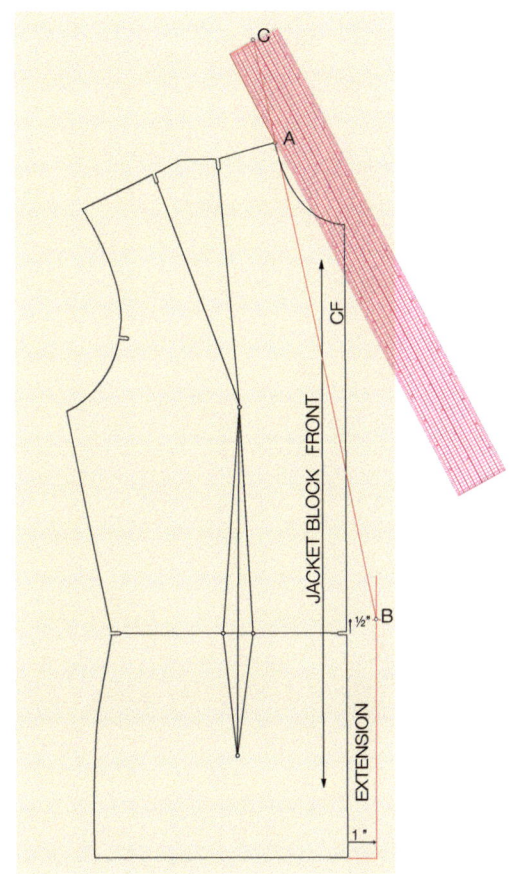

1. Trace the front pattern, leaving enough space for shawl collar development.

2. Label high-point shoulder A.

3. Draw the button extension (red line) 1 ⅛ inch (2.75cm) parallel to the center front line (CF).
   Note: The size of the extension will equal the diameter of your button.

4. Mark the breakpoint, B, ½ inch (1.2cm) up from waist and notch.

5. A to C = back neckline measurement plus ⅛ inch (3mm), record _____.

6. Draw a line from A through B to C.

7. Using the same back neck measurement, place ruler on A and draw a new line 1 inch (2.5cm) to the left of C.

**CHAPTER TWO:
THE TUXEDO**

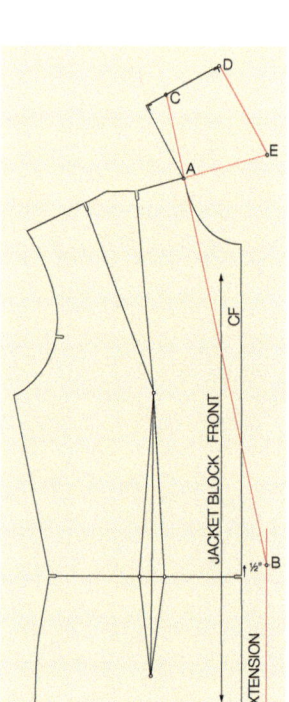

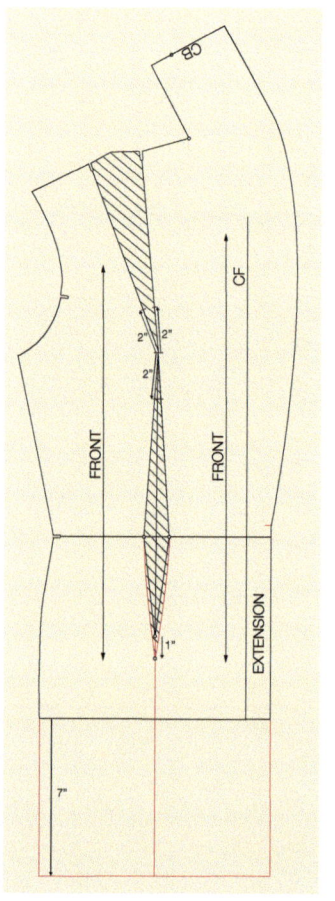

8. Square a line 3 ¾ inches (9.25cm), label D.
   Note: This is the center back of the collar.

9. Extend shoulder line out 3 ¾ inches (9.25cm), label E (red dotted line).
   Note: This is where the collar hits the shoulder.

10. Draw a line (red line) from D to E.

11. Draw a straight line from B to E.

12. Draw a curved line (red curved line) the desired shape to finish the shawl collar.
    Note: The straight line is used as a reference point for the curve of the collar.

Classic princess front

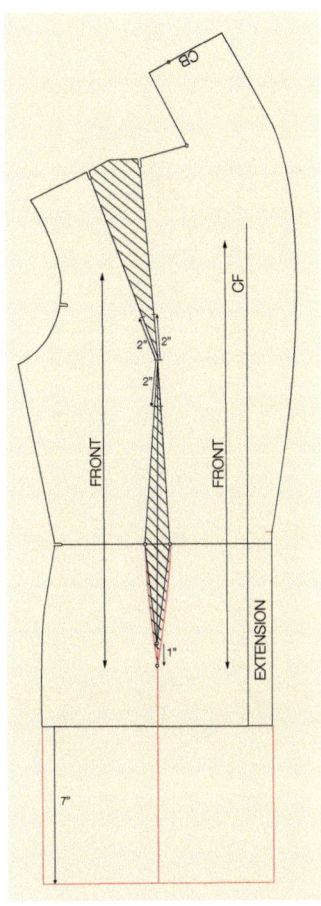

1. Lengthen torso 7 inches (17.5cm).
2. Extend line (red line) to hem through center of contour dart.
3. Lengthen contour dart 1 inch (2.5cm).
4. Mark control notches 2 inches (5cm) from apex on all lines.
5. Draw a ⅛ inch (3mm) curve down both dart legs starting at notches under apex and ending at waist. **Note: This will add shape to the bodice under bust.**
6. Mark grainline on side back perpendicular to waist.
7. Cut front and side front pieces apart making sure to cut out the darts.
8. Smooth out the bust-line and hip area if it looks too pointy or uneven.
9. Walk the pattern with an awl starting at the waist; adjust pattern as needed to balance style-line at shoulder and hem.

Back vent

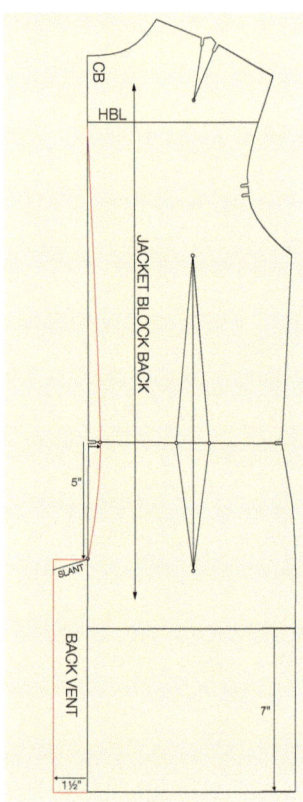

1. Trace back pattern.
2. Lengthen torso 7 inches (17.5cm).
3. Mark down 5 inches (12.5cm) from waist at the center back (CB).
4. For back vent, measure out from CB 1 ½ inches (3.75cm) and draw a line (red line).
5. Draw a slanted line at top to connect.
6. Measure ½ inch (1.2cm) in from waist at CB.
7. Draw a curved line (curved red line) down 5 inches (12.5cm) ending at vent opening.
8. Draw a curved line (curved red line) up to horizontal balance line (HBL).

Classic princess back

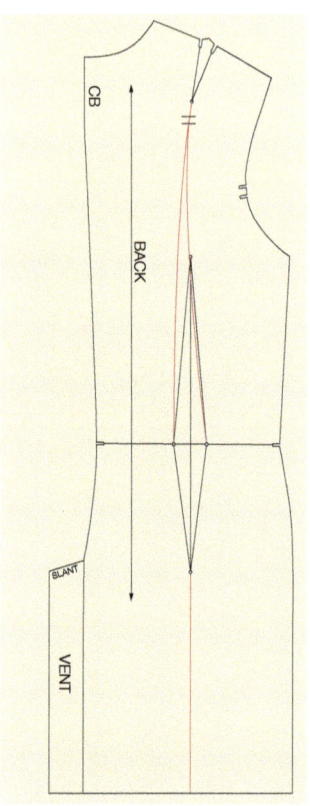

1. Extend line (red line) to hem through center of contour dart.
2. Starting at tip of shoulder dart, draw desired curve (red curve) for princess line, shifting the top contour dart point up and over if necessary.
3. Mark a double-notch where style-lines meet.
   Note: It is fine if the new lines are a bit wider than the original contour dart.

| THE HISTORY OF THE TUXEDO | CONTEMPORARY TUXEDOS | THE PATTERN | MUSLIN OR TOILE FITTING | PRODUCTION PATTERN | TECHNICAL FLATS AND FINISHED PATTERN PIECES |

Welt pocket with flap placement

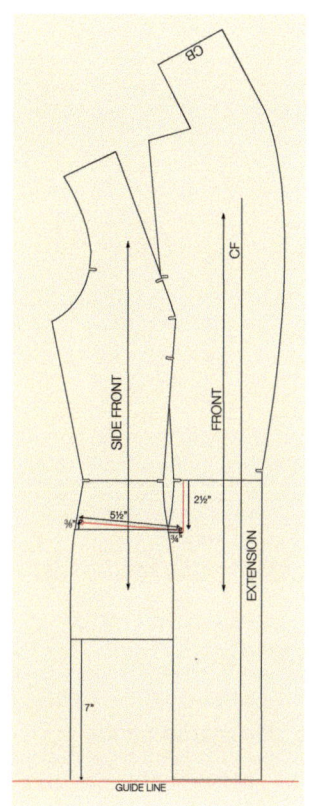

4. Mark grainline on side back perpendicular to waist.

5. Cut back and side back pieces apart making sure to cut out the darts.

6. Smooth out any areas if they look too pointy or uneven.

7. Walk the pattern with an awl starting at the waist; adjust pattern as needed to balance style-line at shoulder and hem.

1. Draw a horizontal guideline (red line) on paper.

2. Place the front pattern on guideline.

3. Measure 2 ½ inches (6.2cm) down from front dart at waistline and ¾ inch (1.75cm) towards CF and draw a line parallel to waist.

4. Place side panel on horizontal guideline with patterns touching where line is drawn.

5. Draw a new line (red line) 5 ½ inches (13.7cm) long, raising it ⅜ inch (1cm) towards the waist at side seam (this will give the illusion of the pocket being straight).

6. Circle and drill ⅛ inch (6mm) into the pocket.
   Note: Make sure the pocket ends at least ½ inch (2.5cm) from side seam; adjust pocket size if necessary.

MUSLIN OR TOILE FITTING

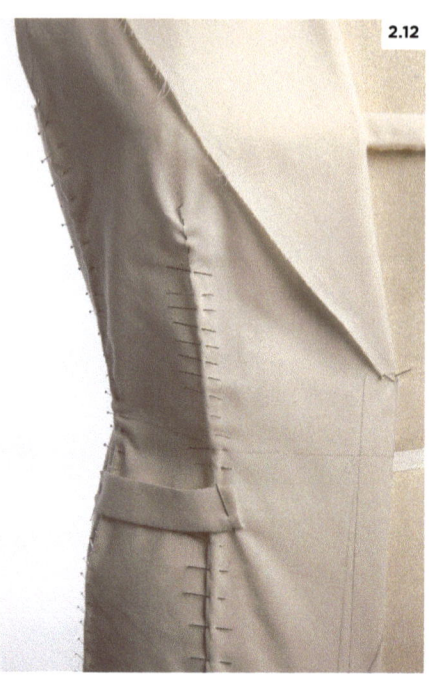

- Before you draft the facing, pocket, and lining patterns, prepare a muslin for fit.

- Do not add seam allowance (SA) to pattern as you will most likely be adjusting the muslin for fit.

- Trace the jacket 2-piece sleeve block for the muslin.

- Draw the seam allowance (SA) directly onto the muslin after tracing the working pattern.

- Make any necessary fit corrections to pattern.

- Now you can move on to the facing, pocket, and lining patterns.

2.10 Checking muslin for fit.
2.11 Shawl collar detail.
2.12 Pinning detail.

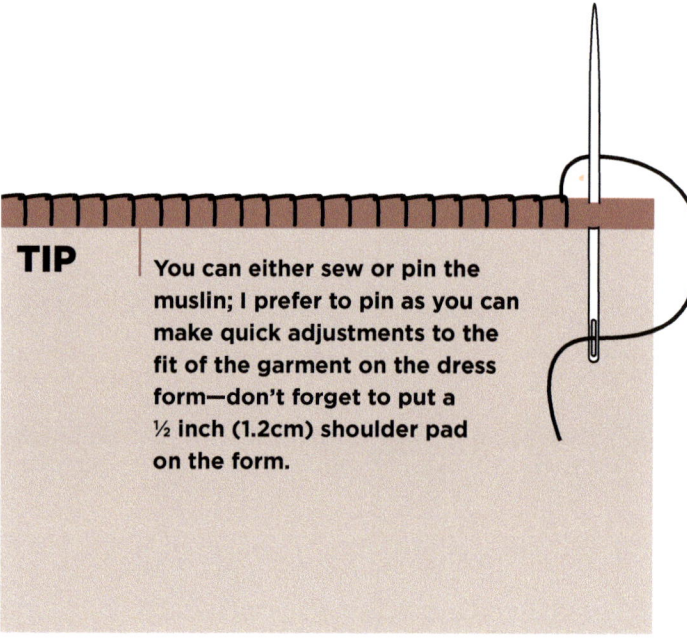

TIP You can either sew or pin the muslin; I prefer to pin as you can make quick adjustments to the fit of the garment on the dress form—don't forget to put a ½ inch (1.2cm) shoulder pad on the form.

Front facing

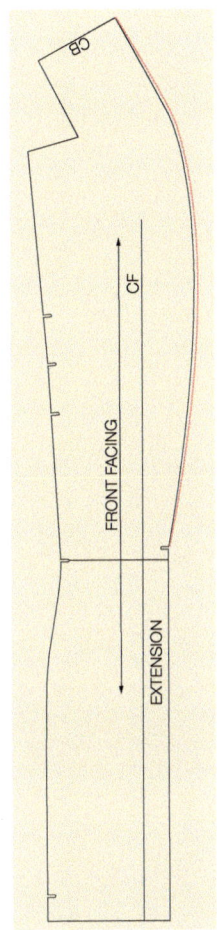

Back facing

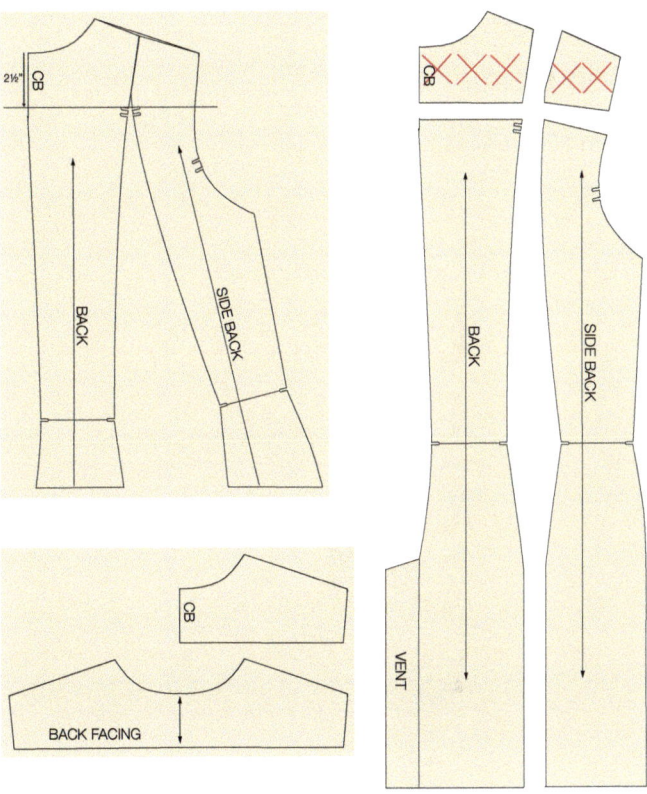

1. Trace front pattern.

2. Add ⅛ inch blending from breakpoint to edge of lapel at CB (red dotted line).

3. Mark notches 2 inches (5cm) above and 2 inches (5cm) below bust point (apex) and 1 inch (2.5cm) up from hem.
   Note: This is so lapel can be pressed under the ⅛ inch (3mm) so the stitching line does not show on the garment.

1. Place back and side back pattern pieces together so they line up at shoulder.

2. Square a 2 ½ inch (6.2cm) line down from CB neckline.

3. Trace pattern above this line; this becomes your back facing.

4. Fold pattern paper in half and trace back facing pattern; set aside.

5. Cut out and discard top of back and side back patterns; the remaining patterns will be developed into your lining pieces.

**CHAPTER TWO:
THE TUXEDO**

Left and right back lining

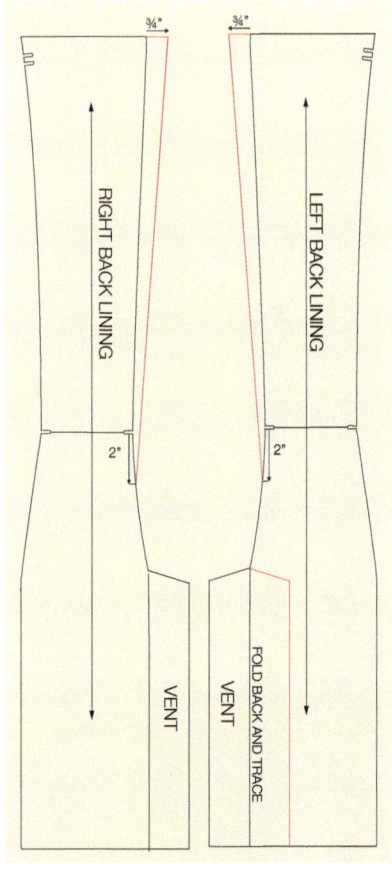
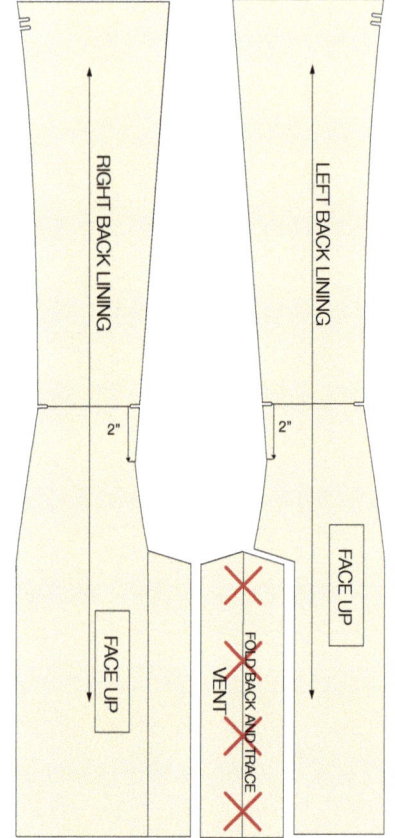

1. Trace remaining back piece, turn over and trace again.

2. Create an action pleat down the CB on both patterns by drawing a straight line 2 inches (5cm) down from CB waistline and ¾ inch (1.75cm) out from top of lining piece; notch.

3. Right back lining piece remains the same.

4. For left back lining, fold pattern back at vent fold line and trace.

5. Cut out vent piece and discard as shown.

6. Write "face-up" on both pattern pieces.

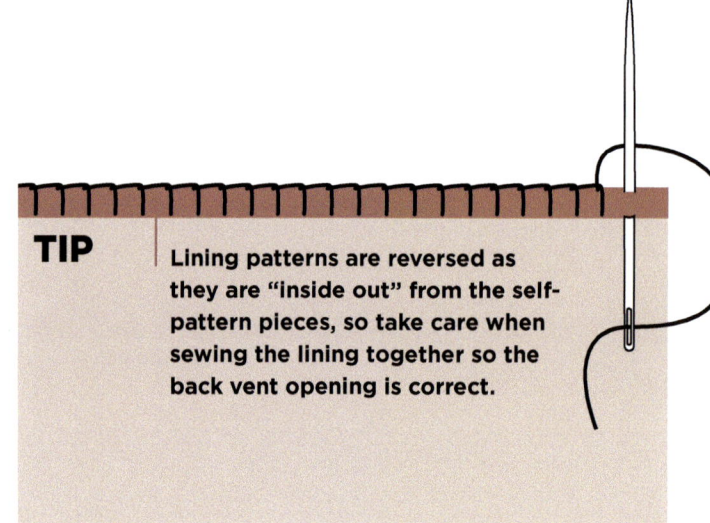

TIP | Lining patterns are reversed as they are "inside out" from the self-pattern pieces, so take care when sewing the lining together so the back vent opening is correct.

Side back and side front lining

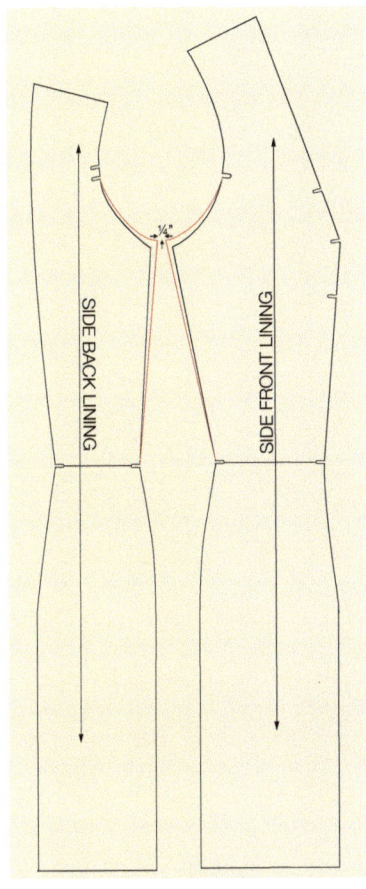

1. Starting at waistline—draw a line (red line) up and out and up ¼ inch (6mm) to allow for ease in the lining pieces.
2. Blend (red curve) to armhole notches.

Upper and under-sleeve lining

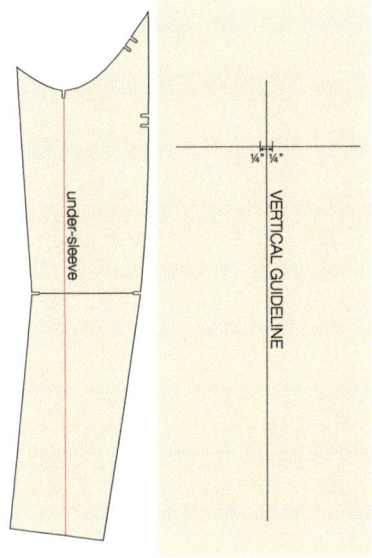

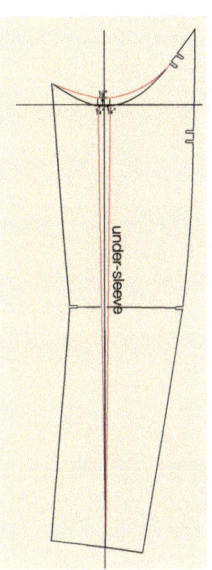

1. Trace upper-sleeve pattern and set aside.
2. Trace under-sleeve pattern and cut out.
3. Square a slash-line (red line) down from under-arm notch to hem and cut to—not through to—hem.
4. On paper, draw a vertical guideline; mark out ¼ inch (6mm) on either side of the guideline.
5. Place side panel on the guideline and spread open to meet the marks, tape down and trace pattern.
6. At new under-arm notch, mark up ¼ inch (6mm) and blend to front edge and back notches (red curve).

Note: The guideline becomes your new grainline and under-arm notch.

CHAPTER TWO:
THE TUXEDO

PRODUCTION PATTERN

Seam allowances and hems

Front pattern seam allowance and hem

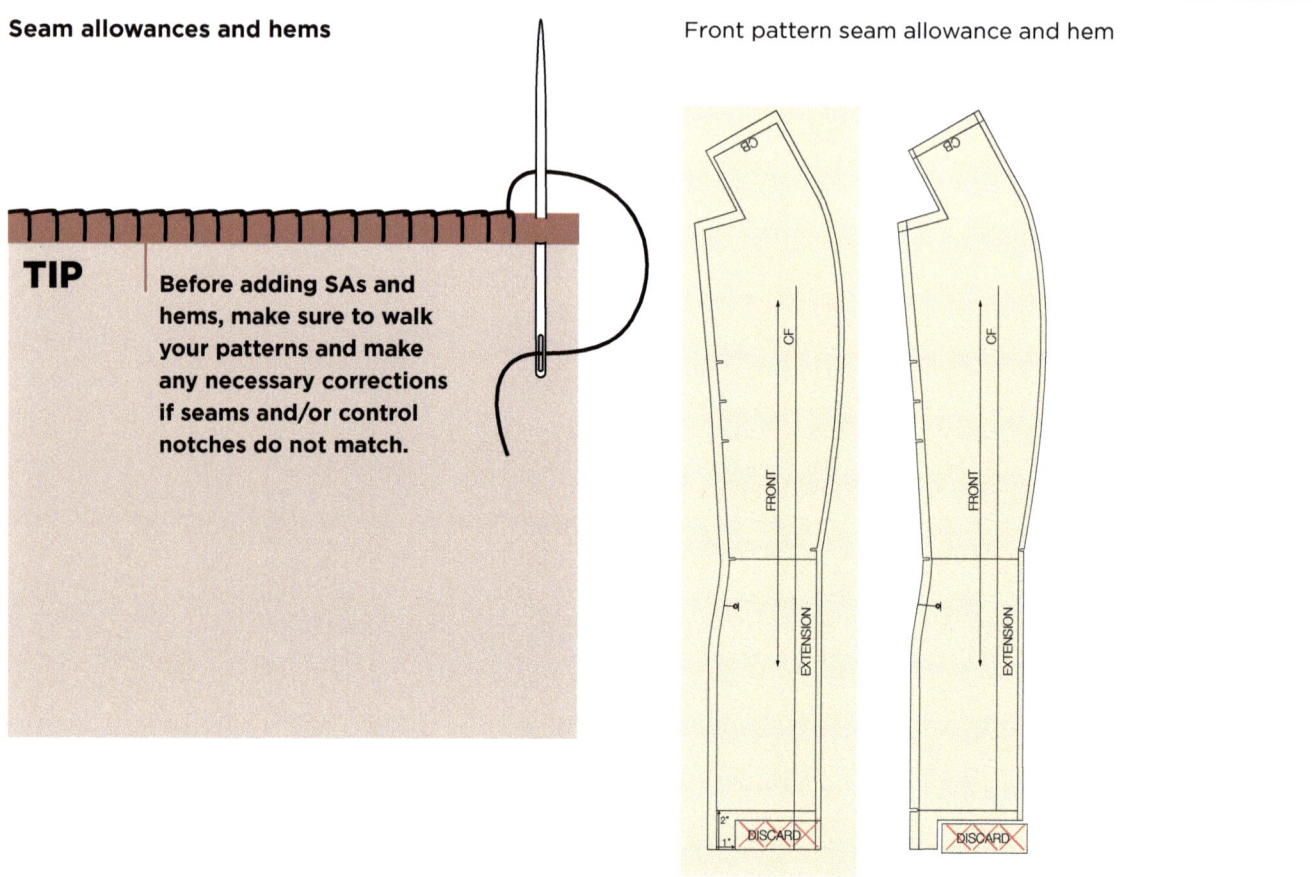

TIP | Before adding SAs and hems, make sure to walk your patterns and make any necessary corrections if seams and/or control notches do not match.

1. Trace front pattern.

2. Add ½ inch (1.2cm) SA to all seams with the exception of the front, neckline, and hem.

3. Add ¼ inch (6mm) SA to the front and neckline.

4. Mark hem 2 inches (5cm); this includes the ½ inch (1.2cm) SA.

5. Measure 1 inch (2.5cm) in from side seam and square down to hem.

6. Measure ½ inch (1.2cm) down from original hem and draw line to squared line.
   Note: You will discard this "wedge" when cutting out the pattern.

| THE HISTORY OF THE TUXEDO | CONTEMPORARY TUXEDOS | THE PATTERN | MUSLIN OR TOILE FITTING | **PRODUCTION PATTERN** | TECHNICAL FLATS AND FINISHED PATTERN PIECES |

Back, side back, and side front seam allowance and hems

Sleeve patterns seam allowance and hems

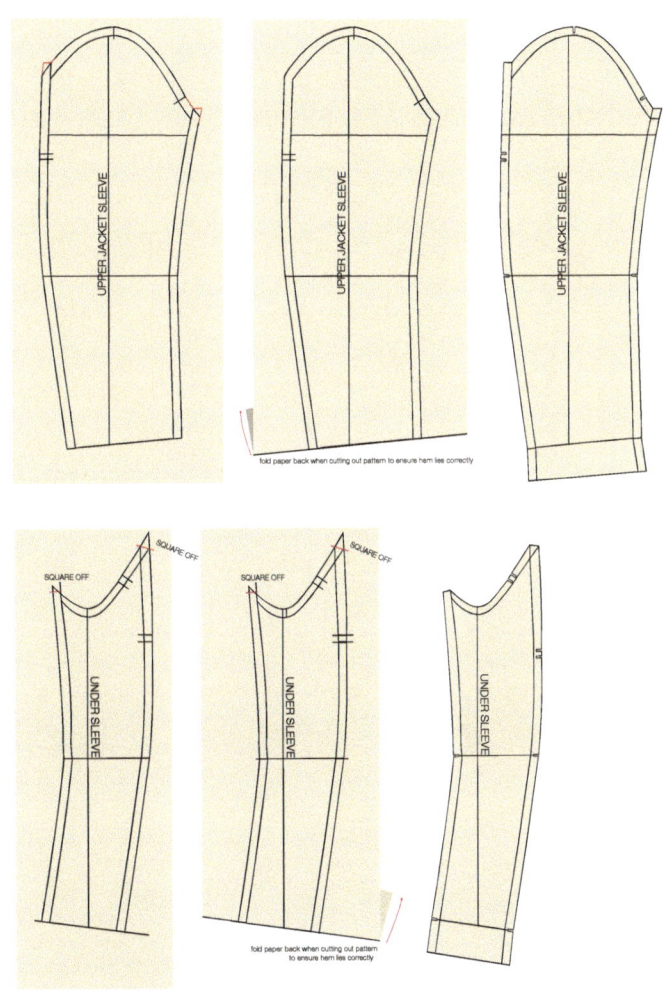

1. Add ½ inch (1.2cm) SA to all seams with the exception of the back neckline, vent, and hems.
2. Add ¼ inch (6mm) SA to back neckline and vent.
3. Mark hems 2 inches (5cm); this includes the ½ inch (1.2cm) SA.

1. Add ½ inch (1.2cm) SA to all seams with the exception of the hem.
2. Mark hems 2 inches (5cm); this includes the ½ inch (1.2cm) SA.
   Note: Make sure to fold paper back at hemline when cutting out to ensure the hem lies correctly on garment.

**CHAPTER TWO:
THE TUXEDO**

Front and back facing seam allowance

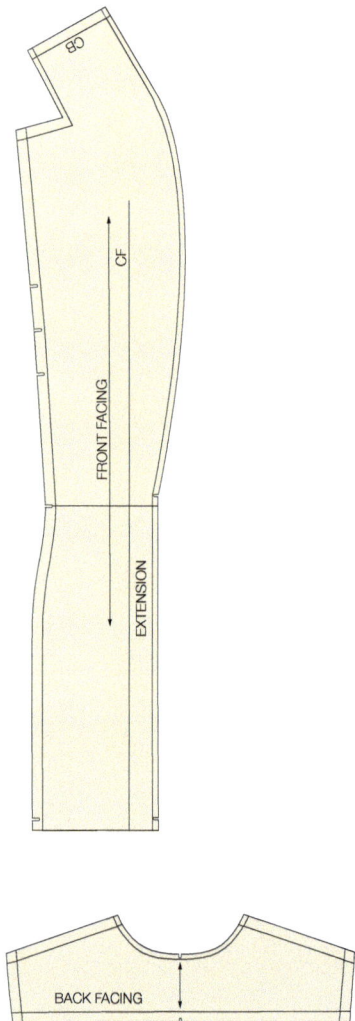

Back, side back, side front, and sleeve linings seam allowance and hems

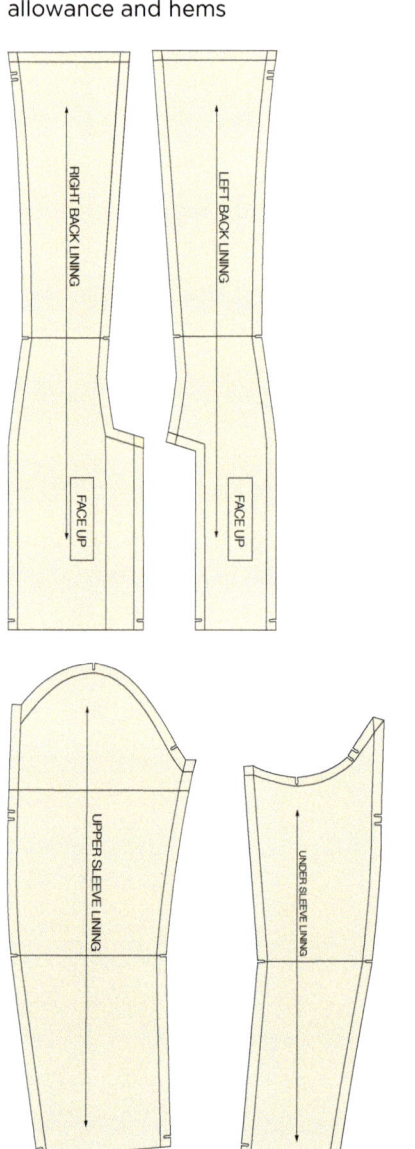

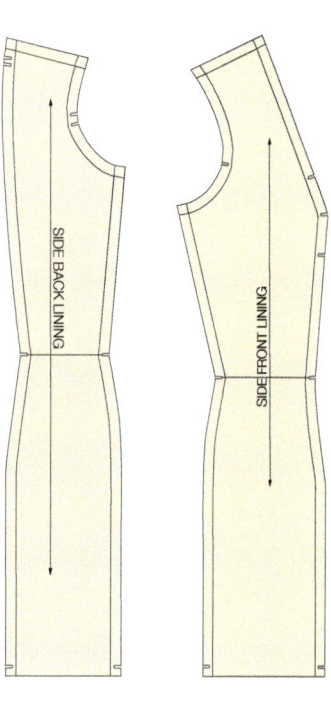

1. Add ¼ inch (6mm) SA to back and front necklines and down CF.
2. Add ½ inch (1.2cm) SA to all other seams.

1. Add ½ inch (1.2cm) SA to all seams with the exception of the hem.

2. You do not add a SA to the hem as it is already "built in"; mark and notch up ½ inch (1.2cm).

				PRODUCTION PATTERN	TECHNICAL FLATS AND FINISHED PATTERN PIECES
THE HISTORY OF THE TUXEDO	CONTEMPORARY TUXEDOS	THE PATTERN	MUSLIN OR TOILE FITTING		

Welt pocket with flap

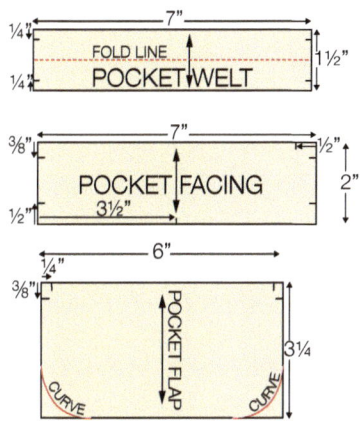

Pocket lining

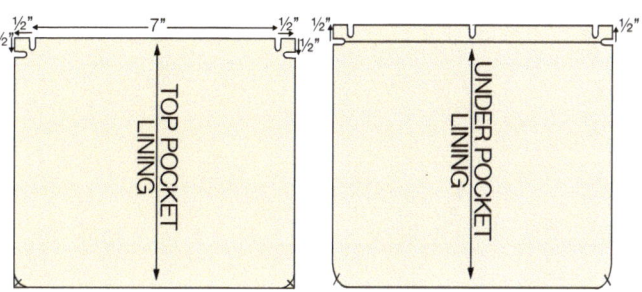

1. Pocket welt—square off a rectangle 7 inches (17.5cm) by 1 ½ inches (3.75cm).
   Note: All seam allowances (SA) are included in pocket directions.

2. Mark dotted line (red dotted line) for fold-line at ¾ inch (1.75cm) and notch.

3. Pocket facing—square off a rectangle 7 inches (17.5cm) by 2 inches (5cm).

4. Mark 3 ½ inches (8.75cm) on length of facing and notch.

5. Pocket flap—square off a rectangle 6 inches (15cm) by 3 ¼ inches (8cm).

6. Curve pocket flap at corners to desired shape.

7. Notch all SA as shown.

1. For top-pocket lining, measure the length of the welt, 7 inches (17.5cm).

2. Square down 6 inches (15cm) for the pocket depth.
   Note: This measurement can be changed depending on how deep you want your pocket to be, but make sure that the pocket is at least 1 inch (2.5cm) shorter than the finished hem of the jacket.

3. Curve pocket bag at corners and place a control notch on the curve.

4. For under-pocket bag, trace top-pocket bag and add ½ inch (1.2cm) to the length of the bag.

5. Notch under-pocket bag as shown (under-pocket will be sewn to pocket facing).

6. Notch all SA as shown.

TIP The depth of the pocket can be changed depending on how deep you want it to be, but make sure that the pocket is at least 1 inch (2.5cm) shorter than the finished hem of the jacket.

**CHAPTER TWO:
THE TUXEDO**

TECHNICAL FLATS AND FINISHED PATTERN PIECES

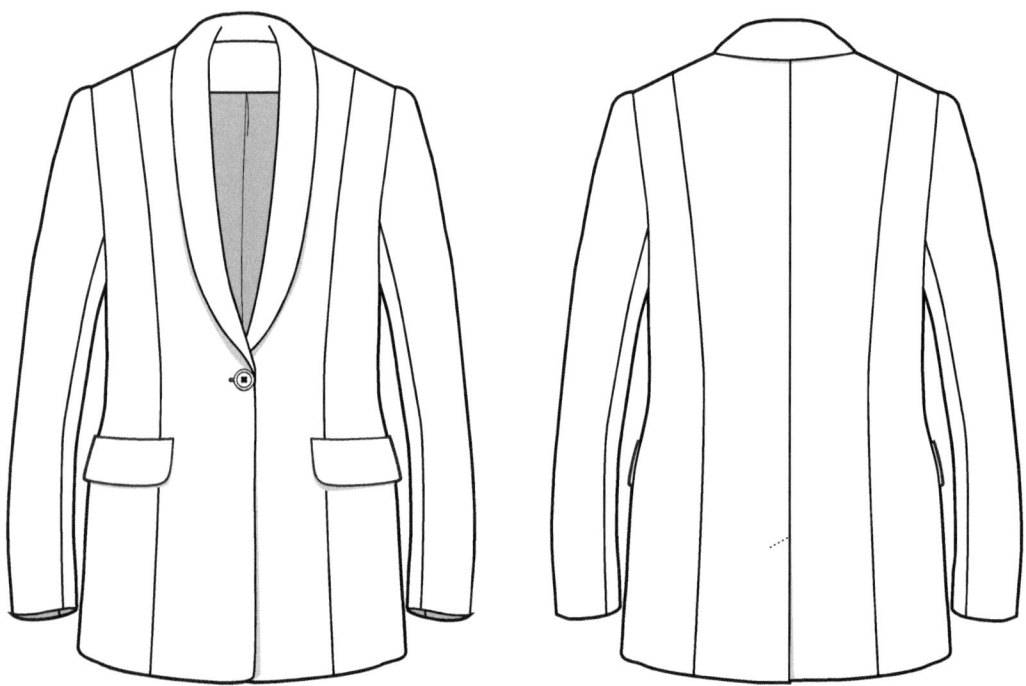

Self:

1. Front (cut 2).
2. Side front (cut 2).
3. Back (cut 2).
4. Side back (cut 2).
5. Upper-sleeve (cut 2).
6. Under-sleeve (cut 2).
7. Front facing (cut 2).
8. Back facing (cut 1).
9. Pocket flap (cut 4).
10. Welt (cut 2).

Lining:

1. Front (cut 2).
2. Side front (cut 2).
3. Left back (cut 1).
4. Right back (cut 1).
5. Side back (cut 2).
6. Upper-sleeve (cut 2).
7. Under-sleeve (cut 2).
8. Top-pocket bag (cut 2).
9. Under-pocket bag (cut 2).

"You can have anything you want if you dress for it."

Edith Head

| THE HISTORY OF THE TUXEDO | CONTEMPORARY TUXEDOS | THE PATTERN | MUSLIN OR TOILE FITTING | PRODUCTION PATTERN | **TECHNICAL FLATS AND FINISHED PATTERN PIECES** |

2.13
Front detail of tuxedo.

CHAPTER THREE

THE MILITARY JACKET

Patterning concepts learned:
- cutaway style-line with faced hem
- armhole princess style-line with front contour dart
- mandarin collar
- 1-piece sleeve with flared cuff

3.1
Designed military jacket front.

THE HISTORY OF THE MILITARY JACKET

Fashion has always been connected with military style. Long before military-inspired garb strutted down the runway, civilian clothing influenced what a soldier wore simply because there was no standard uniform required. The men outfitted themselves in the stylish clothing of the day and frequently tried to outdo each other with elaborate embellishments and colorful fabrics.

In the nineteenth century, the most ostentatious form of regimental dress was the uniform of the Royal Hussars, who were known more for their opulent uniforms adorned with gold braid and buttons than for their fighting. These soldiers were known for their "dandyism" and their uniforms were so stylish it would have been nearly impossible to wage battle while wearing them.

With few exceptions, standardized uniforms didn't have a place in the military until the reign of Louis XIV. With the formation of standing armies, matching uniforms were essential to help identify the enemy on the battlefield.

It was not until the early twentieth century and the introduction of camouflage uniforms that function took the place of fashion on the battlefield, with embellished dress uniforms being regulated for formal occasions only.

3.2
Painting of English explorer Captain James Cook, 1775–1776, wearing captain's full-dress uniform.

"Knowledge speaks, but wisdom listens."

Jimi Hendrix

| THE HISTORY OF THE MILITARY JACKET | CONTEMPORARY MILITARY JACKETS | THE PATTERN | MUSLIN OR TOILE FITTING | PRODUCTION PATTERN | TECHNICAL FLATS AND FINISHED PATTERN PIECES |

3.3
Colonel of the 10th Hussars, H.R.H. the Prince of Wales, George Frederick Ernest Albert, later King George V, c. 1800.

3.4
Jimi Hendrix at Monterey Pop Festival, June, 1967, wearing his vintage Royal Hussar jacket.

3.5
Chris Martin of Coldplay performs in concert, 2008, during the period of their album *Viva La Vida*. The colorful military style jacket was one of a series worn by Chris Martin and was inspired by the painting *La Liberté guidant le peuple* by Eugène Delacroix.

So, when did wearing military jackets become cool? Fast-forward to 1960s London and a little shop on Portobello Road named "I was Lord Kitchener's Valet", which sold vintage military uniforms to civilians. Musicians of the day, including Eric Clapton, John Lennon, Mick Jagger, and Jimmy Hendrix, were all known to shop there.

Jagger purchased a red Grenadier guardsman drummer's jacket and wore it while performing with the Rolling Stones on the television program *Ready Steady Go!*. The fans took notice and lined up around the block the next morning in order to purchase a vintage military piece for themselves.

One of the most iconic images of military style, and adding to the hip-factor, is that of Jimmy Hendrix in 1967 performing bare-chested in a vintage Royal Hussar jacket purchased from the boutique. It is also said that the costumes for the cover image of the Beatles' *Sgt. Pepper's Lonely Hearts Club Band* album were inspired by the merchandise on display at the shop.

Fashion designers quickly got on board and started showing military-inspired pieces in their collections, with musicians helping to keep the look popular for generations to come.

73

CHAPTER THREE:
THE MILITARY JACKET

CONTEMPORARY MILITARY JACKETS

3.6
Gucci: Runway, Milan Fashion Week
Womenswear Spring/Summer 2015.

3.7
Ulyana Sergeenko: Runway,
Paris Fashion Week Haute Couture Fall/Winter 2012/13.

| THE HISTORY OF THE MILITARY JACKET | **CONTEMPORARY MILITARY JACKETS** | THE PATTERN | MUSLIN OR TOILE FITTING | PRODUCTION PATTERN | TECHNICAL FLATS AND FINISHED PATTERN PIECES |

3.8
Chanel: Runway, Paris Fashion Week Womenswear Fall/Winter 2015/2016.

3.9
Gucci: Runway, Milan Fashion Week Womenswear Spring/Summer 2015.

CHAPTER THREE:
THE MILITARY JACKET

THE PATTERN

Start with basic torso and sleeve blocks

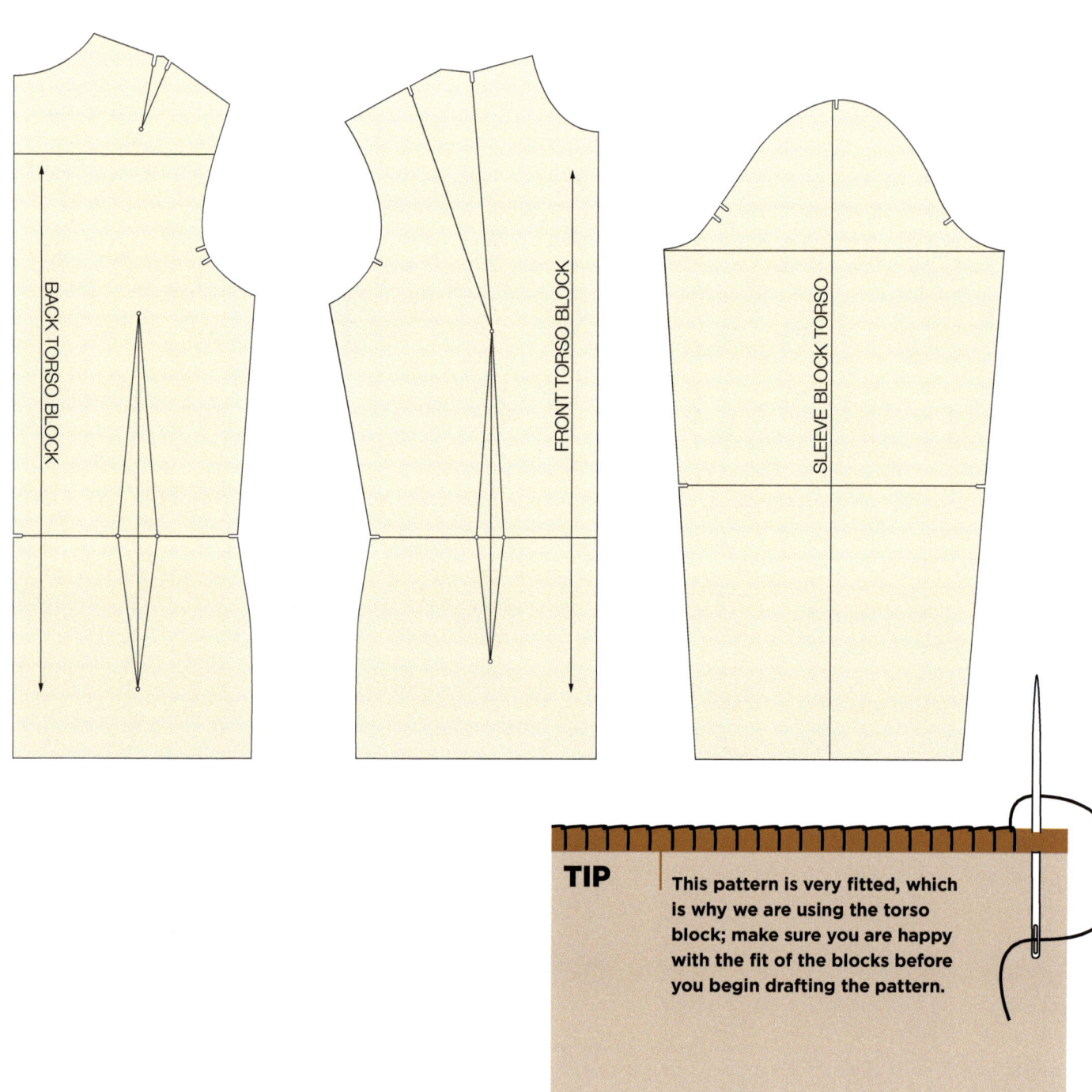

TIP This pattern is very fitted, which is why we are using the torso block; make sure you are happy with the fit of the blocks before you begin drafting the pattern.

| THE HISTORY OF THE MILITARY JACKET | CONTEMPORARY MILITARY JACKETS | **THE PATTERN** | MUSLIN OR TOILE FITTING | PRODUCTION PATTERN | TECHNICAL FLATS AND FINISHED PATTERN PIECES |

Lengthen pattern and lower neckline

Temporarily move front shoulder dart to side seam

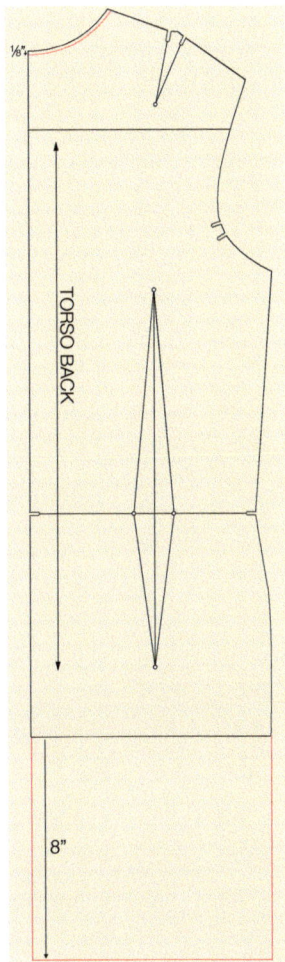
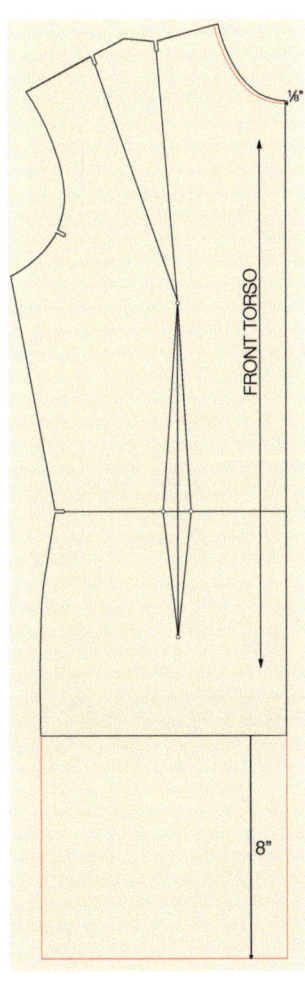
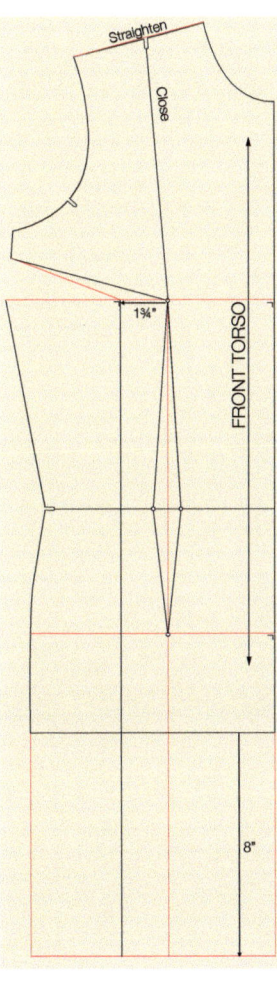

1. Trace front and back patterns.
2. Lengthen torso 8 inches (20cm).
3. Lower front and back neckline ⅛ inch (3mm).
4. Redraw necklines (red dotted lines) using a French curve.
5. Measure front neckline, record _____.
6. Measure back neckline, record _____.

1. Temporarily move shoulder dart to side seam using the slash and spread method.
2. Square a slash line (red line) perpendicular to the center front, passing through the apex (bust point) to the side seam.
3. Cut slash line to the edge of the apex.
4. Cut shoulder dart leg to the edge of the bust point (apex).
5. Close shoulder dart and tape shut.
6. Move bust point in 1 ¾ inch (4.25cm) and redraw dart legs (red).
7. Square a line (red line) perpendicular to the center front, passing through the bottom contour dart point.
8. Square a line perpendicular to the center front from new bust point to hemline.
9. Extend contour dart center line (red line) to the hemline.
10. Straighten shoulder seam (red line) if necessary.

Divide front contour dart and adjust for shoulder pad

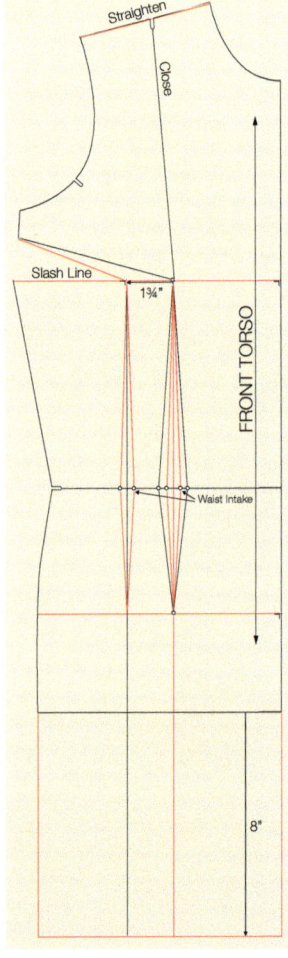 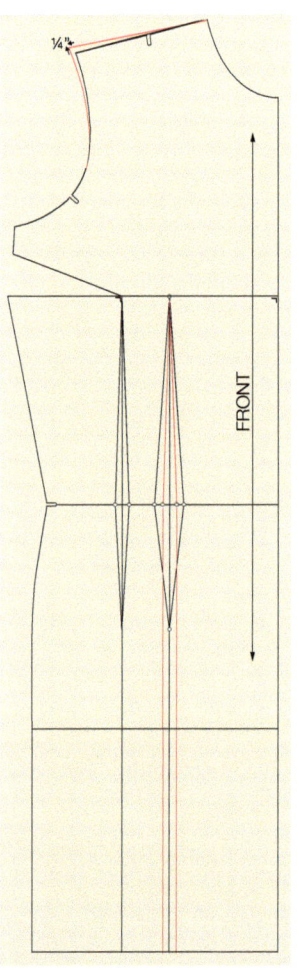

1. Measure contour dart intake at waist, record_____.
2. Divide dart intake in two and reduce this amount on the existing dart by decreasing ½ of this measurement on both sides of the dart intake at the waist.
3. Draw new dart legs to waist and extend legs to hemline to create an open-ended dart (red).
4. Create a new contour dart (red) using the remaining dart intake.
5. For ½ inch (1.2cm) shoulder pad, raise shoulder (red line) up and out ¼ inch (6mm), record front shoulder measurement_____.
6. True up armhole curve (red curve) with a French curve.

Move back shoulder dart to armhole and adjust for shoulder pad

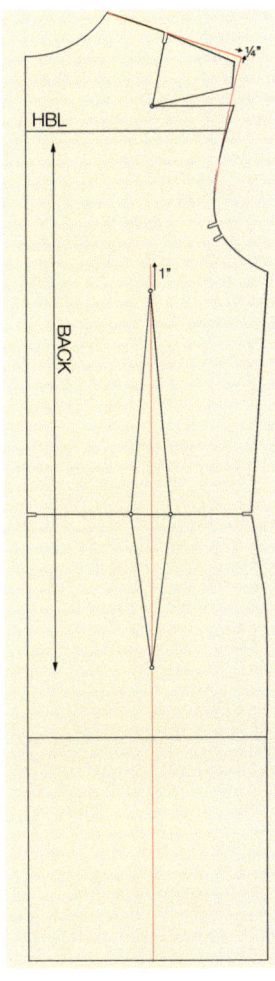

Adjust sleeve for shoulder pad

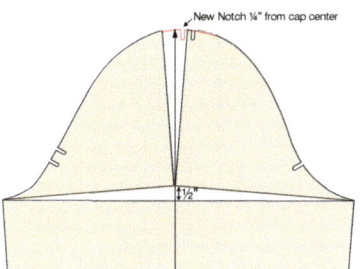

1. For the back block transfer the shoulder dart to the armhole using the slash and spread method.

2. Square a slash line perpendicular to the center back from the shoulder dart point to the armhole.

3. Cut slash line to the edge of the dart point.

4. Cut shoulder dart leg to the edge of the dart point.

5. Close shoulder dart and tape shut.

6. Raise shoulder (red line) up and out ¼ inch (6mm), making sure front and back shoulder measurements are the same.

7. True up armhole curve with French curve.

8. Extend contour dart center line (red line) up 1 inch (2.5cm) from top dart point and continue down to hem.

1. Slash sleeve pattern at center of cap and through biceps line.

2. Lift the pattern up ½ inch (1.2cm) (the size of your shoulder pad) and tape down.

3. True up cap with French curve and re-mark center of cap.

4. Move shoulder notch so it is ¼ inch (6mm) from cap center.

Front princess style-line

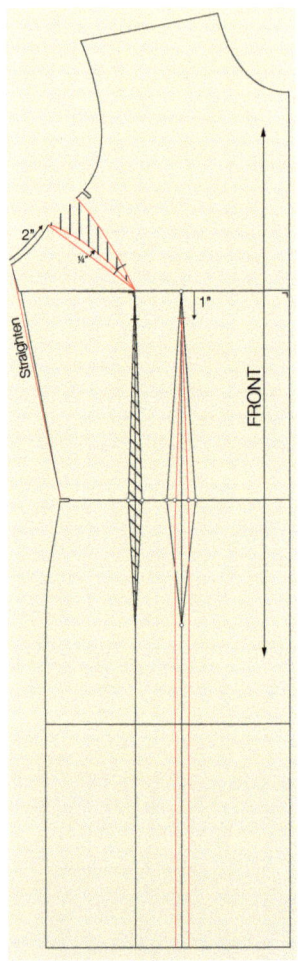
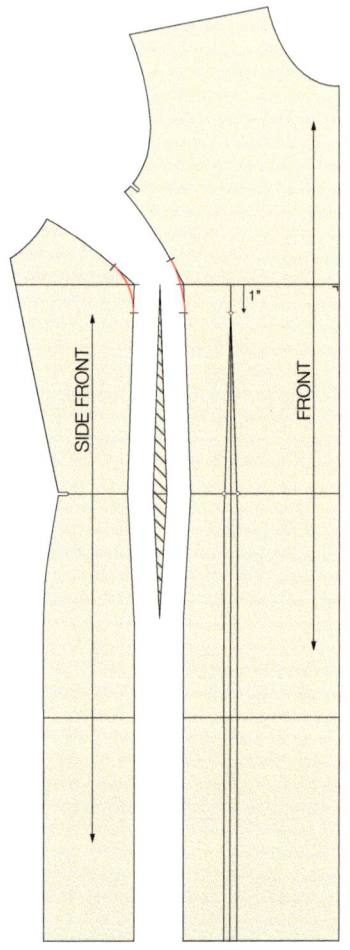

1. Lower open-ended contour dart point 1 inch (2.5cm) and redraw dart legs (red).
2. Draw a straight line (red line) 2 inches (5cm) from armhole.
3. Draw a curved slash line (red curved line) above straight line.
4. Close the temporary armhole dart by using the slash and spread method.
5. Cut curved slash line to the edge of the dart point.
6. Cut dart leg to the edge of the dart point.
7. Close dart and tape shut.
8. Mark control notches 1 inch (2.5cm) above and below dart point.
9. Cut front and side front pieces apart making sure to cut out the darts.
10. Mark grainline for side front pattern perpendicular to waistline.
11. Smooth out the bust-line if it looks too pointy or uneven.
12. Walk the pattern from the waist up and waist down using an awl, adjusting pattern as needed to balance style-line at armhole and hemline.

Armhole princess back

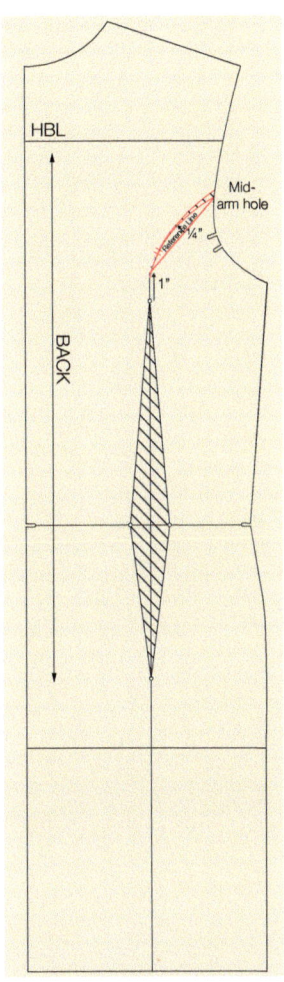 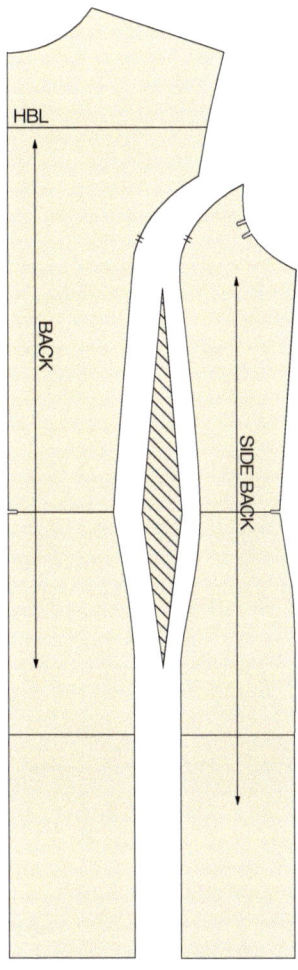 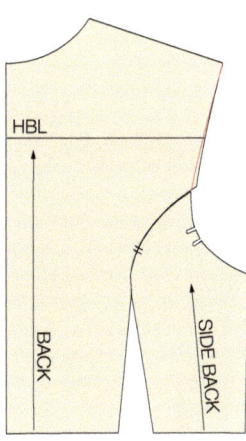

1. Draw a straight line from extended center line of the dart point to mid-armhole (this gives you a reference point for the princess line).
   Note: You can mark this point wherever you like, but remember, the closer to the under-arm, the more curved the princess line will be.

2. Draw a curved line from armhole to dart point; double-notch for back.

3. Draw another curved line ¼ inch (6mm) down from princess line connecting with the original curve equal to the length of the original back shoulder dart.

4. Cut out back and side back patterns making sure to eliminate the darts (shaded area).

5. Smooth out princess style-line if necessary.

6. Walk the pattern from the waist up and the waist down using an awl, adjusting the pattern as needed to balance style-line at armhole and hemline.

Cutaway style-line

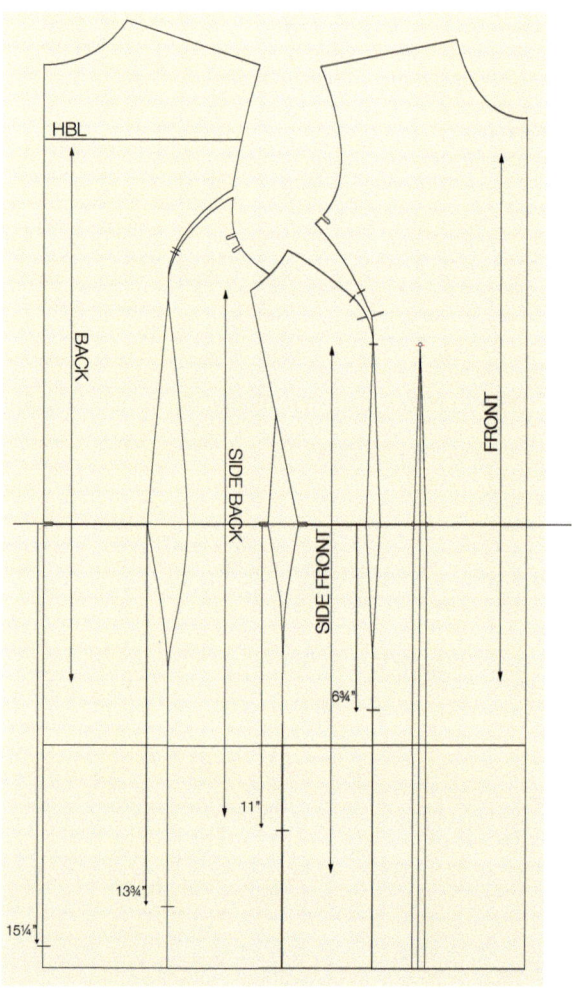

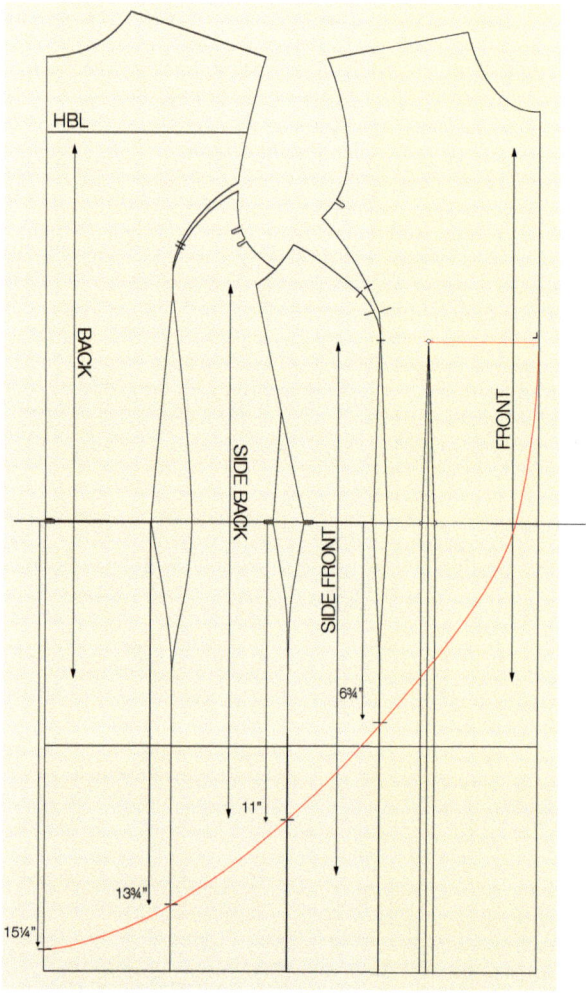

1. Draw a horizontal reference line on pattern paper.
2. Place pattern pieces in order starting at the center back using the reference line as a guide at the waistline and matching patterns up at the hem so they do not overlap. **Note: The patterns will overlap at the top.**

3. Mark the cutaway style-line as shown, squaring off at the center front from the bust point and using the measurements indicated as a guide for the curve.

| THE HISTORY OF THE MILITARY JACKET | CONTEMPORARY MILITARY JACKETS | **THE PATTERN** | MUSLIN OR TOILE FITTING | PRODUCTION PATTERN | TECHNICAL FLATS AND FINISHED PATTERN PIECES |

HBL

BACK | SIDE BACK | SIDE FRONT | FRONT

4. Cut out the cutaway style-line.

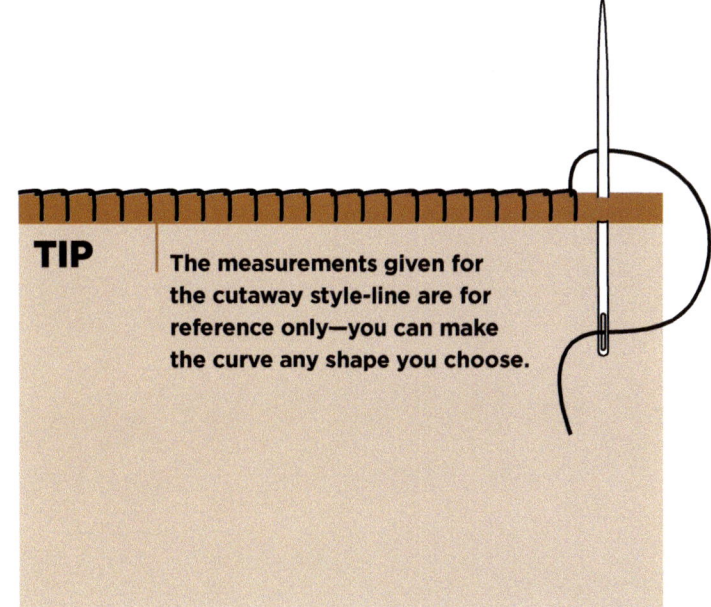

TIP — The measurements given for the cutaway style-line are for reference only—you can make the curve any shape you choose.

Adjusting the front curve

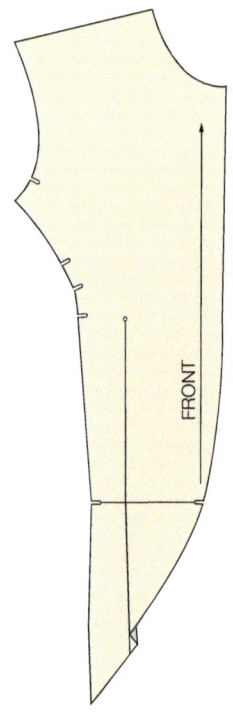
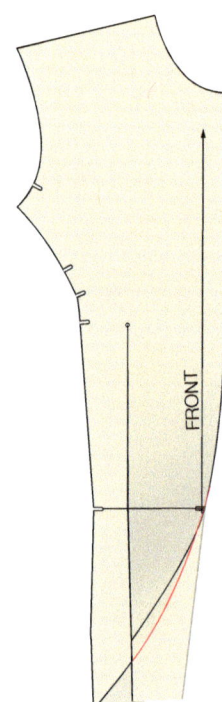
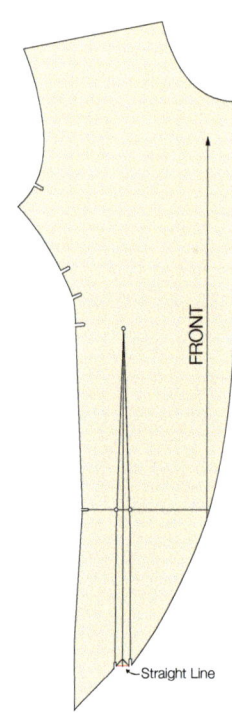

1. On the front pattern, fold the open-ended contour dart towards the center front.

2. The front pattern piece curve needs to be adjusted because of the dart intake.

3. Open the pattern up and tape a piece of paper to the end of the contour dart.

4. Re-fold the dart towards the center front.

5. Draw a new curved line (red curved line) while the paper is still folded.

6. Cut out the new curved line (red curved line) while the paper is still folded.

7. The end of the contour dart will "v" up; draw a straight line and notch dart legs.

Mandarin collar

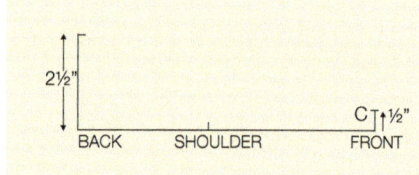
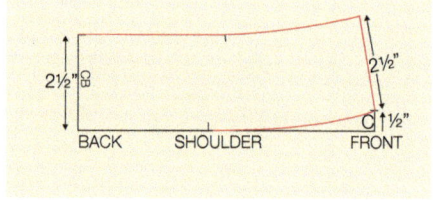

1. Draw a horizontal line equal to the front and back neckline measurement.

2. Mark center back (CB) and center front (CF).

3. Using back neckline measurement mark shoulder S.

4. Square a line 2 ½ inches (3.2cm) up from CB.

5. Square up ½ inch (1.2cm) from CF and label C.

6. Draw a curved line (red curved line) from S to C and square a line (red line) 2 ½ inches (3.2cm) up from C.

7. Draw a line (red line) parallel to the neckline from the CB to the CF to complete the collar.

Sleeve with flared cuff

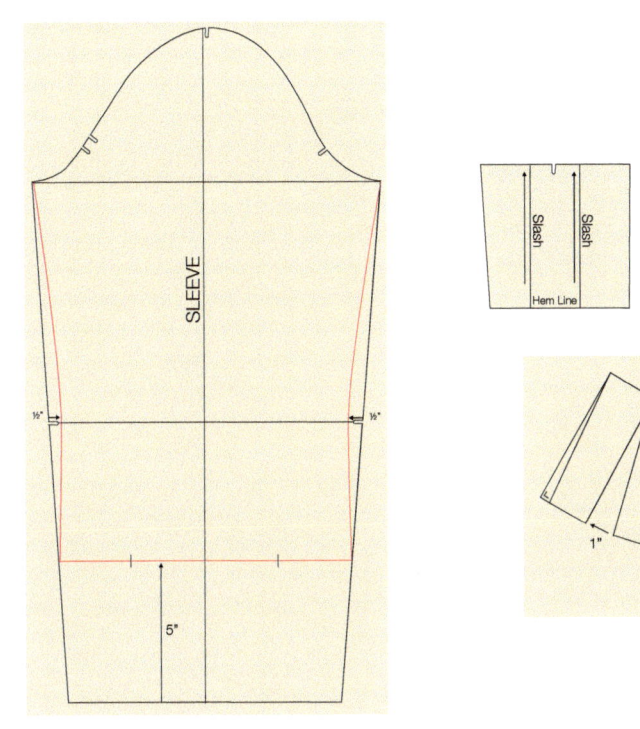
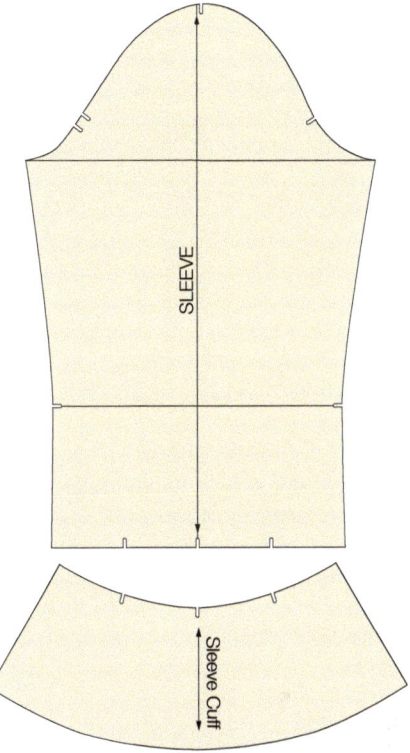

1. Trace sleeve pattern.

2. For flared cuff, measure a line 5 inches (12.5cm) up from hemline.

3. Mark notches at midpoint from center line.

4. Contour top sleeve by marking in ½ inch (1.2cm) at elbow and drawing curved lines (red curved lines) as shown.

5. Cut out cuff and cut in half lengthwise at center line.

6. For flare divide the half cuff into three parts and slash from hemline.

7. Fold pattern paper in half and spread half cuff ½ inch (1.2cm) on fold and 1 inch (2.5cm) on the slashed lines.

8. Square off the corner at hemline.

9. Smooth out curves if needed and cut out, retaining all notches.

MUSLIN OR TOILE FITTING

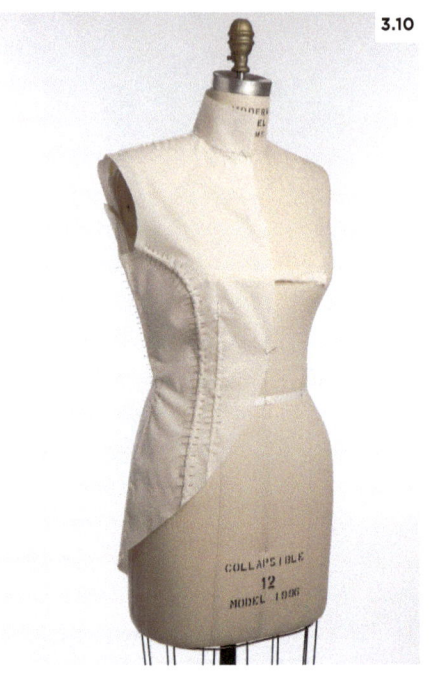  

- Before you draft the facings and lining patterns, prepare a muslin for fit.
- Do not add SAs to pattern as you will most likely be adjusting the muslin for fit—draw the SAs directly onto the muslin.
- Make any necessary fit corrections to pattern.
- Now you can move on to the facings and lining patterns.

3.10 Checking muslin fit before sleeve is added.
3.11 Muslin fit with sleeve added.
3.12 Pinning detail.

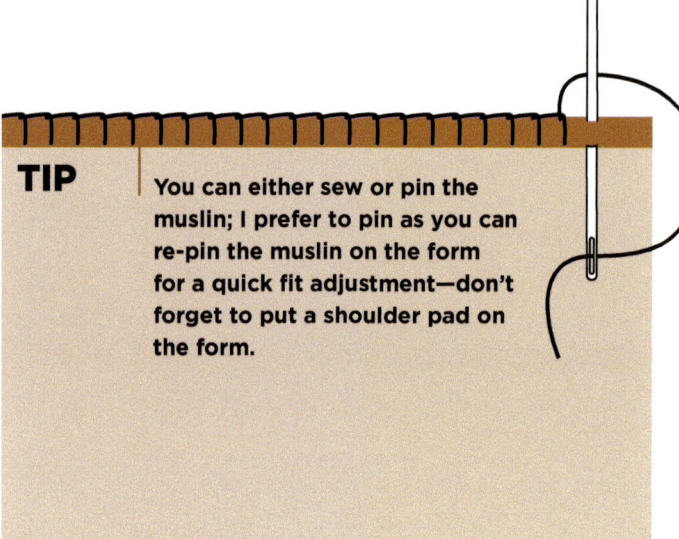

TIP You can either sew or pin the muslin; I prefer to pin as you can re-pin the muslin on the form for a quick fit adjustment—don't forget to put a shoulder pad on the form.

Front facing and side front lining

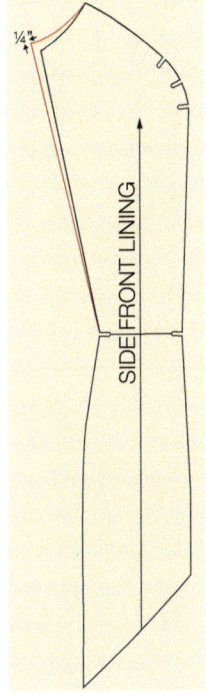
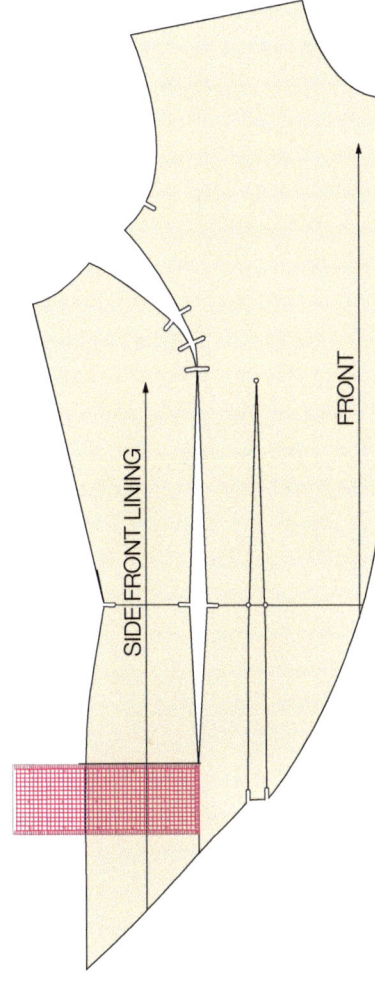

1. Trace front and side front pattern pieces.

2. Starting at waistline on the side front pattern, draw new seam-line (red line) out and up ¼ inch (6mm) to allow for ease in the lining pieces.

3. Blend (red curve) to front princess line.

4. Cut out side front lining piece and align with the front pattern at hemline and trace bottom part of side front pattern.

5. Place a ruler where patterns start to separate and square off from grainline, making sure that the line is marked on both top and bottom patterns.

6. Remove side front lining piece and cut off at squared-off line; discard bottom part of pattern.

7. Draw squared-off line on front facing pattern.

8. Measure side seam length on front facing, record_____.

9. Notch 1 inch (2.5cm) up from squared-off line on both pattern pieces and 2 inches (5cm) down on side seam of front-facing piece.

Back hem facing, back, and side back lining

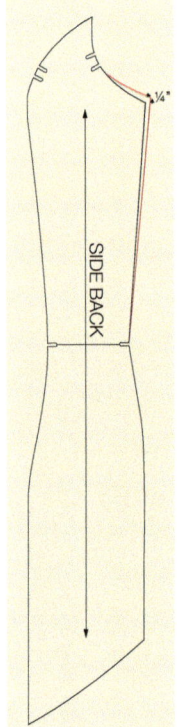
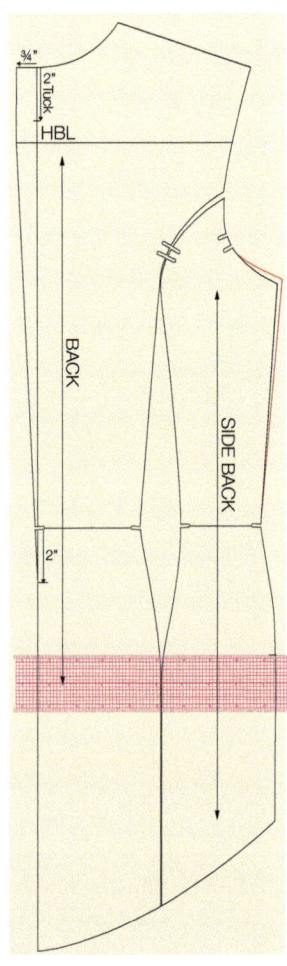
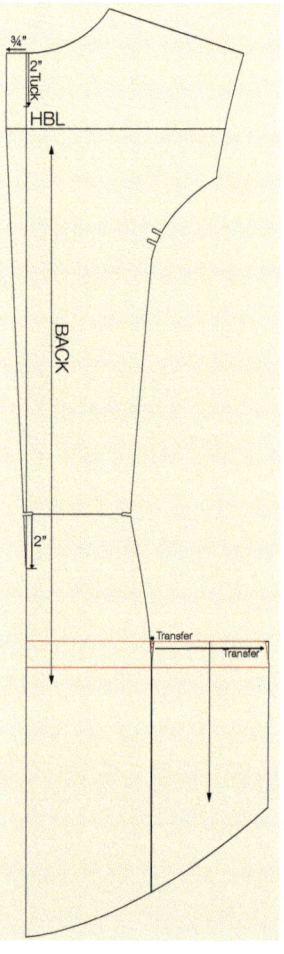

1. Trace back and side back pattern pieces.
2. Starting at waistline on the side back pattern, draw new seam-line (red line) out and up ¼ inch (6mm) to allow for ease in the lining pieces.
3. Blend (red curve) to back armhole notches.
4. Create an action pleat on the back pattern.
5. Mark out ¾ inch (1.75cm) from CB and square down to HBL.
6. Mark 2 inches (5cm) down from waist at CB and continue line to meet HBL.
7. At CB neckline seam, mark 2 inches (5cm) down for tuck.
8. Cut out side back lining piece and align with the back pattern at hemline and trace bottom part of side back pattern.
9. Place a ruler to match front-facing side seam measurement squaring off from center back seam-line, making sure that the line is marked on both top and bottom patterns.
10. Remove side back lining piece and cut off at squared-off line; discard bottom part of pattern.

Sleeve lining

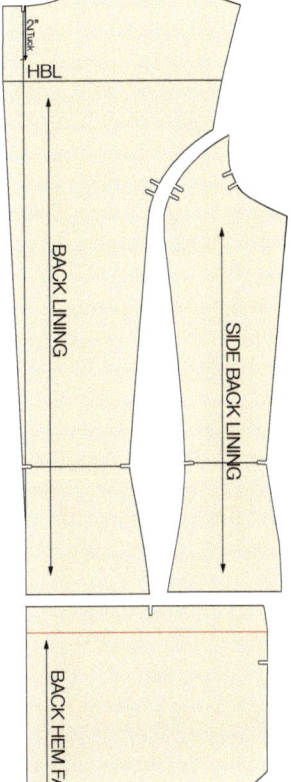

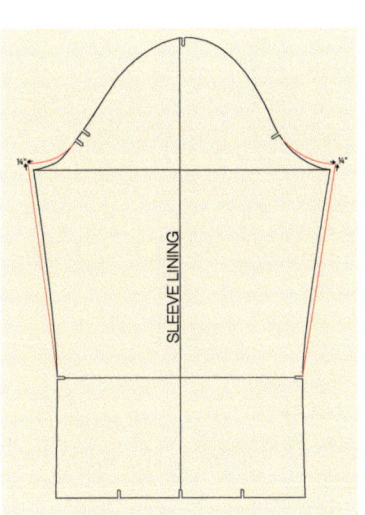

11. Draw the squared-off line on back pattern; there will be a space where the pattern no longer joins—measure the width and length of the space and transfer the measurement to the side seam and smooth line.

12. Notch 2 inches (5cm) down on side seam.
    Note: Grainline does not change, which means you must cut two back lining patterns to allow for the action pleat.

1. Trace top sleeve pattern.

2. Starting at elbow draw out and up ¼ inch (6mm) to allow for ease in the lining pieces.

3. Blend armhole curves to notches.

CHAPTER THREE:
THE MILITARY JACKET

PRODUCTION PATTERN

Seam allowances and hems

TIP
- Before adding SAs and hems make sure to walk your pattern and make any necessary corrections if seams or control notches do not match.
- Now you can make your production pattern.

Mandarin collar seam allowance

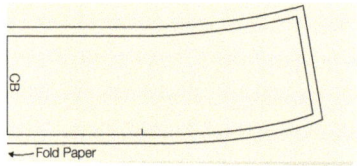

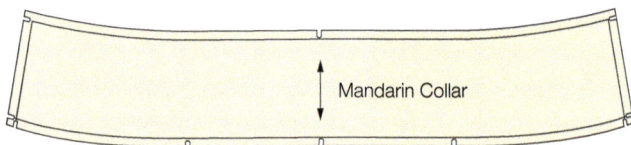

1. Fold paper in half and trace the collar; don't forget to mark your shoulder seam notch.
2. Add ¼ inch (6mm) SA to all seams.
3. Open pattern up and mark CB notch.
4. Mark grainline parallel to CB.
   Note: Mark SAs and cut out pattern while paper is still folded!

Front and front-facing pattern seam allowance

Side back and side front pattern seam allowance

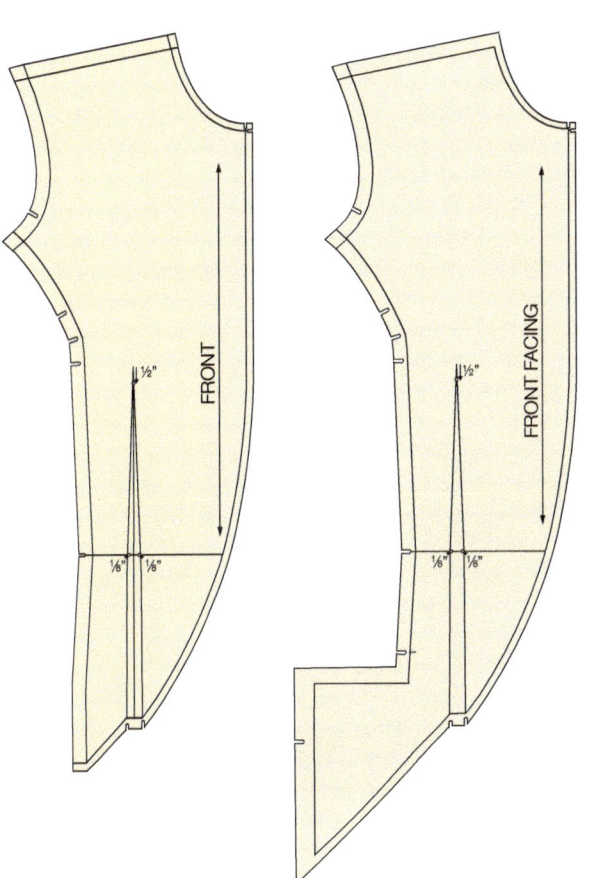
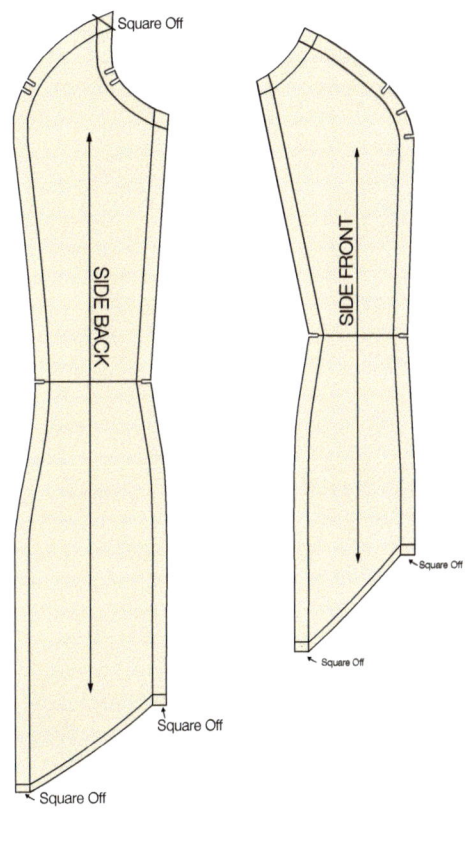

1. Trace front and front-facing patterns.
2. Add ½ inch (1.2cm) SA to all seams with the exception of the front and neckline.
3. Add ¼ inch (6mm) SA to the front and neckline.
4. Circle and drill vertical dart points ½ inch (1.2cm) into the dart and horizontal dart points ⅛ inch (3mm) into the dart.
5. Make sure you square off SAs.

1. Trace side back and side front patterns.
2. Add ½ inch (1.2cm) SA to all seams with the exception of the faced hemline.
3. Add ¼ inch (6mm) SA to the faced hemline curve making sure to square off SA.
   Note: Squaring off SAs ensures precision when sewing.

Back pattern seam allowance

Back hem facing pattern seam allowance

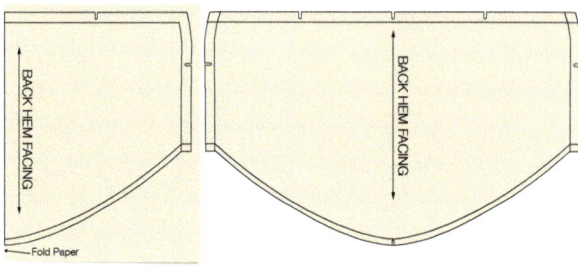

1. Fold pattern paper in half and trace the back pattern.
2. Add ½ inch (1.2cm) SA to all seams with the exception of the back neckline and faced hemline.
3. Add ¼ inch (6mm) SA to the back neckline and faced hemline curve making sure to square off SA.
4. Cut out pattern.
5. Notch pattern while still folded.

1. Fold pattern paper in half and trace the back hem facing pattern.
2. Add ½ inch (1.2cm) SA to all seams with the exception of the faced hemline curve.
3. Add ¼ inch (6mm) SA to the back hemline curve making sure to square off SA.
4. Cut out pattern.
5. Notch pattern while still folded.

| THE HISTORY OF THE MILITARY JACKET | CONTEMPORARY MILITARY JACKETS | THE PATTERN | MUSLIN OR TOILE FITTING | **PRODUCTION PATTERN** | TECHNICAL FLATS AND FINISHED PATTERN PIECES |

Top sleeve and sleeve cuff pattern seam allowance

Back, side back, side front, and sleeve lining pattern seam allowance and hem

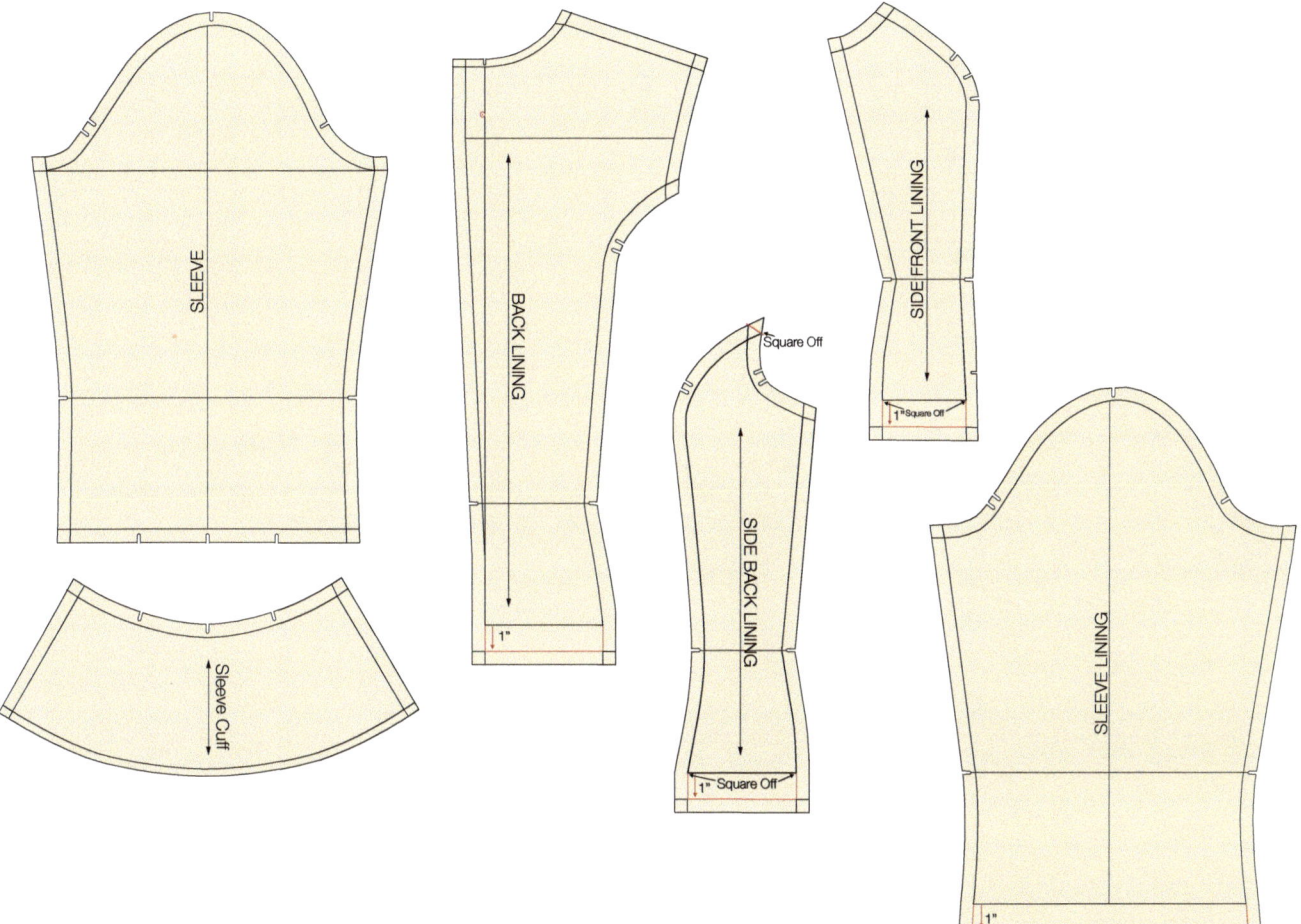

1. Add ½ inch (1.2cm) SA to top sleeve.
2. Add ½ inch (1.2cm) SA to sleeve cuff with the exception of the hemline.
3. Add ¼ inch (6mm) SA to hemline.

1. Add ½ inch (1.2cm) SA to all seams with the exception of the back neckline and hem.
2. Add ¼ inch (6mm) SA to the back neckline.

3. Circle and drill ⅛ inch (3mm) into the tuck.
4. Add 1 inch (2.5cm) ease to all hems plus ½ inch (1.2cm) SA. **Note: You need to add the 1 inch (2.5cm) of ease to the hemline because the patterns are faced and there is no hem uptake; this ease prevents the lining from "riding up" so the garment will hang properly.**

**CHAPTER THREE:
THE MILITARY JACKET**

TECHNICAL FLATS AND FINISHED PATTERN PIECES

Self:

1. Front (cut 2).
2. Side front (cut 2).
3. Back (cut 1).
4. Side back (cut 2).
5. Sleeve (cut 2).
6. Sleeve cuff (cut 4).
7. Mandarin collar (cut 2).
8. Front facing (cut 2).
9. Back hem facing (cut 1).

Lining:

1. Side front (cut 2).
2. Back (cut 2).
3. Side back (cut 2).
4. Sleeve (cut 2).

"Vain trifles as they seem, clothes have, they say, more important offices than to merely keep us warm. They change our view of the world and the world's view of us."

Virginia Woolf, *Orlando*

| THE HISTORY OF THE MILITARY JACKET | CONTEMPORARY MILITARY JACKETS | THE PATTERN | MUSLIN OR TOILE FITTING | PRODUCTION PATTERN | **TECHNICAL FLATS AND FINISHED PATTERN PIECES** |

3.13
Front detail of military jacket.

CHAPTER FOUR

THE MOTORCYCLE JACKET

Patterning concepts learned:
- asymmetrical exposed front zipper closure
- convertible collar
- armhole princess style-line
- 2-piece contoured sleeve
- welt pockets with exposed zippers
- exposed zipper sleeve vent with godet

4.1
Designed military jacket front.

CHAPTER FOUR:
THE MOTORCYCLE JACKET

THE HISTORY OF THE MOTORCYCLE JACKET

The motorcycle jacket has long been associated with youth and rebellion and is synonymous with depicting an outsider image. The Schott Perfecto®, introduced in 1928, was not only the first motorcycle jacket to incorporate zippers into its design, but was also the symbol of defiance for numerous youth movements in both the United States and Great Britain.

Motorcycle clubs existed with little recognition until the summer of 1947 when a group of 4,000 motorcycle enthusiasts rode into Hollister, California for a motorcycle rally and wreaked so much havoc on the town that state troopers had to be called in. *Life* magazine ran a story on the "riot" as it was now being called and referred to these leather-clad men as outlaw bikers.

America's fascination with the motorcycle jacket continued when Hollywood loosely based the 1953 film *The Wild One* starring Marlon Brando on the Hollister riots. Brando's portrayal of the reluctant antihero helped to cement the jacket's outsider image and rebel vibe, which had already begun to take shape in the years following the riots.

Influenced by *The Wild One*, artist Tom of Finland's erotic drawings of S/M gay culture depicted bikers in black leather motorcycle gear. His art not only boosted the subversive image of the jacket, but also helped to dispel common gay stereotypes that were prevalent at the time.

4.2
Marlon Brando in *The Wild One* wearing a Schott Perfecto®, 1953, the first motorcycle jacket to incorporate zippers into its design and a symbol of youth defiance.

"Please bury me next to my baby. Bury me in my leather jacket, jeans, and motorcycle boots. Goodbye."

Sid Vicious

4.3
A gang of Rockers at the Ace Cafe in London, 1963.

4.4
The Ramones, 1970, who helped make the biker jacket a fashion staple of the punk scene.

4.5
Punk rockers in London, 1980, wearing biker jackets, which have become the symbol of punk rock.

Biker jackets became so identified with gangs and hoodlums that they were banned in American high schools in 1955. Add rock and roll to the mix and the motorcycle jacket came to embody the anti-establishment faction even more.

The UK also had its own fascination with the motorcycle jacket. In the 1960s, the Rockers, a youth subculture, known for their clashes with the Mods, had an affinity for 1950s American rock and roll, motorcycles, and wearing their leather motos.

The 1970s and 1980s brought the punk rock movement into the mix. Punk's underground music scene was a backlash against the uninspiring mainstream music that was popular at the time. The motorcycle jacket became a uniform of sorts for bands such as the Ramones, Blondie, the Sex Pistols, and Television, adding a cool factor to the already rebellious image of the jacket.

Today motorcycle jackets have become a fashion staple, but if you dig deep, the spirit of the rebel still remains.

CONTEMPORARY MOTORCYCLE JACKETS

4.6
Yohji Yamamoto: Runway, Paris Fashion Week
Spring/Summer 2015.

4.7
Louis Vuitton: Runway, Paris Fashion Week
Spring/Summer 2016.

| THE HISTORY OF THE MOTORCYCLE JACKET | **CONTEMPORARY MOTORCYCLE JACKETS** | THE PATTERN | MUSLIN OR TOILE FITTING | PRODUCTION PATTERN | TECHNICAL FLATS AND FINISHED PATTERN PIECES |

4.8
Saint Laurent: Runway, Paris Fashion Week Fall/Winter 2015/2016.

4.9
Bouchra Jarrar: Runway, Paris Haute Couture Fashion Week Spring/Summer 2015.

CHAPTER FOUR:
THE MOTORCYCLE JACKET

THE PATTERN

Start with basic torso and 2-piece sleeve blocks

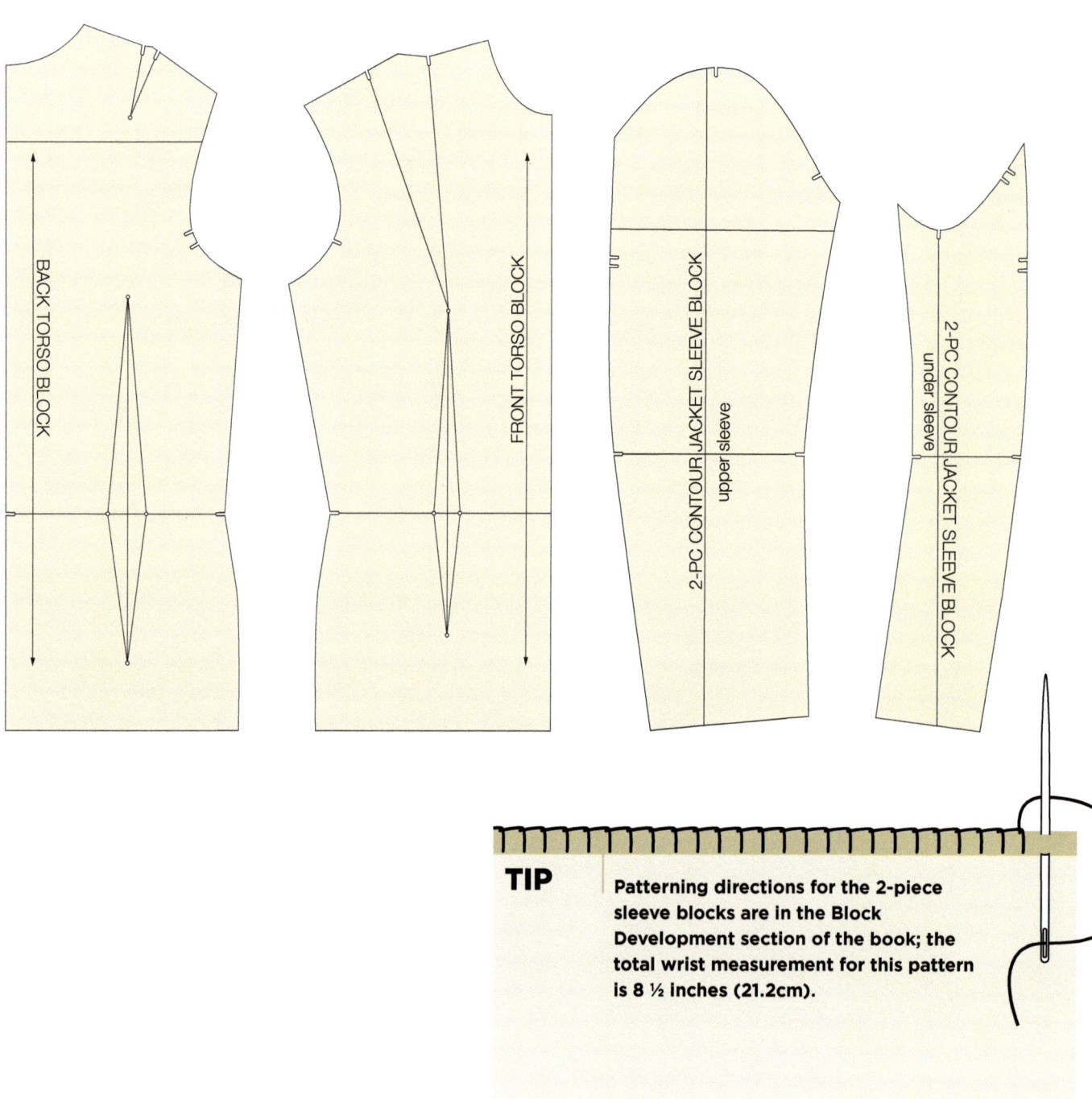

TIP | Patterning directions for the 2-piece sleeve blocks are in the Block Development section of the book; the total wrist measurement for this pattern is 8 ½ inches (21.2cm).

Shorten pattern and lower neckline

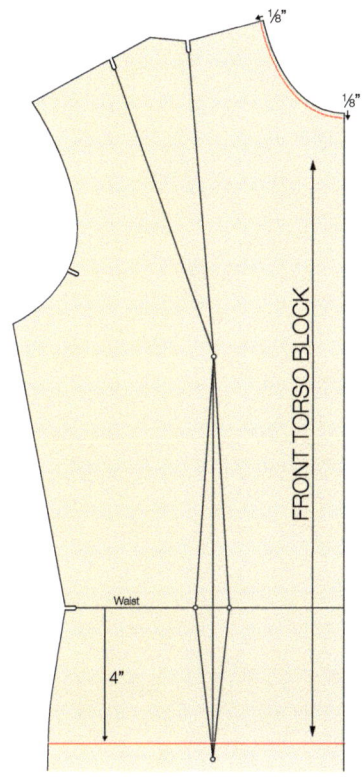
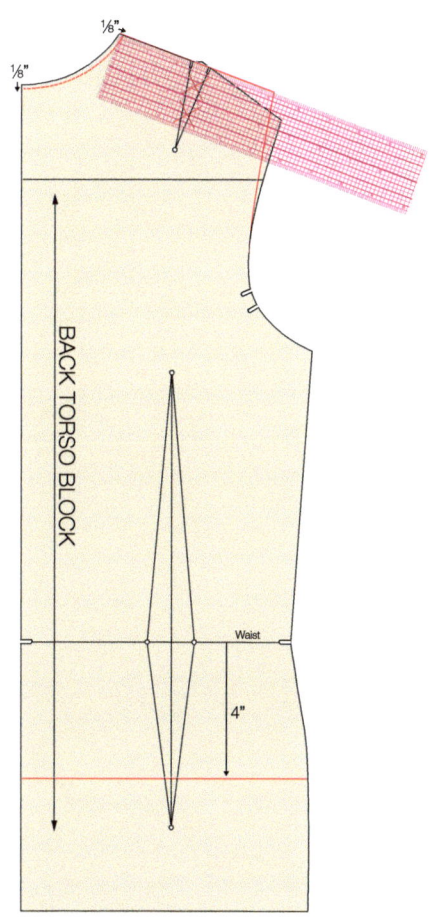

1. Trace front and back patterns.
2. For the back block, you must first eliminate the shoulder dart.
3. Place ruler even with shoulder line at the neckline and draw a straight line.
4. Use the front shoulder measurement and mark the back shoulder to match.
5. True up armhole curve with French curve.
6. Shorten torso 4 inches (10cm).
7. Lower front and back neckline ⅛ inch (3mm).
8. Redraw necklines (red dotted lines) using a French curve.
9. Measure front neckline, record _____.
10. Measure back neckline, record _____.
    Note: You will cut through the contour darts when cropping the pattern.

Armhole princess front

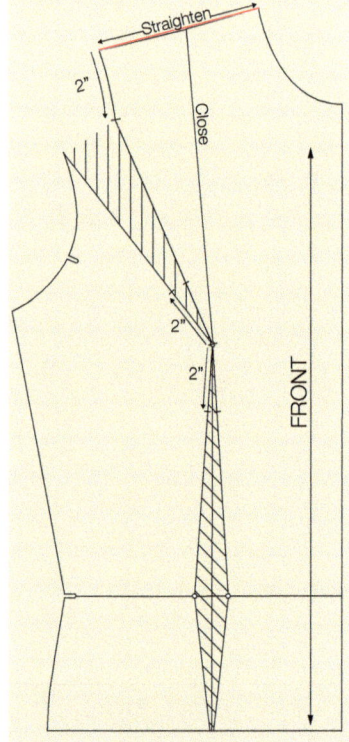
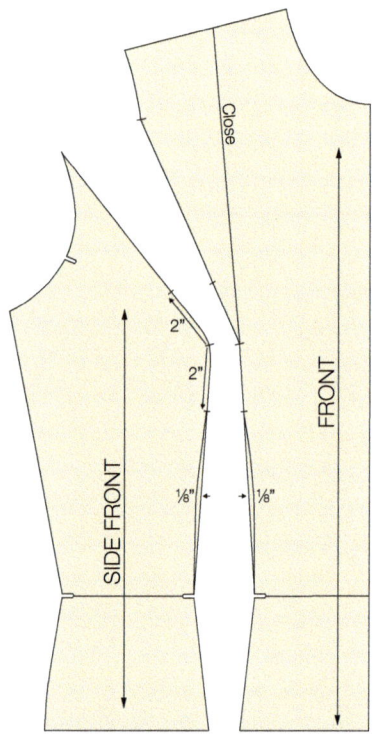

1. Move shoulder dart to armhole using the slash and spread method.
2. Draw a slash-line 2 inches (5cm) below shoulder edge.
3. Cut slash-line to the edge of the bust point (apex).
4. Cut shoulder dart leg to the edge of the bust point (apex).
5. Close shoulder dart and tape shut.
6. Mark control notches 2 inches (5cm) from apex on all lines.
7. Draw a ⅛ inch (3mm) curve down both dart legs starting at notches.
8. Straighten shoulder seam if necessary.
9. Cut front and side front pieces apart making sure to cut out the dart.
10. Smooth out the bust-line if it looks too pointy or uneven.
11. Walk the pattern using an awl starting at the waist; adjust pattern as needed to balance style-line at armhole and hemline.

Exposed zipper pocket placement

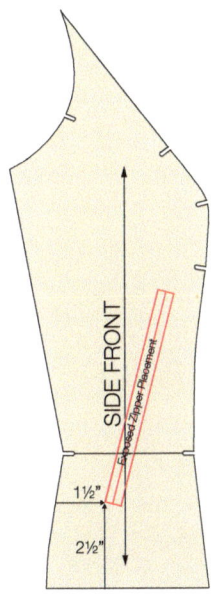

1. Measure the length of your zipper plus ½ inch (1.2cm)—a 6 inch (15cm) zipper was used for this pattern.
2. Mark the exposed zipper opening 6 ½ inches (16.2cm) by ½ inch (1.2cm).
3. Mark zipper placement 2 ½ inches (6.2cm) up from hemline and 1 ½ inches (3.75cm) over from side seam.
4. Angle pocket opening as desired.

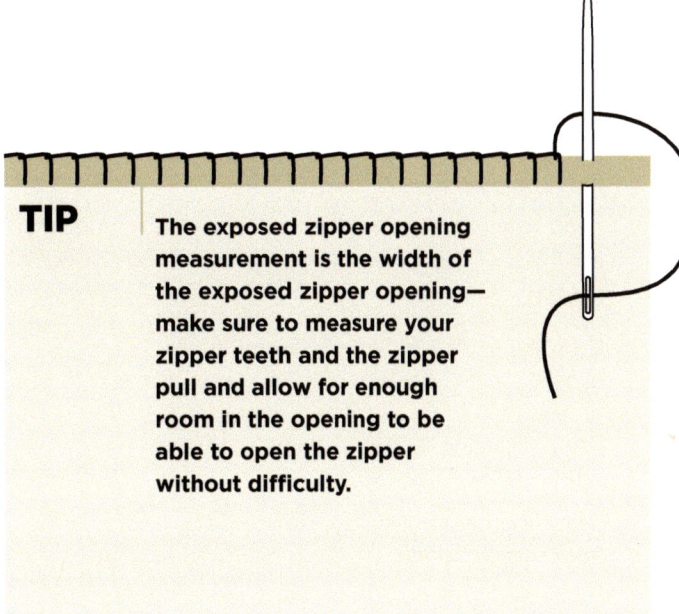

TIP — The exposed zipper opening measurement is the width of the exposed zipper opening—make sure to measure your zipper teeth and the zipper pull and allow for enough room in the opening to be able to open the zipper without difficulty.

CHAPTER FOUR:
THE MOTORCYCLE JACKET

Armhole princess back

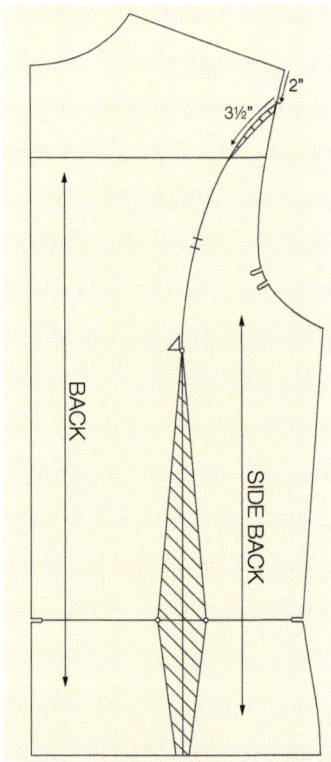
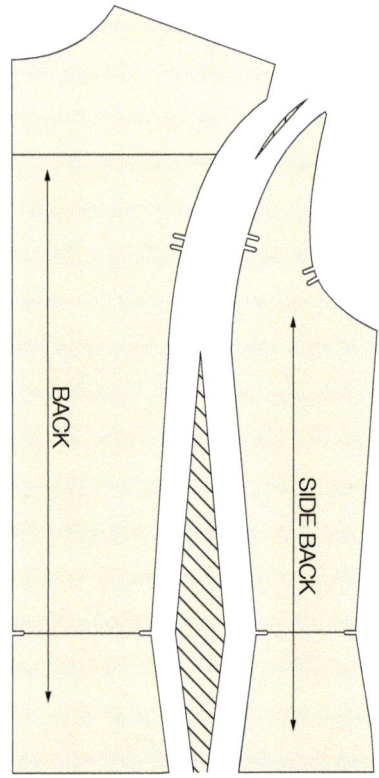
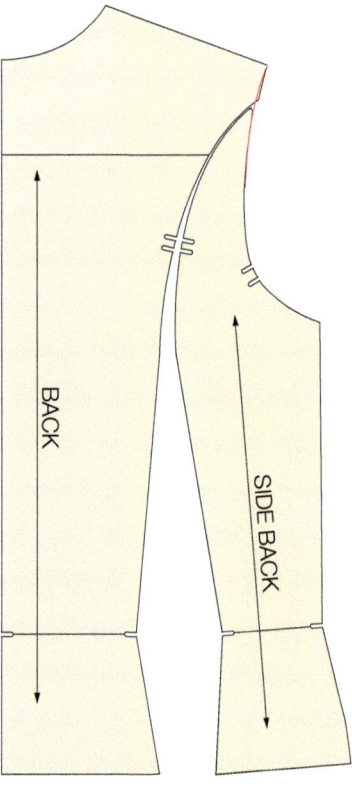

1. Mark grainline for side back pattern piece parallel to CB.

2. Draw a straight line from dart point to 2 inches (5cm) below shoulder seam (this gives you a reference point for princess line).

3. Draw a curved line from armhole to dart point—double-notch for back.

4. Draw another curved line ¼ inch (6mm) down from princess line connecting with the original curve 3 ½ inches (8.75cm) down (the length of the shoulder dart).

5. Cut out back and side back patterns making sure to eliminate the darts (shaded area).

6. Walk the pattern using an awl starting at the waist; adjust pattern as needed to balance style-line at armhole and hemline.

Front lapel and exposed zipper placement

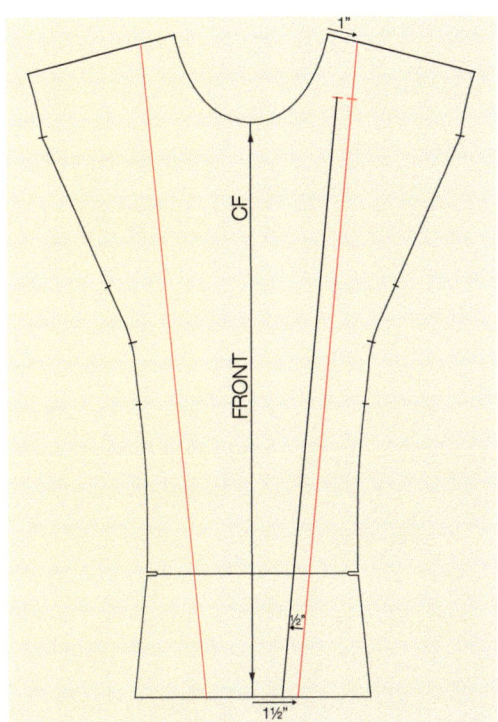
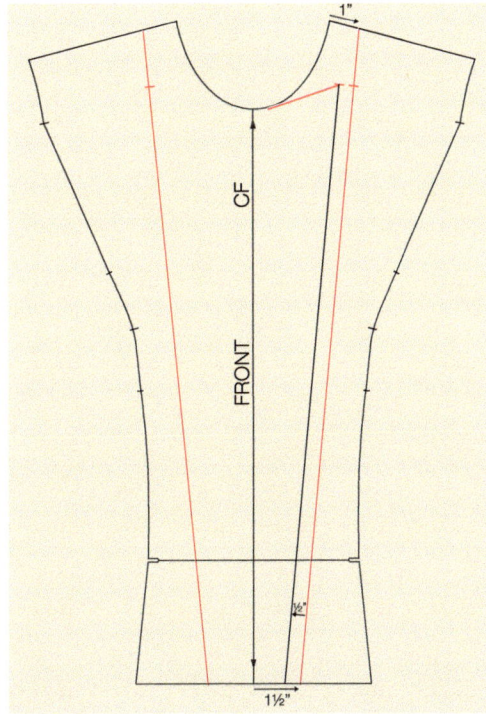
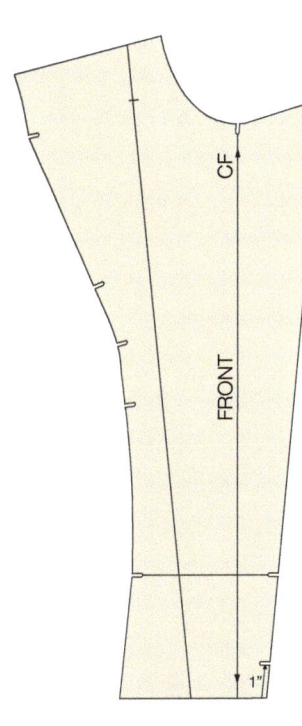

1. Trace both left and right front patterns together to open up the pattern.

2. Draw zipper placement line (red line) 1 ½ inches (3.75cm) over from center front (CF) at hemline and 1 inch (2.5cm) over from shoulder point.

3. Mark a notch the length of zipper plus 1 ½ inches (3.75cm)—an 18 inch (45cm) zipper was used for this pattern.
   Note: You will want the zipper to be at least the length of the CF measurement.

4. Transfer zipper placement line (red line) to the right side of the pattern—this will be used as a reference point.

5. Draw a parallel line ½ inch (1.2cm) to the left of the zipper placement line on the left side of the pattern and notch; this is the edge of the lapel.
   Note: This measurement is the width of the exposed zipper opening—it should be the same as the pocket opening measurement.

6. Draw a line (red line) connecting the CF neckline to the notch on the lapel edge.

7. Cut out front pattern making sure to retain CF notch.

Asymmetrical front pattern development

Convertible collar development

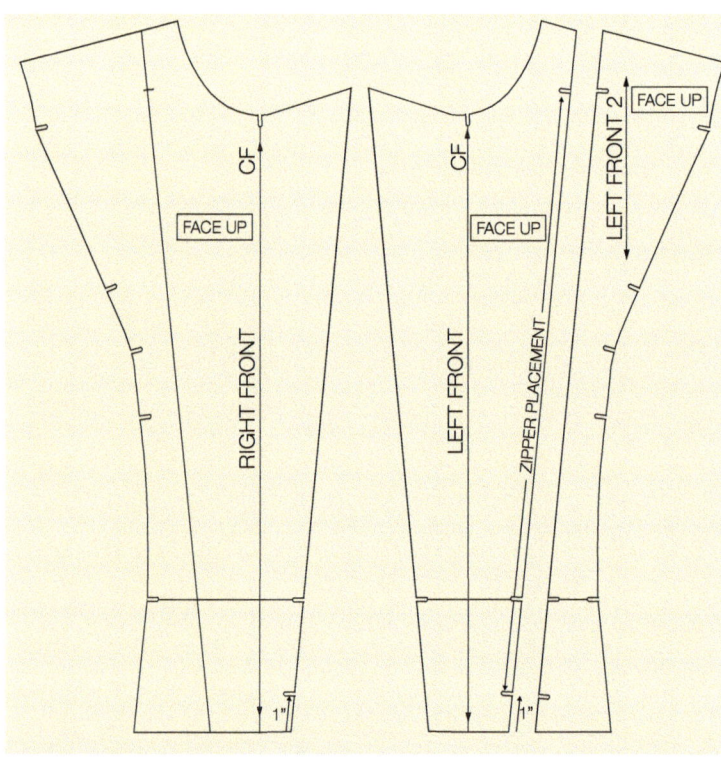

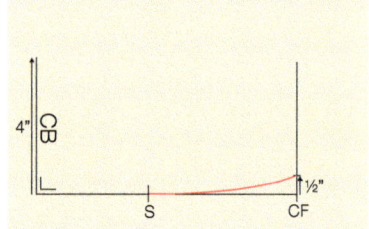

1. Trace a left and right front pattern retaining zipper guideline.
2. Cut out left pattern piece along the zipper guideline notching 1 inch (2.5cm) up from hemline for zipper placement.
3. Mark the zipper placement notch on the right front pattern as indicated 1 inch (2.5cm) up from hemline.
4. Label patterns as indicated with "face-up" on each pattern piece.
5. Draw grainline for left-front-2-pattern piece perpendicular to the waistline.
   Note: You must mark "face-up" on asymmetrical pattern pieces to ensure the correct side of the fabric is cut out.

1. Draw a horizontal line equal to the front and back neckline measurement.
2. Mark center back (CB) and center front (CF).
3. Using back neckline measurement mark shoulder S.
4. Square a line 4 inches (10cm) up from CB.
5. Square another line at CB.
6. Square a line up from CF.
7. Mark a point ½ inch (1.2cm) up from CF.
8. Draw a curved line (red curved line) from shoulder S to point.
9. Extend collar edge 1 ¼ inch (3cm) from CF line.
10. Connect CF to end of collar edge.
11. Adjust shape of collar (red) curving a line ½ inch (1.2cm) down from collar edge.
12. Notch shoulder S.
    Note: This jacket can be worn completely or partially zipped which is why a convertible collar was used for the pattern.

Exposed zipper sleeve vent with godet

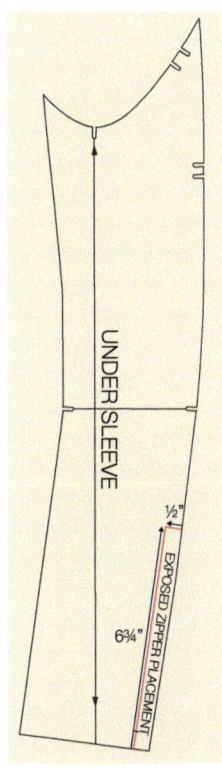

1. Trace two under-sleeve patterns—set one aside for lining development.

2. Measure the length of your zipper plus ¾ inch (1.75cm)—a 6 inch (15cm) zipper was used for this pattern.

3. Mark the exposed zipper opening on the under-sleeve pattern 6 ¾ inches (16.75cm) by ½ inch (1.2cm).

4. Cut out from pattern and discard.

5. Mark zipper placement notch ½ inch (1.2cm) up from the hemline.

6. For the godet backing for the zipper opening, draw a vertical line 6 ¾ inches (16.75cm) long.

7. At the top of the line, measure ¼ inch (6mm) on either side of line (this is the same measurement as the exposed zipper opening).

8. For the width of the godet, measure 1 inch (2.5cm) on either side line of the bottom of the pattern and connect top and bottom lines to complete the godet.

9. Mark a zipper placement notch ½ inch (1.2cm) up from godet opening.

MUSLIN OR TOILE FITTING

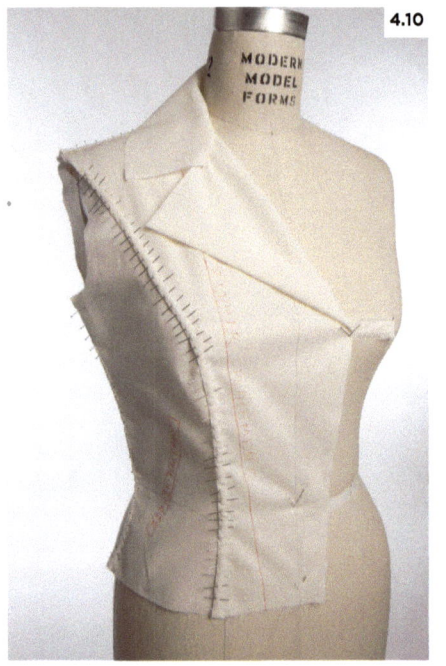

- Before you draft the facings and lining patterns, prepare a muslin for fit.
- Do not add SAs to pattern as you will most likely be adjusting the muslin for fit—draw the SAs directly onto the muslin.
- Make any necessary fit corrections to pattern.
- Adjust exposed zipper pocket placement if necessary.
- Now you can move on to the facing and lining patterns.

4.10 Checking muslin fit before sleeve is added.
4.11 Muslin fit with sleeve added.
4.12 Collar/lapel detail.

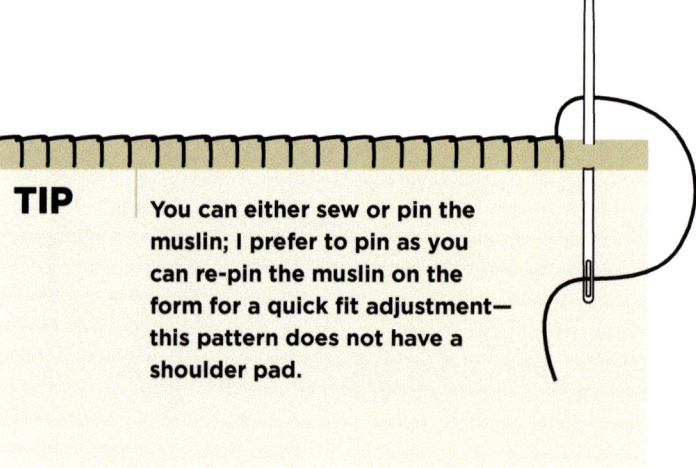

TIP You can either sew or pin the muslin; I prefer to pin as you can re-pin the muslin on the form for a quick fit adjustment—this pattern does not have a shoulder pad.

Completing the upper- and under-collar

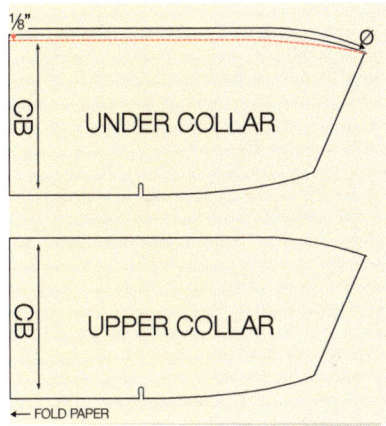

Front facing

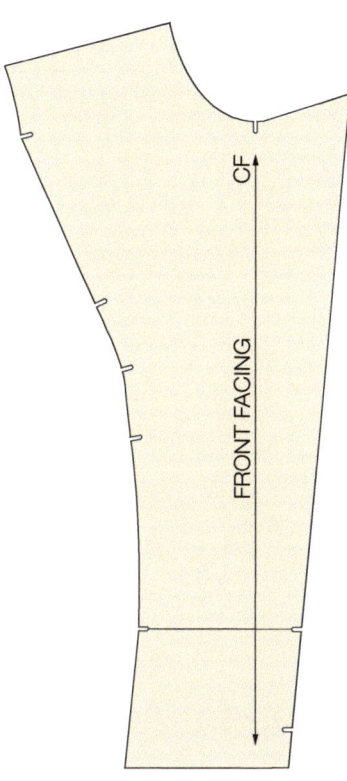

1. Fold paper in half and trace the collar twice—don't forget to mark your shoulder seam notch.
2. Mark the first pattern the upper-collar.
3. On the second pattern, draft under-collar by reducing the out-seam of the collar by ⅛ inch (3mm) at the CB and blending to zero at the collar point (red dotted line).
4. Mark grainlines parallel to CB.

1. Trace the right front pattern piece for both left and right facing patterns; set aside.

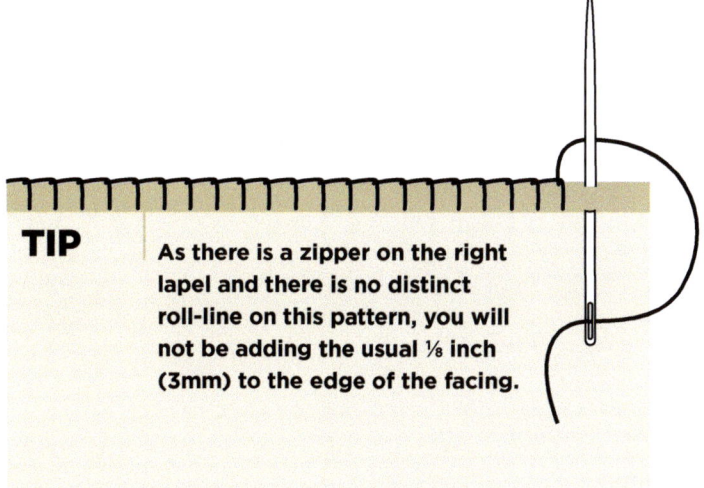

TIP As there is a zipper on the right lapel and there is no distinct roll-line on this pattern, you will not be adding the usual ⅛ inch (3mm) to the edge of the facing.

Side front and side back lining

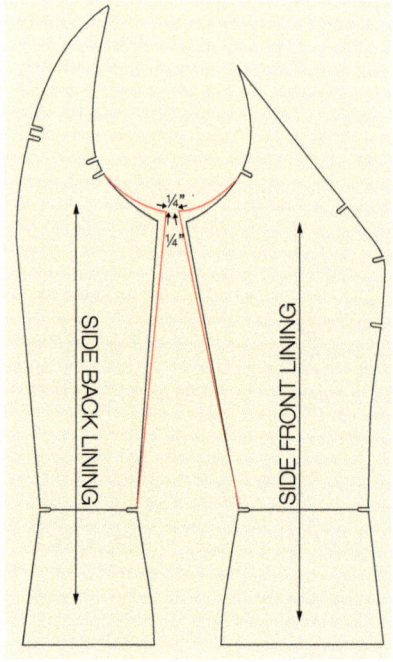

1. Starting at waistline draw a line (red line) out and up ¼ inch (6mm) to allow for ease in the lining pieces.
2. Blend (red curved lines) to armhole notches.

Back lining

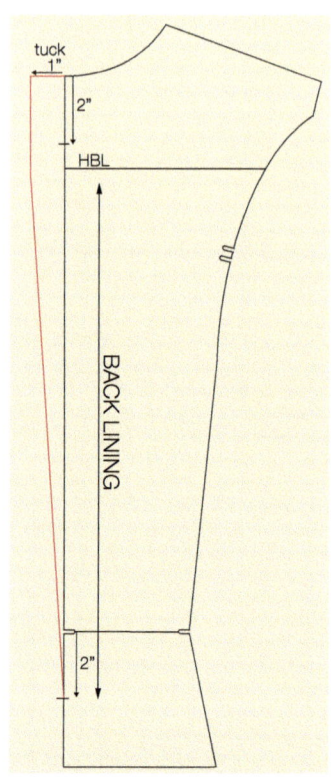

1. Trace back pattern.
2. Mark out 1 inch (2.5cm) from CB and square down to HBL.
3. Mark 2 inches (5cm) down from waist at CB and continue line to meet HBL.
4. At CB seam, mark 2 inches (5cm) down for tuck.
5. Mark grainline perpendicular to waistline.
   Note: Grainline does not change which means you must cut two back patterns to allow for the action pleat.

Upper- and under-sleeve lining with built-in godets

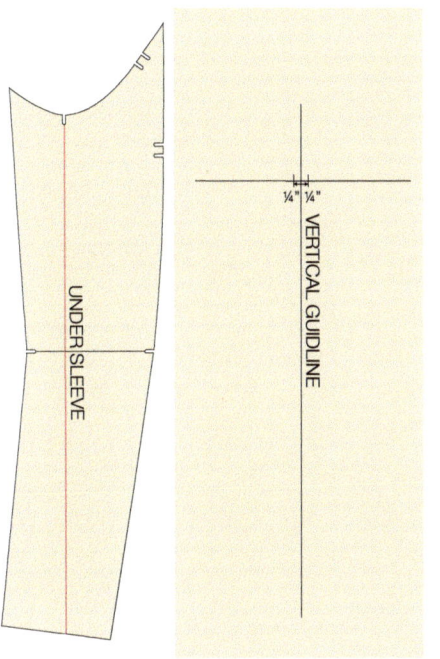
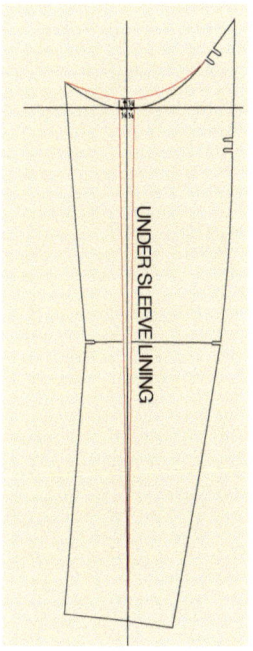
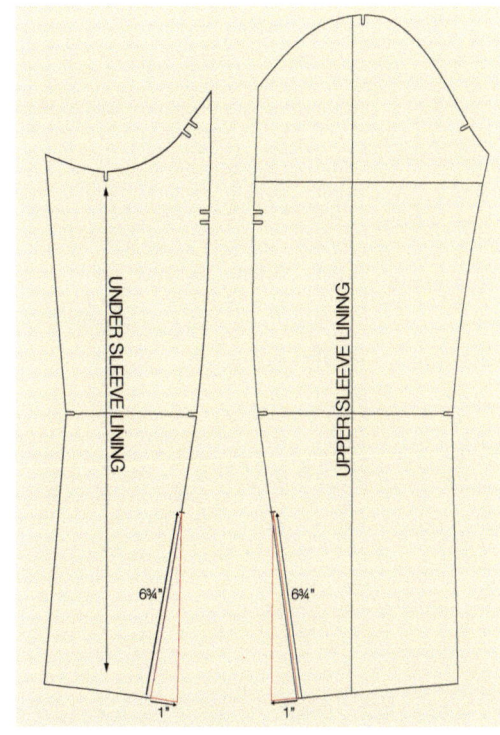

1. Cut out the under-sleeve pattern that was set aside.
2. Square a slash-line (red line) down from under-arm notch to hem and cut to—not through to—hem.
3. On paper, draw a vertical guideline; mark out ¼ inch (6mm) on either side of the guideline.
4. Place side panel on the guideline and spread open to meet the marks, tape down and trace pattern.
5. At new under-arm notch, mark up ¼ inch (6mm) and blend to front edge and back notches (red curved line). **Note: The guideline becomes your new grainline and under-arm notch.**
6. Trace the upper-sleeve pattern.
7. Measure up 6 ¾ inches (16.75cm) on both upper- and under-sleeve pattern hemlines as shown for the built-in godet.
8. Extend hemline 1 inch (2.5cm) on both upper- and under-sleeve lining patterns (these measurements equal the size of the godet) and connect these two points to create the built-in godet.

CHAPTER FOUR:
THE MOTORCYCLE JACKET

PRODUCTION PATTERN

Seam allowances and hems

TIP
- Before adding SAs and hems make sure to walk your pattern and make any necessary corrections if seams or control notches do not match.
- Now you can make your production pattern.

Upper-collar seam allowance

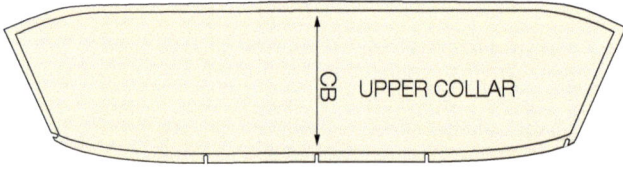

Under-collar seam allowance

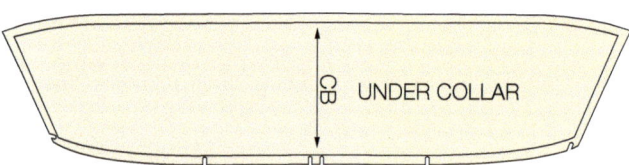

1. Add ¼ inch (6mm) SA to all seams for upper-collar.
2. Notch at CB, shoulder, and the SA.
3. Mark grainline parallel to CB.

1. Add ¼ inch (6mm) SA to all seams for the under-collar.
2. Make a double-notch at back (one on each side of the CB).
3. Notch shoulder and the SA.
4. Mark grainline parallel to CB.
   Note: Mark SAs and cut out pattern while paper is still folded!

Front and front facing pattern seam allowance and hems

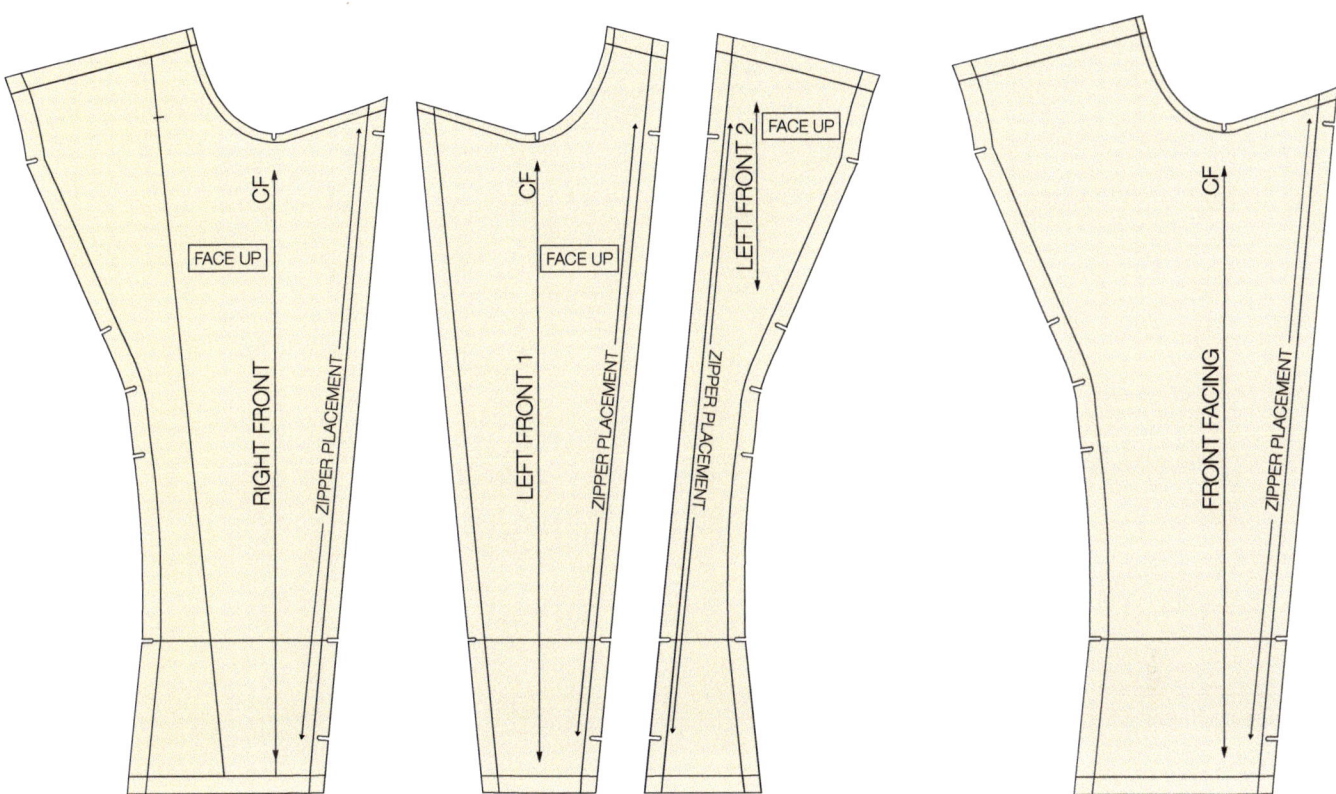

1. Trace right-front, left-front-1, left-front-2, and front facing patterns.

2. Add ½ inch (1.2cm) SA to all seams with the exception of the necklines.

3. Add ¼ inch (6mm) SA to the necklines.
   Note: The front-edge pattern SAs are ½ inch (1.2cm) because of the zipper; I have made the left-front edge the same as the right-front edge so there is no confusion when sewing.

CHAPTER FOUR:
THE MOTORCYCLE JACKET

Side back and side front pattern seam allowance and hems

Back pattern seam allowance and hems

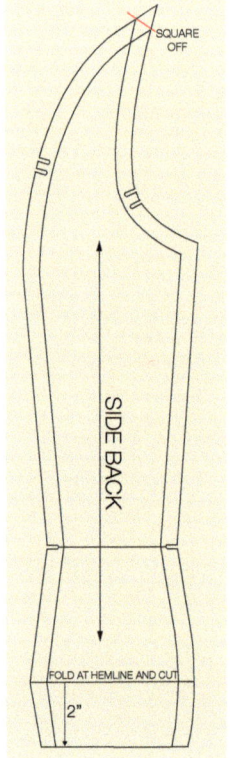 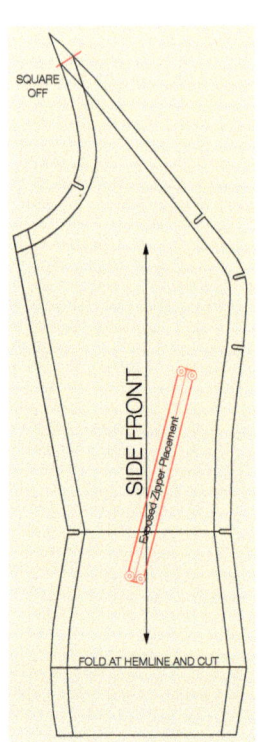 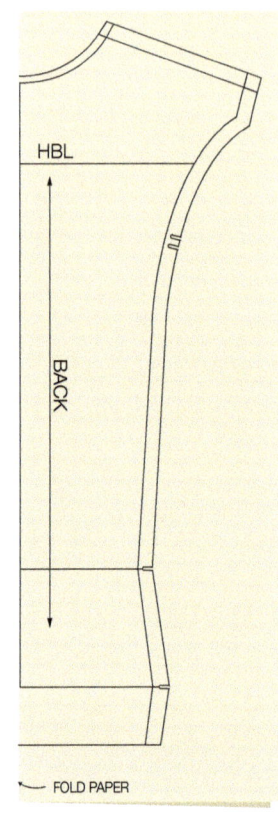 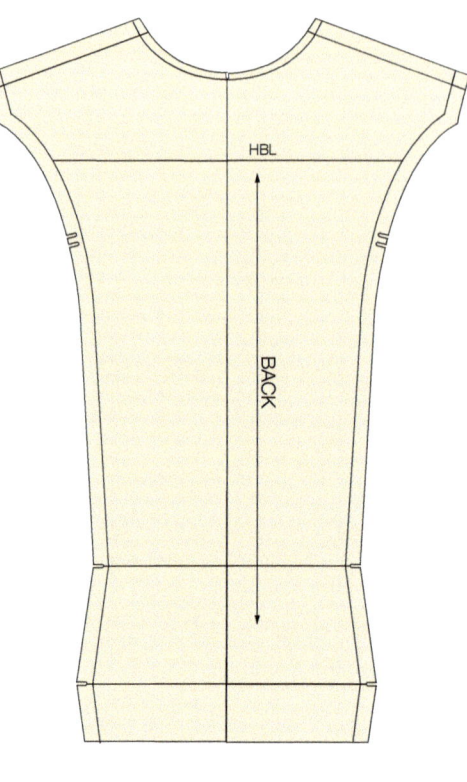

1. Trace side back and side front patterns.
2. Add ½ inch (1.2cm) SA to all seams with the exception of the hem.
3. Mark hems 2 inches (5cm): this includes the ½ inch (1.2cm) SA.
4. Circle and drill ⅛ inch (3mm) into the pocket opening.
   Note: Make sure to fold paper back at hemline when cutting out to ensure the hem lies correctly on garment.

1. Fold pattern paper in half and trace the back pattern.
2. Add ½ inch (1.2cm) SA to all seams with the exception of the back neckline and hem.
3. Add ¼ inch (6mm) SA to the back neckline.
4. Mark hem 2 inches (5cm): this includes the ½ inch (1.2cm) SA.
5. Cut out pattern, folding back at hemline when cutting.
6. Retain all notches.

Sleeve patterns seam allowance and hems

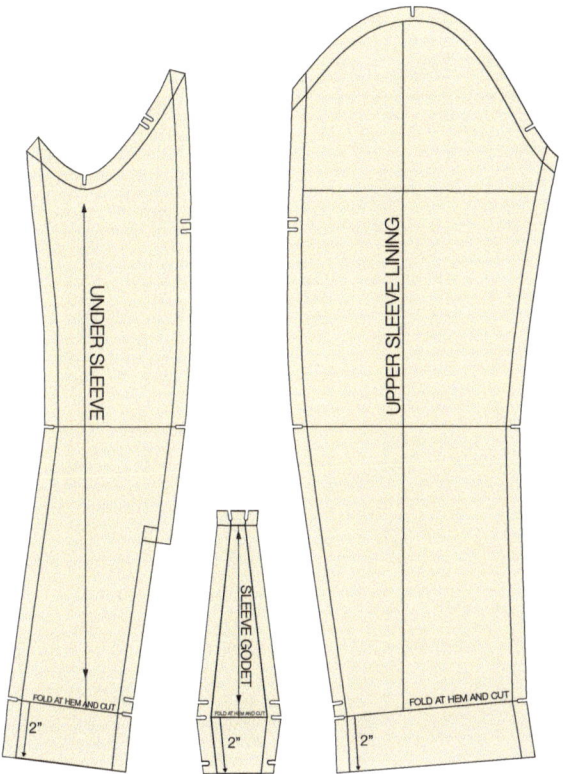

1. Add ½ inch (1.2cm) SA to all seams with the exception of the hem.
2. Mark hems 2 inches (5cm): this includes the ½ inch (1.2cm) SA.

TIP Make sure to fold paper back at hemline when cutting out to ensure the hem lies correctly on garment.

Back, side back, side front, and sleeve linings seam allowance and hems

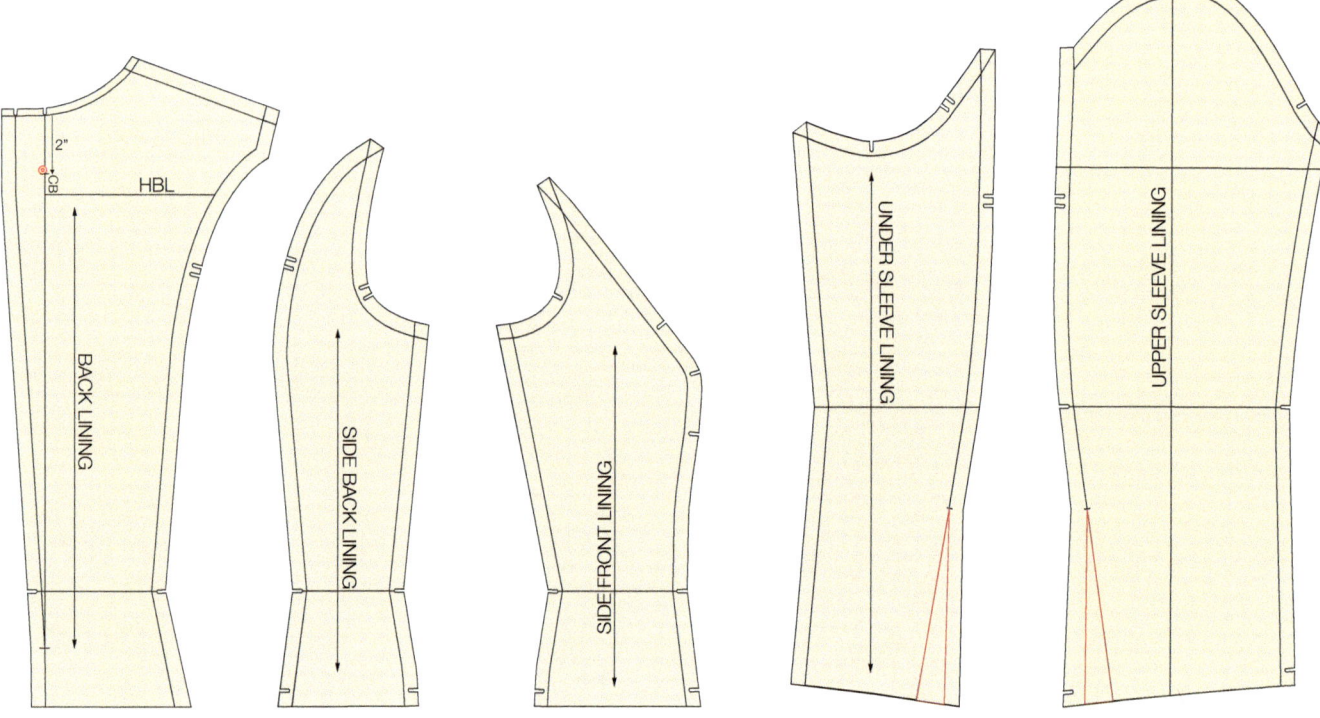

1. Add ½ inch (1.2cm) SA to all seams with the exception of the back neckline and hem.

2. Add ¼ inch (6mm) SA to the back neckline.

3. You do not add a SA to the hem as it is already "built in"; mark and notch up ½ inch (1.2cm).

4. Circle and drill ⅛ inch (3mm) into the tuck.

Pocket lining

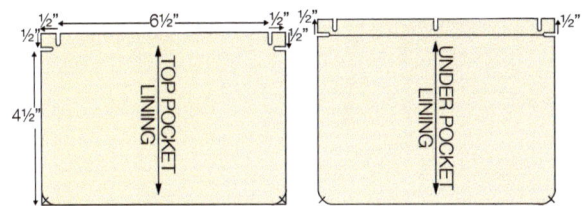

1. For top-pocket bag, measure the length of the welt (6 ½ inches) + 1 inch (2.5cm) for SA (18.7cm).
2. Square down 4 ½ inches (5.2cm) for the pocket depth.
3. Notch top-pocket bag as shown.
4. Curve pocket bag at corners and place a control notch on the curve.
5. For under-pocket bag, trace top-pocket bag and add ½ inch (1.2cm) to the length of the bag.
6. Notch under-pocket bag as shown.

Pocket and sleeve vent facings

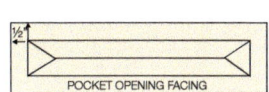
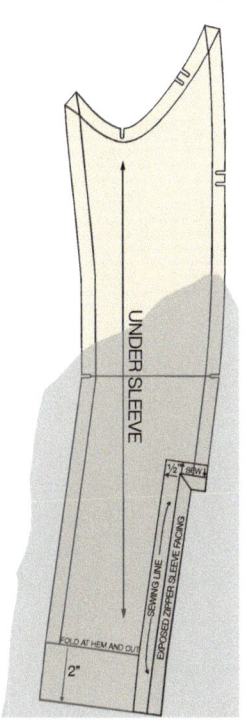

1. Trace pocket and under-sleeve vent openings—make sure you trace the under-sleeve pattern with the SA and hem added.
2. Add ½ inch (1.2cm) SA as shown and cut out.

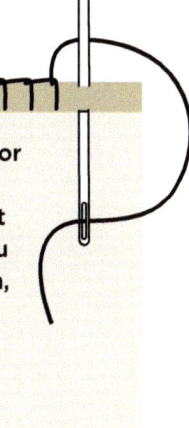

TIP — A silk organza in a matching color is a good choice for the sleeve and pocket opening facings as it is lightweight and durable; if you are using leather for this pattern, you do not need to face the openings as they can be cut to size and glued.

CHAPTER FOUR: THE MOTORCYCLE JACKET

TECHNICAL FLATS AND FINISHED PATTERN PIECES

Self:

1. Right-front (cut 1).
2. Left-front-1 (cut 1).
3. Left-front-2 (cut 1).
4. Side front (cut 2).
5. Back (cut 1).
6. Side back (cut 2).
7. Upper-sleeve (cut 2).
8. Under-sleeve cuff (cut 2).
9. Under-sleeve godet (cut 2).
10. Upper-collar (cut 1).
11. Under-collar (cut 1).
12. Front facing (cut 2).

Contrast:

1. Pocket facing (cut 2).
2. Sleeve vent facing (cut 2).

Lining:

1. Side front (cut 2).
2. Back (cut 2).
3. Side back (cut 2).
4. Upper-sleeve (cut 2).
5. Under-sleeve (cut 2).
6. Top-pocket (cut 2).
7. Under-pocket (cut 2).

> "The novelties of one generation are only the resuscitated fashions of the generation before last."
>
> George Bernard Shaw

| THE HISTORY OF THE MOTORCYCLE JACKET | CONTEMPORARY MOTORCYCLE JACKETS | THE PATTERN | MUSLIN OR TOILE FITTING | PRODUCTION PATTERN | **TECHNICAL FLATS AND FINISHED PATTERN PIECES** |

4.13
Front detail of motorcycle jacket.

CHAPTER FIVE

THE MAO JACKET

Patterning concepts learned:
- **tunic-style jacket**
- **collar with stand**
- **2-piece contour sleeve with vent, and breast and hip patch pockets with flaps**

5.1
Designed Mao jacket front.

**CHAPTER FIVE:
THE MAO JACKET**

THE HISTORY OF THE MAO

The Zhongshan suit, as it's known in the East, first became popular as the national costume of China in the early twentieth century. The suit's design was first introduced as a way of embodying both Eastern and Western philosophies of dress in order to represent the mindset of a new and modern China. It is no coincidence that the original suit, which came to symbolize the spirit and political ideals of the newly formed nation, shares its name with the leader of the time, Sun Yat-sen (Romanized as Sun Zhongshan). Unfortunately, during China's Cultural Revolution, the suit was identified to such a large extent with communist revolutionary Mao Zedong, that it has since become known as the "Mao suit" in the West.

The design originated in 1911 when Sun overthrew the imperial Qing dynasty and established the Republic of China. He wanted to establish a new national identity by doing away with the traditional garb of the time, which included ornately embroidered silk robes, in favor of a simpler mode of dress. The end result was a combination of Japanese cadet uniforms and Western business suits, which blended the best of both Eastern and Western dress, and helped to modernize the customs of "old-world" China.

5.2
A gallery assistant poses in front of Andy Warhol's *Mao* (1972) at Sotheby's auction house in London, 2013.

Symbolic meaning is inherent in every detail of the jacket and its early political relevance makes this jacket rife with social significance. The five buttons down the center front symbolize the five branches of government, while those attached to the pocket flaps represent the four ancient virtues enjoyed by the people: propriety, justice, honesty, and honor. The "People's Principles", which consist of nationalism, democracy, and the people's livelihood, are exemplified by the three buttons attached to the sleeve placket. Lastly, there is no seam down the center back of the jacket to show the peaceful reunification of the nation. This intriguing use of a garment to represent the philosophy of an entire nation gives a whole new meaning to fashion theory.

"What a strange power there is in clothing."

Isaac Bashevis Singer

| THE HISTORY OF THE MAO | CONTEMPORARY MAO JACKETS | THE PATTERN | MUSLIN OR TOILE FITTING | PRODUCTION PATTERN | TECHNICAL FLATS AND FINISHED PATTERN PIECES |

5.3
A group of Chinese children in uniform in front of a picture of Chairman Mao Zedong, 1968.

5.4
Chinese revolutionary and political leader Sun Yat-sen who introduced the Zhongshan suit early in the twentieth century.

5.5
Young woman in army uniform standing in front of the Forbidden Palace, Beijing, China.

Today, the suit which once signified the democracy of the nation is now mostly associated with China's Communist Party and Mao. Ironically, at the same time the suit was becoming the symbol of working-class identity in China, the Mao jacket became fashionable among the European and American artists and intellectuals of the day.

Politics aside, today many contemporary designers continue to reinterpret the clean lines of the jacket into their collections.

CONTEMPORARY MAO JACKETS

5.6
Yohji Yamamoto: Runway, Paris Fashion Week Womenswear Fall/Winter 2015/2016.

5.7
AF Vandevorst: FASHION-FRANCE Fall/Winter 2013–2014.

| THE HISTORY OF THE MAO | CONTEMPORARY MAO JACKETS | THE PATTERN | MUSLIN OR TOILE FITTING | PRODUCTION PATTERN | TECHNICAL FLATS AND FINISHED PATTERN PIECES |

5.8
Yohji Yamamoto: Runway, Paris Fashion Week Womenswear Fall/Winter 2015/2016.

5.9
Marc Jacobs: Runway, Mercedes-Benz Fashion Week Spring 2015.

CHAPTER FIVE:
THE MAO JACKET

THE PATTERN

Start with jacket front, back, and 2-piece sleeve blocks

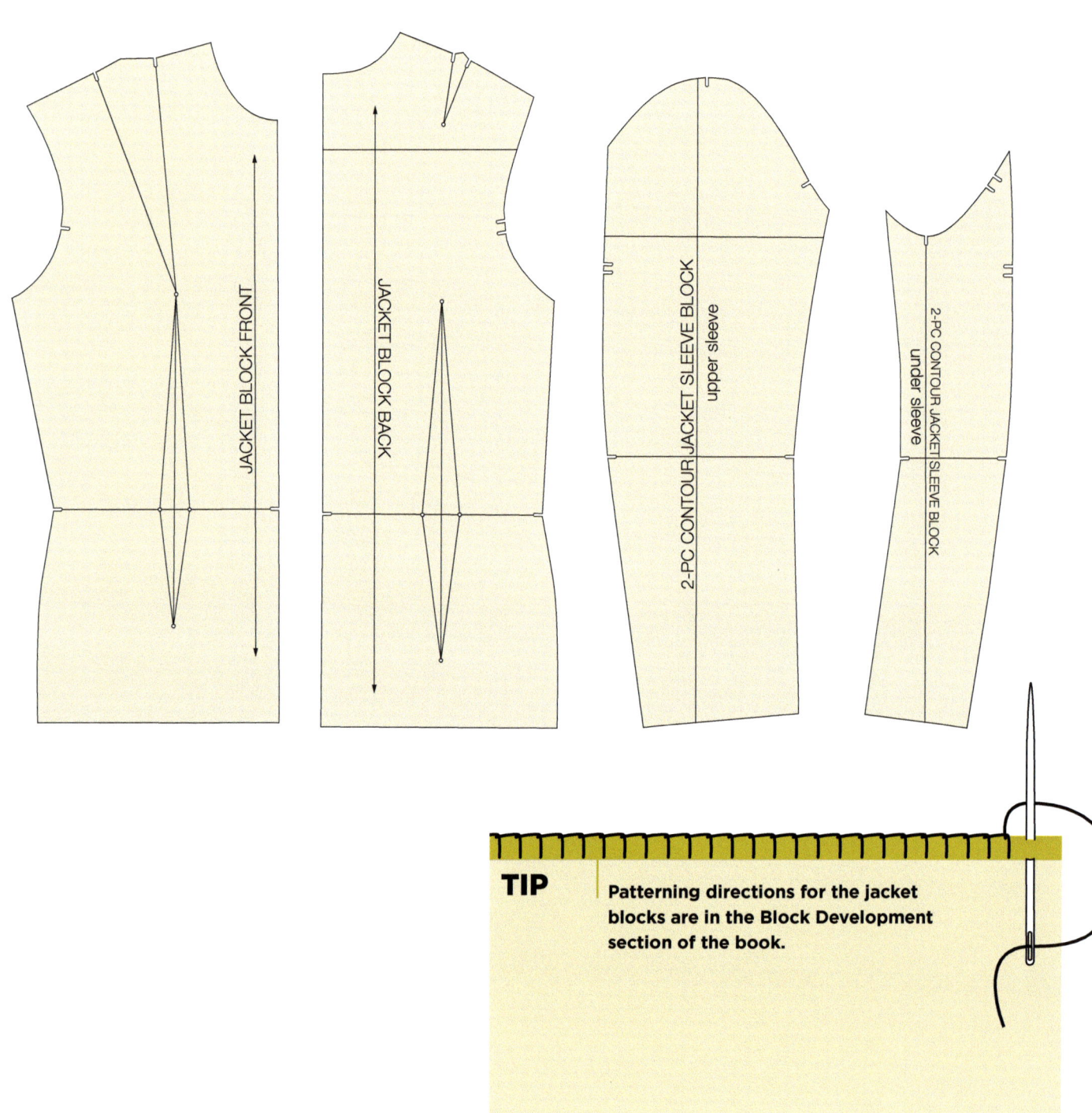

TIP Patterning directions for the jacket blocks are in the Block Development section of the book.

Front and back tunic style

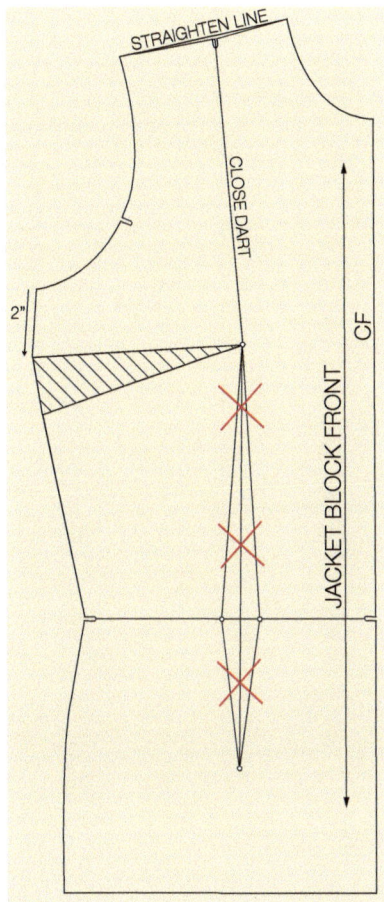

1. Trace front jacket block.
2. Transfer shoulder dart to side seam by the slash and spread method.
3. Draw a line from the apex (dart point) to the side seam 2 inches (5cm) below armhole.
4. Cut slash-line from this line to apex.
5. Cut another slash-line down dart leg on shoulder.
6. Close shoulder dart and tape shut.
7. Straighten shoulder line if not straight.
8. Release contour dart (red Xs).
9. Retain waist dart mark closest to center front (CF) as it will be used for pocket placement.
   Note: Releasing a dart simply means to ignore it.

**CHAPTER FIVE:
THE MAO JACKET**

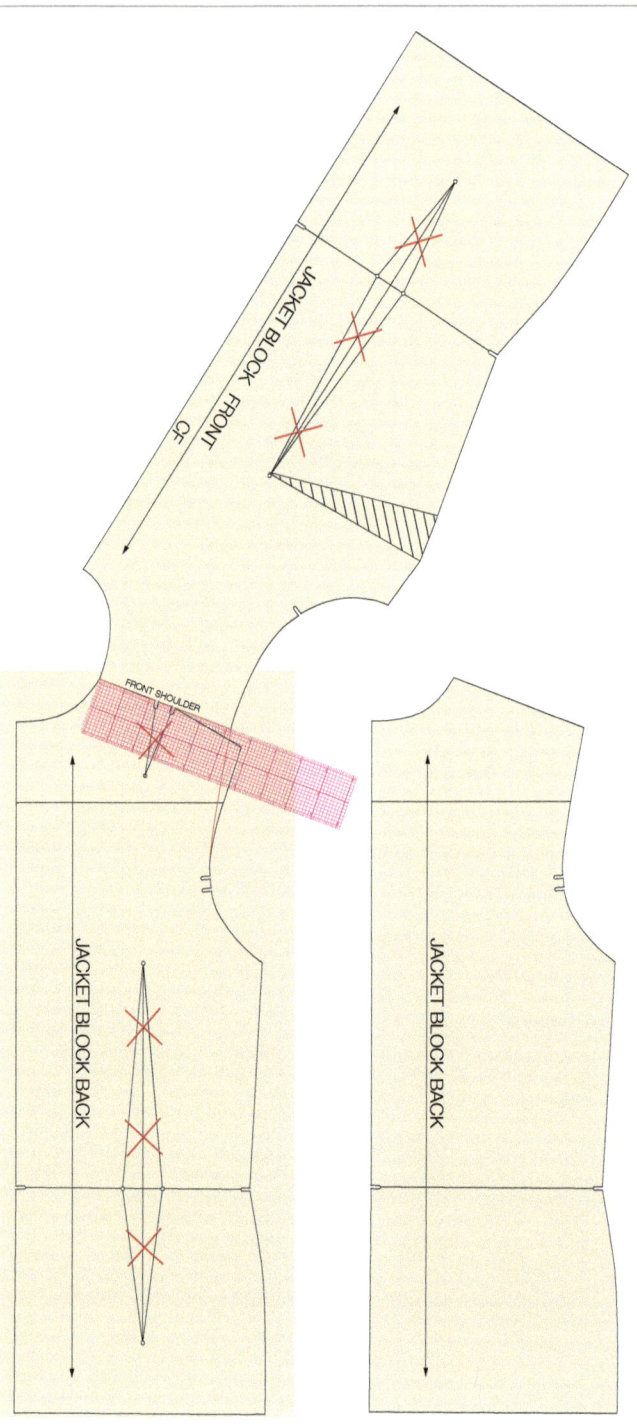

1. Trace back jacket block.
2. For the back block, you must first eliminate the shoulder dart.
3. Place ruler even with shoulder line at the neckline and draw a straight line.
4. Use the front shoulder measurement and mark the back shoulder to match.
5. True up armhole curve with French curve.
6. Release contour dart (red Xs).

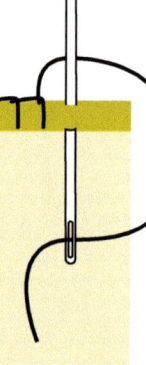

TIP | I've retained the bust dart for a better fit; if you want to completely eliminate all darts, it is best to draft the pattern from measurements instead of manipulating a block.

Lengthen pattern, lower neckline, front extension, and front dart

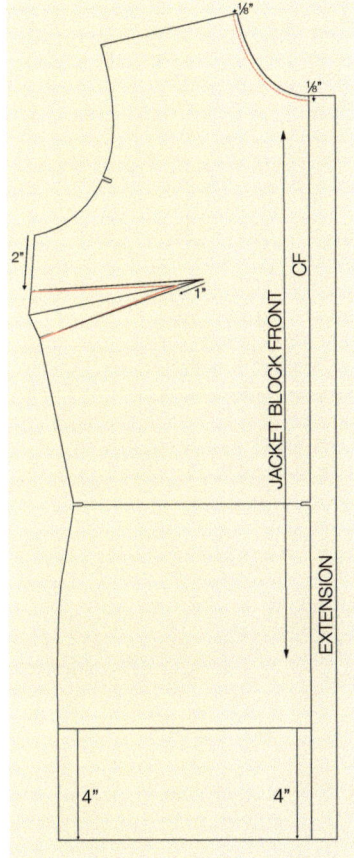

1. Lengthen front and back pattern 4 inches (10cm).
2. Lower front and back neckline ⅛ inch (3mm) (red dotted line).
3. Redraw necklines using a French curve.
4. Measure front neckline, record_____.
5. Measure back neckline, record_____.
6. Add 1 inch (2.5cm) for button/hole extension parallel to center front.
   Note: Make sure that your extension matches the diameter of the buttons that you are using.
7. Move front dart point 1 inch (2.5cm) in from apex (bust point).
8. Draw new dart legs (red lines).

Collar stand

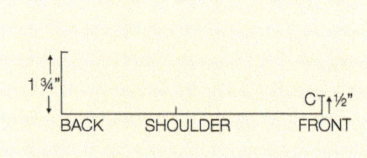 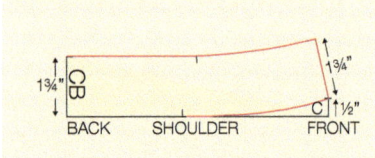

1. For collar stand, draw a horizontal line equal to the front and back neckline measurement.
2. Mark center back (CB) and center front (CF).
3. Using back neckline measurement mark shoulder S.
4. Square a line 1 ¾ inches (4.25cm) up from CB.
5. Square up ½ inch (1.2cm) from CF and label C.
6. Draw a curved line (curved red line) from S to C and square a line (red line) 1 ¾ inches (4.25cm) up from C.
7. Draw a line (red line) parallel to the neckline from the CB to the CF to complete the collar stand.
8. Mark a control notch at the midpoint of the upper edge of the collar stand.

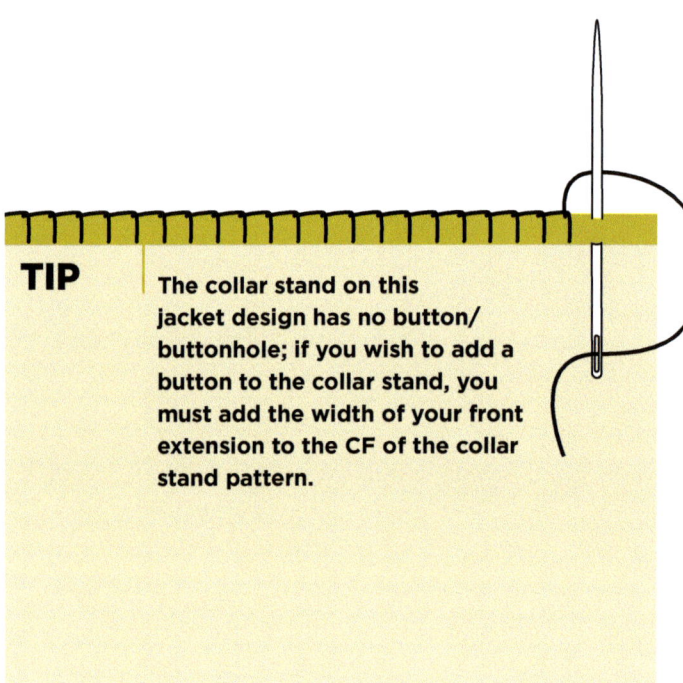

TIP The collar stand on this jacket design has no button/buttonhole; if you wish to add a button to the collar stand, you must add the width of your front extension to the CF of the collar stand pattern.

Collar

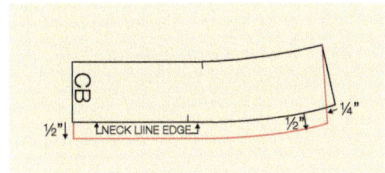

1. Collar is developed from the collar stand pattern.
2. Trace collar stand.
3. Draw a parallel line (red line) ½ inch (1.2cm) down from neckline edge: this is your collar edge.
4. Mark a point ¼ inch (6mm) in from CF neckline edge and draw a line (red line) from top of stand to meet with the collar edge.

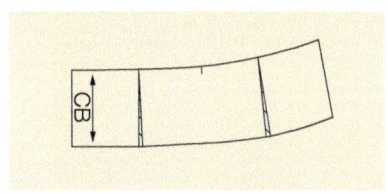

5. Cut out collar, retaining upper-edge notch.
6. Mark two slash-lines midpoint between upper-edge notch.
7. Using the slash-and-spread method, open collar ⅛ inch (3mm).
8. Mark grainline parallel to CB.
9. Trace, smoothing out curves if necessary.
   Note: Adding this extra ease helps the collar to lie flat on the garment.

Breast pocket with flap

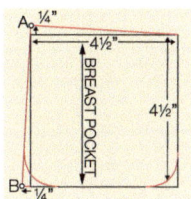 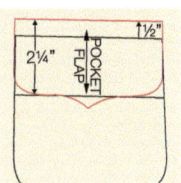

1. Make a 4 ½ inch (11.2cm) square for breast pocket.
2. Angle top pocket line (red line) up ¼ inch (6mm), mark A.
3. Measure ¼ inch (6mm) over from bottom pocket, mark B.
4. Draw a line (red line) connecting A to B.
5. Curve bottom of the pocket to desired shape.
6. Trace breast pocket for breast pocket flap.
7. Draw a parallel line (red line) ½ inch (2.5cm) up from top of pocket.
8. Draw another parallel line 2 ¼ inches (6.2cm) down from this new line.
9. Connect the endpoints to make a rectangle.
10. Make flap desired shape and cut out.

**CHAPTER FIVE:
THE MAO JACKET**

Hip pocket with flap

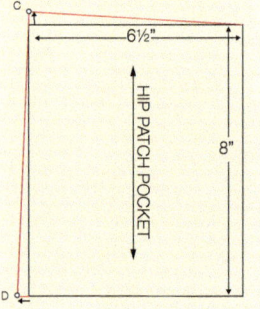 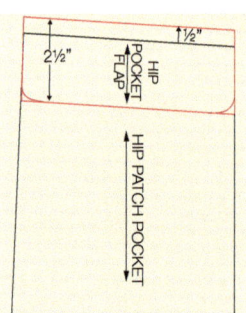

1. Make a rectangle 6 ½ inches (16.2cm) wide by 8 inches (20cm) long for hip pocket.
2. Angle top pocket line (red line) up ⅜ inch (1cm), mark C.
3. Measure ⅜ inch (1cm) over from bottom pocket, mark D.
4. Draw a line (red line) connecting C to D.
5. Trace hip pocket for hip pocket flap.
6. Draw a parallel line (red line) ½ inch (1.2cm) up from top of pocket.
7. Draw another parallel line 2 ½ inches (6.2cm) down from this new line.
8. Connect the endpoints to make a rectangle.
9. Make flap desired shape and cut out.
   Note: Angling the pocket up helps it to conform to the curves of the body giving the illusion of it lying straight.

Pocket placement

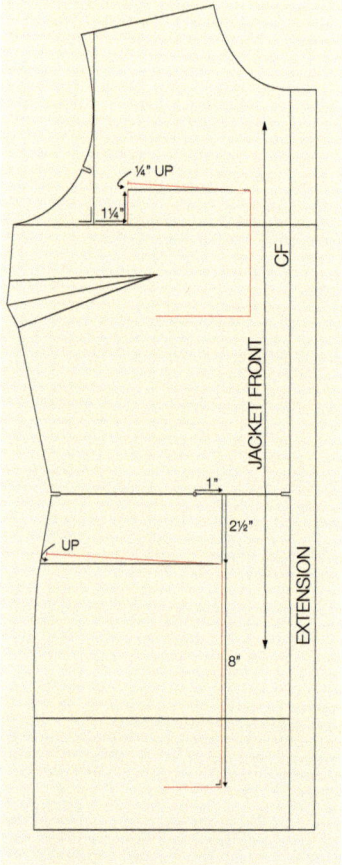

1. Draw a guideline from the under-arm perpendicular to the CF.
2. Square a line up from guideline, hitting the midpoint of armhole.
3. Measure over and up 1 ¼ inches (2.75cm) for breast pocket placement.
4. Draw a 4 ½ (11.2cm) inch line parallel to guideline.
5. Square down a 4 ½ inch (11.2cm) line (red line) for side-pocket placement.
6. Square a short line (red line) from this for bottom-pocket placement.

2-piece sleeve with vent

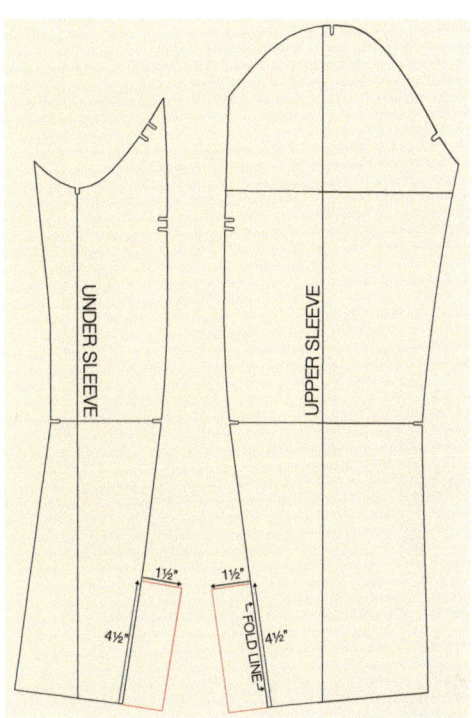

7. Slant top-pocket placement line (red line) up ¼ inch (6mm) towards armhole.

8. For hip pocket placement, measure 2 ½ inches (6.2cm) down from saved dart point at waistline and 1 inch (2.5cm) towards CF and mark.

9. Draw a 6 ½ inch (16.2cm) guideline parallel to the waist.

10. Square down an 8 inch (20cm) line (red line) for side-pocket placement.

11. Square a short line (red line) from this for bottom-pocket placement.

12. Slant top-pocket placement line (red line) up ⅜ inch (1cm) towards side seam.

1. Trace upper- and under-sleeve blocks.

2. Draw the vent 4 ½ inches (11.2cm) up and 1 ½ inches (3.75cm) out at the hemline of both the upper- and under-sleeve.

3. The upper-sleeve vent will be folded back when sewing. **Note: The length and width of the vent will vary depending on the number of buttons and their size.**

CHAPTER FIVE:
THE MAO JACKET

MUSLIN OR TOILE FITTING

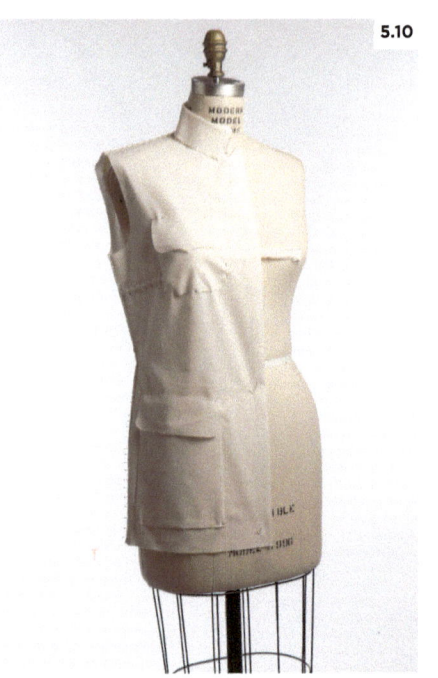
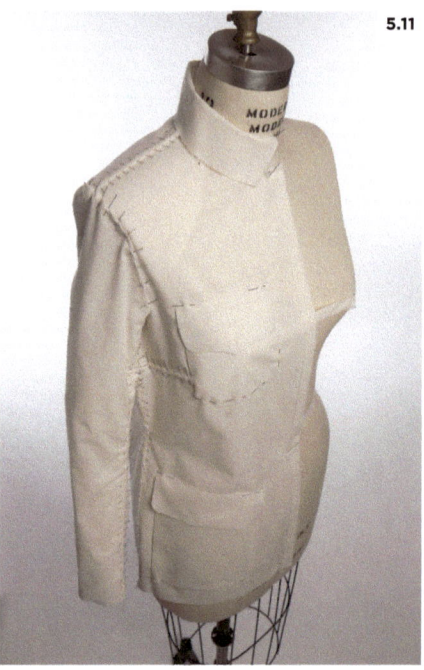

- Before you draft the facing and lining patterns, prepare a muslin for fit.
- Do not add seam allowance (SA) to pattern as you will most likely be adjusting the muslin for fit.
- Draw the seam allowance (SA) directly onto the muslin after tracing the working pattern.
- Make any necessary fit corrections to pattern.
- Make sure that you are happy with the size and placement of the pockets and make adjustments if necessary.
- Now you can move on to the facing and lining patterns.

5.10 Checking muslin fit before sleeve is added.
5.11 Muslin fit with sleeve added.
5.12 Pinning detail.

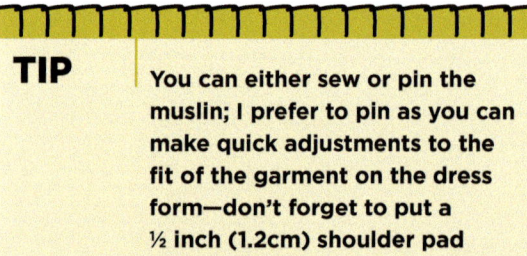

TIP You can either sew or pin the muslin; I prefer to pin as you can make quick adjustments to the fit of the garment on the dress form—don't forget to put a ½ inch (1.2cm) shoulder pad on the form.

Front facing and front lining

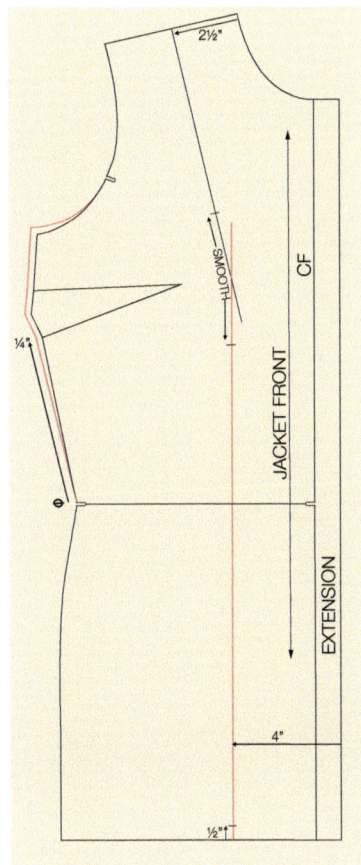
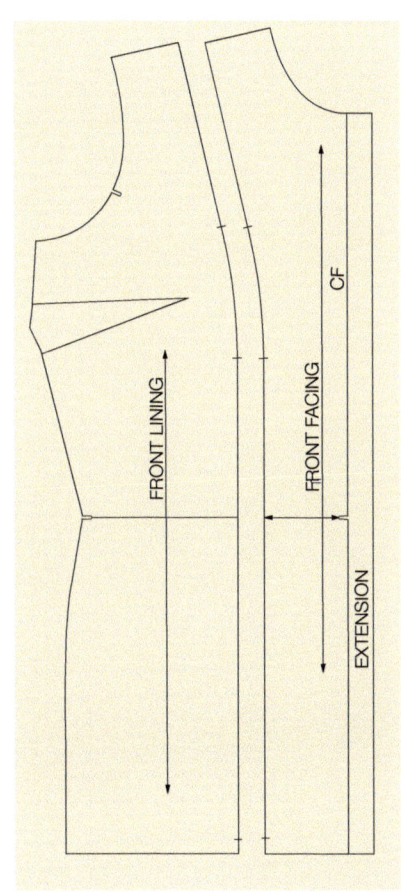

1. Trace front pattern.
2. Draw a parallel line (red line) 4 inches (10cm) from center front extension (CF).
3. Square a line 2 ½ inches (6.2cm) from high-point shoulder until both lines intersect.
4. Smooth out where the two lines intersect.
5. Mark 2 control notches for sewing guide as shown.
6. Notch ½ inch (1.2cm) up from hemline.
7. Starting at side-waistline, draw a line (red line) out and up ¼ inch (6mm) to allow for ease in the lining pattern.
8. Blend to armhole notch.
9. Mark grainlines.
10. Cut apart and label front facing and front lining.

**CHAPTER FIVE:
THE MAO JACKET**

Back facing and back lining

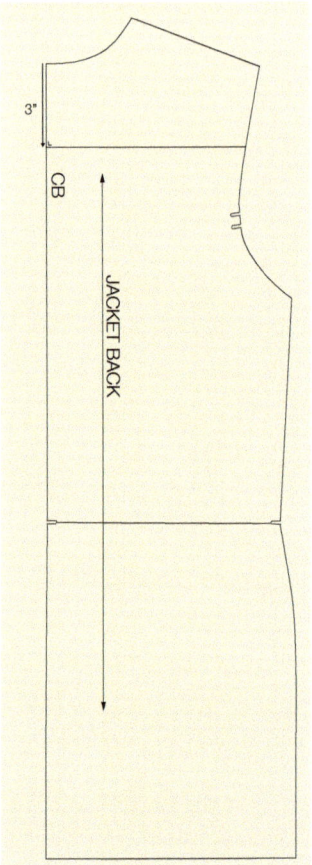
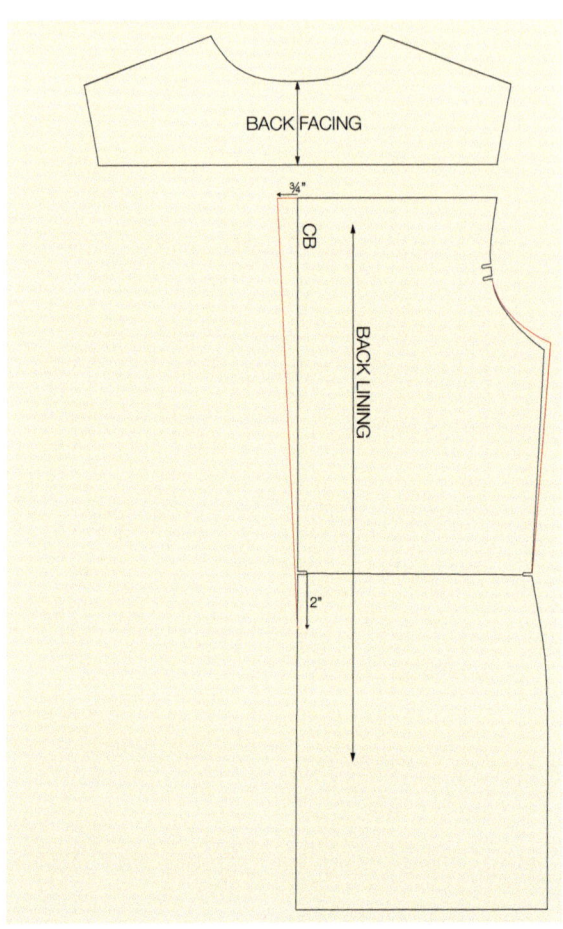

1. Trace jacket back.

2. Square a line 3 inches (7.5cm) down from CB neckline and cut apart.

3. The top pattern is your back facing—open pattern up and redraw.

4. Create an action pleat down the CB of the remaining pattern piece by drawing a straight line (red line) 2 inches (5cm) down from CB waistline and ¾ inch (1.75cm) out from top of lining piece and notch.

5. Starting at side-waistline, draw a line out and up ¼ inch (6mm) to allow for ease in the lining pattern.

6. Blend to back armhole notch.
   Note: Grainline does not change which means you must cut two back patterns to allow for the action pleat.

2-piece sleeve lining

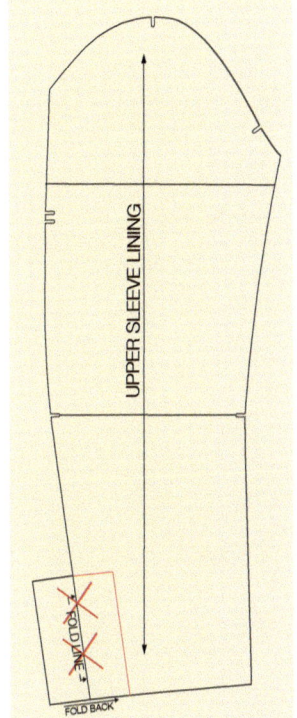
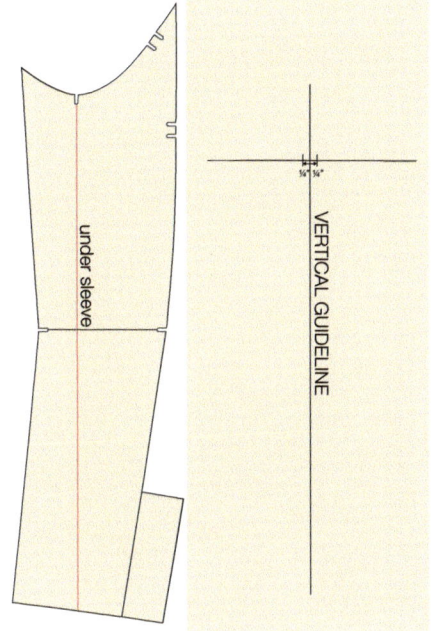
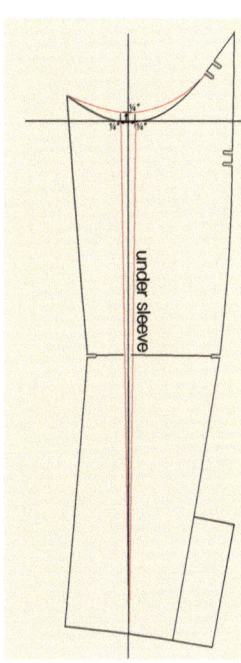

1. Trace upper-sleeve pattern.
2. Fold back vent at fold-line and trace (red lines).
3. Cut out vent piece and discard as shown.

1. Trace under-sleeve pattern and cut out.
2. Square a slash line (red line) down from under-arm notch to hem and cut to—not through to—hem.
3. On paper, draw a vertical guideline; mark out ¼ inch (6mm) on either side of the guideline.
4. Place side panel on the guideline and spread open to meet the marks, tape down and trace pattern.
   Note: The guideline becomes your new grainline and under-arm notch.
5. At new under-arm notch, mark up ¼ inch (6mm) and blend to edges (red curved lines).

PRODUCTION PATTERN

Seam allowances and hems

Front pattern seam allowance and hem

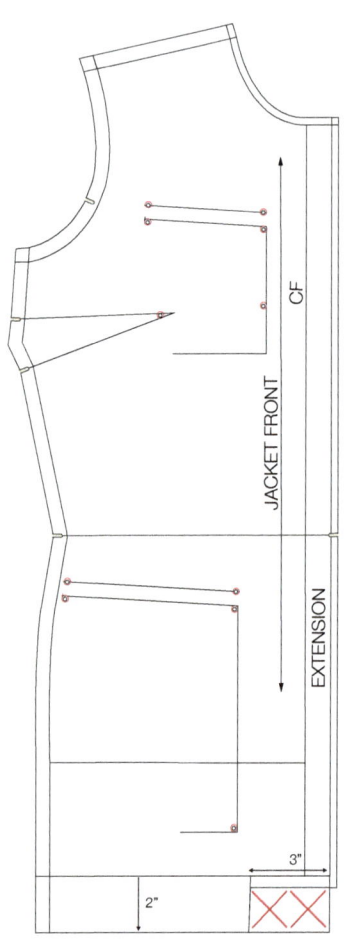 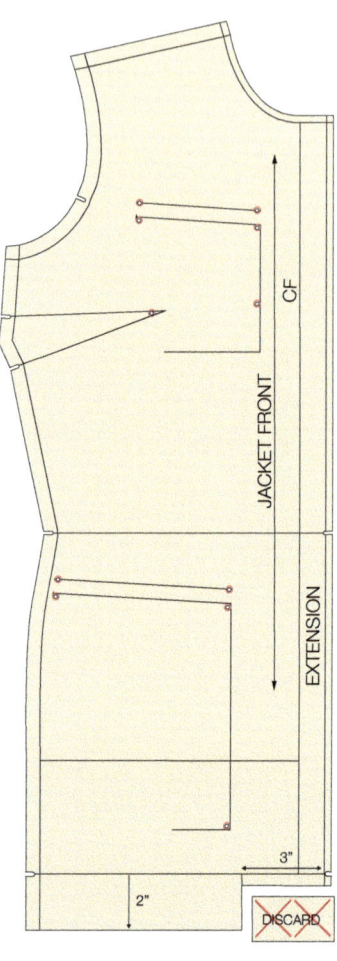

1. Trace front pattern retaining pocket placement lines.
2. Draw a parallel line ½ inch (1.2cm) up from both top pocket placement lines for flap placement.
3. Circle and drill (red circles) ⅛ inch (3mm) into the placement points for the pockets.
4. Circle and drill (red circles) ½ inch (1.2cm) into the bust dart.
5. Add ½ inch (1.2cm) SA to all seams with the exception of the front, neckline, and hem.
6. Add ¼ inch (6mm) SA to the front and neckline.
7. Add 2 inches (5cm) for hem.
8. Measure 3 inches (7.5cm) in from original front hemline and square down to hem.
9. Measure ½ inch (1.2cm) SA down from original hemline and notch.
10. Discard the "wedge" when cutting out the pattern.
    Note: The hem when folded will match the sewing line of your front facing.

Back pattern seam allowance and hem

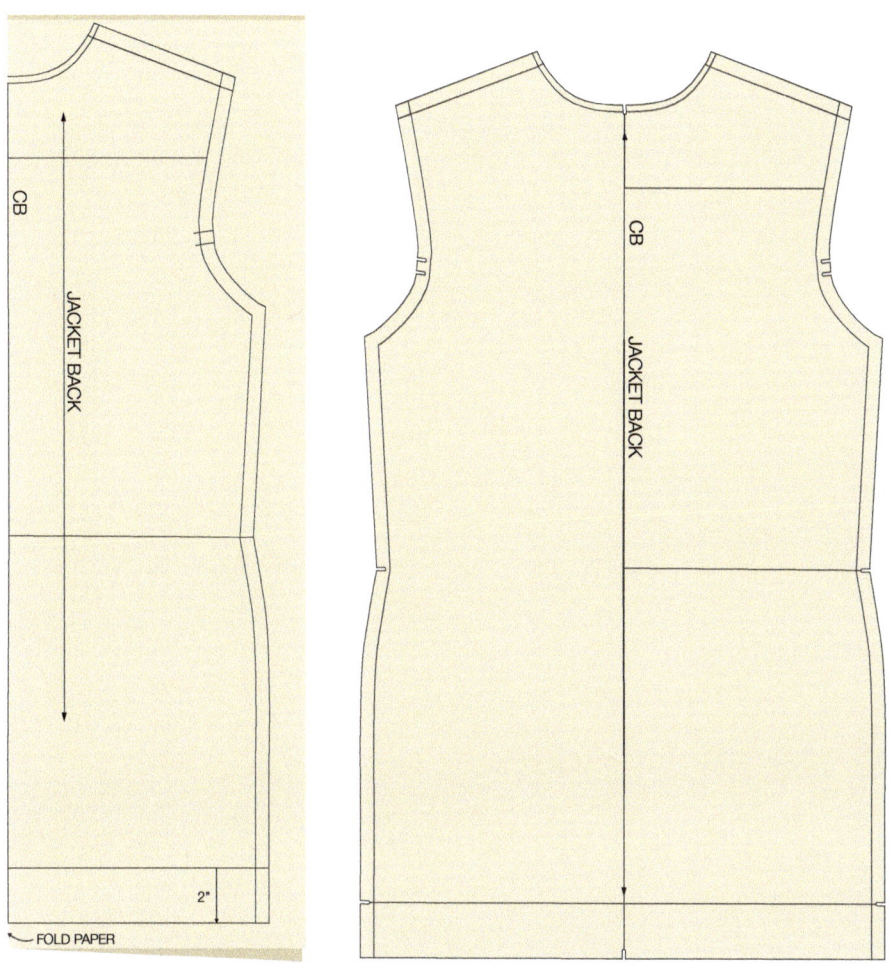

1. Fold pattern paper in half and trace the back pattern.
2. Add ½ inch (1.2cm) SA to all seams with the exception of the back neckline and hem.
3. Add ¼ inch (6mm) SA to the back neckline.
4. Add 2 inches (5cm) for hem.
5. Notch pattern while still folded.

**CHAPTER FIVE:
THE MAO JACKET**

Collar and collar stand seam allowance

Front and back facing seam allowance

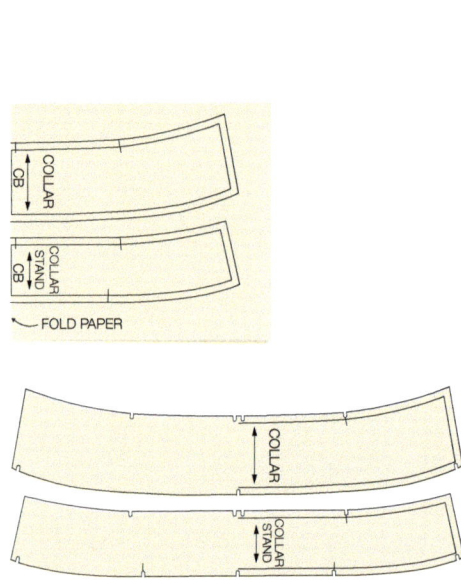

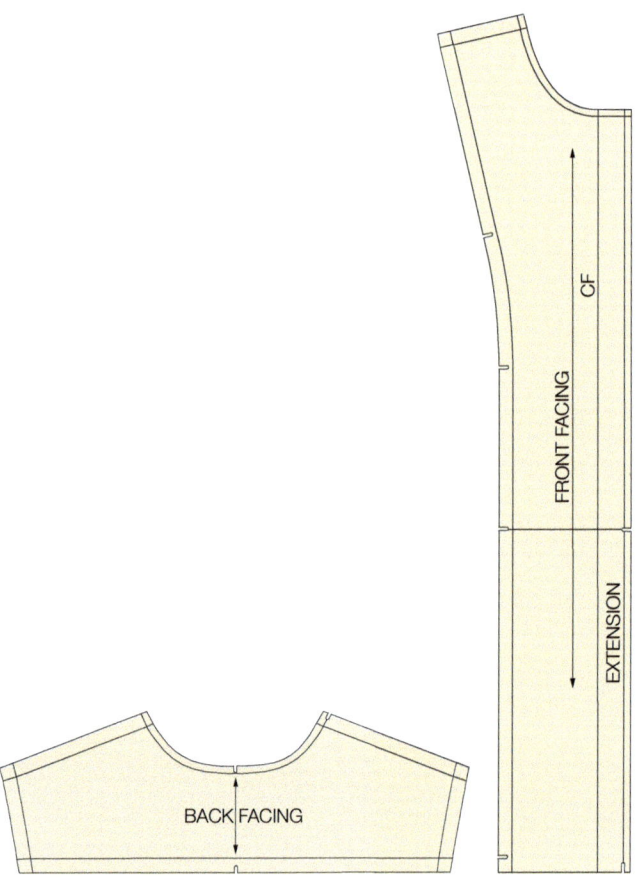

1. Fold pattern paper in half and trace collar and stand.

2. Add ¼ inch (6mm) SA to all seams.

3. Retain all notches.

4. Add a double-notch at the center back (one on each side) of the upper edge of both the collar and the collar stand for sewing guide.

1. Add ¼ inch (6mm) SA to back and front necklines and down CF.

2. Add ½ inch (1.2cm) SA to all other seams.

2-piece sleeve seam allowance and hem

Front and back lining seam allowance and hem

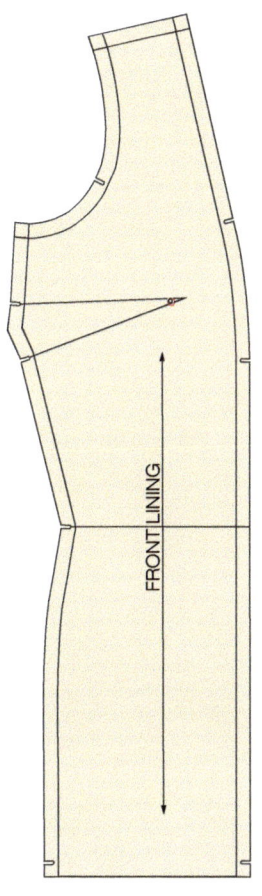

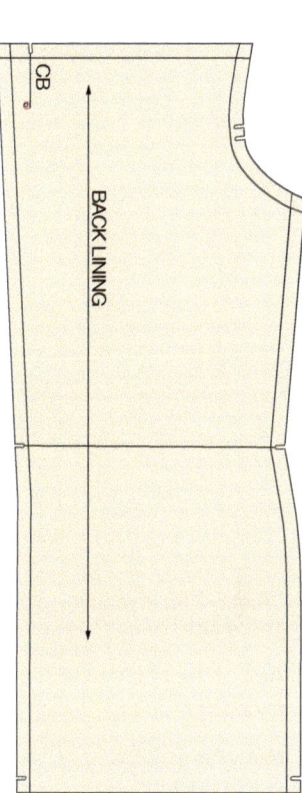

1. Add ½ inch (1.2cm) SA to all seams with the exception of vent and hem.
2. Add ¼ inch (6mm) SA to vent.
3. Mark hems 2 inches (5cm).
4. If you are not planning on making "working" buttonholes, miter upper-sleeve vent (not shown). **Note: Make sure to fold paper back at hemline when cutting out to ensure the hem lies correctly on garment.**

1. Add ½ inch (1.2cm) SA to all seams with the exception of the hem.
2. You do not add a SA to the hem as it is already "built in"; mark ½ inch (1.2cm) up and notch.

2-piece sleeve lining seam allowance and hem

Pocket and pocket lining seam allowances

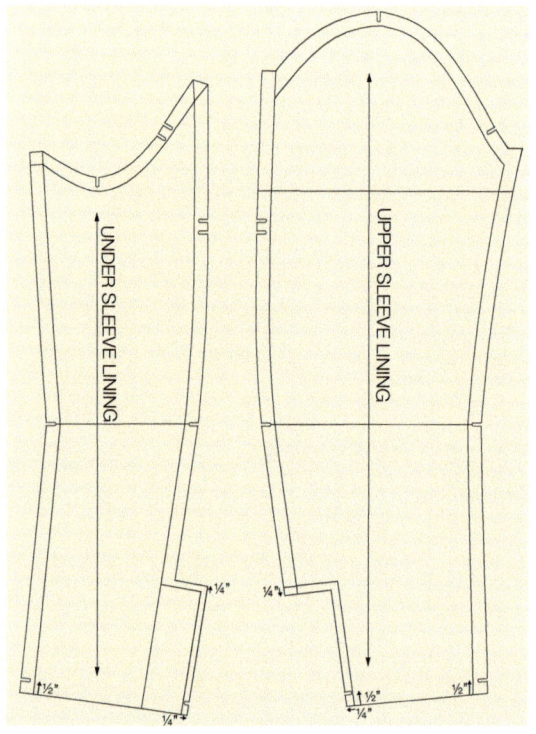

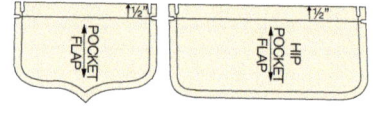

1. Add ½ inch (1.2cm) SA to all seams with the exception of vent and hem.
2. Add ¼ inch (6mm) SA to vent.
3. You do not add a SA to the hem as it is already "built in"; mark ½ inch (1.2cm) up and notch.
4. If you are not making working buttonholes, lining will not have vents; follow the original sleeve-lines of the block (not shown) for your pattern.

1. Add ½ inch (1.2cm) SA to the top of both pocket flaps.
2. Add ¼ inch (6mm) SA to the rest of the pattern.

| THE HISTORY OF THE MAO | CONTEMPORARY MAO JACKETS | THE PATTERN | MUSLIN OR TOILE FITTING | **PRODUCTION PATTERN** | TECHNICAL FLATS AND FINISHED PATTERN PIECES |

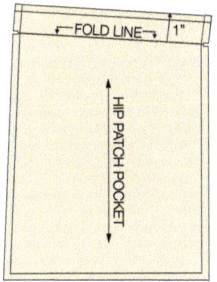 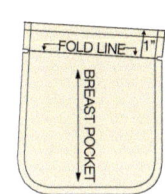 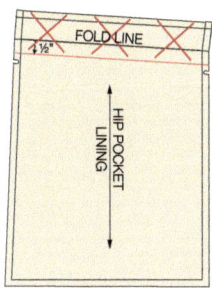 

3. For pocket SA, add 1 inch (2.5cm) to top of pockets (this includes a ¾ inch (1.75cm) fold and ¼ inch (6mm) SA).

4. Add ¼ inch (6mm) SA to the rest of the pattern.

5. To make pocket lining, trace pockets with SA added.

6. Draw a parallel line (red line) ½ inch (1.2cm) down from the fold-line.

7. Cut out pattern at this line and discard the top as shown.

8. Notch ¼ inch (6mm) into pattern as shown for SA.

CHAPTER FIVE:
THE MAO JACKET

TECHNICAL FLATS AND FINISHED PATTERN PIECES

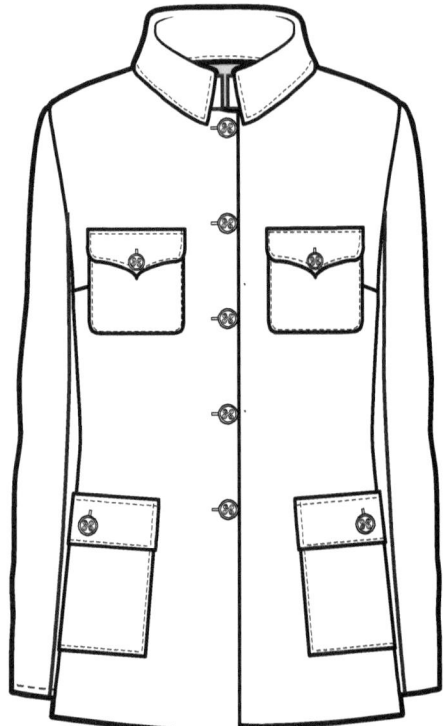
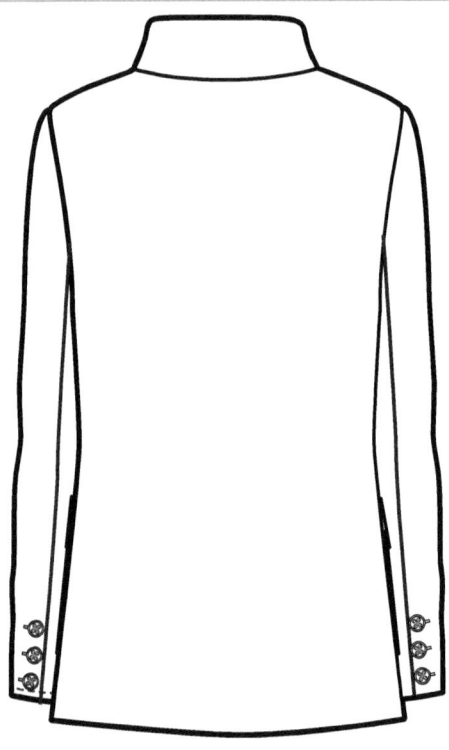

Self:

1. Front (cut 2).
2. Back (cut 1).
3. Upper-sleeve (cut 2).
4. Under-sleeve (cut 2).
5. Collar stand (cut 2).
6. Collar (cut 2).
7. Front facing (cut 2).
8. Back facing (cut 1).
9. Breast pocket (cut 2).
10. Breast pocket flap (cut 2).
11. Hip pocket (cut 2).
12. Hip pocket flap (cut 2).

Lining:

1. Front (cut 2).
2. Back (cut 2).
3. Upper-sleeve (cut 2).
4. Under-sleeve (cut 2).
5. Breast pocket lining (cut 2).
6. Hip pocket lining (cut 2).

"Style is a simple way of saying complicated things."

Jean Cocteau

| THE HISTORY OF THE MAO | CONTEMPORARY MAO JACKETS | THE PATTERN | MUSLIN OR TOILE FITTING | PRODUCTION PATTERN | **TECHNICAL FLATS AND FINISHED PATTERN PIECES** |

5.13
Front detail of Mao jacket.

CHAPTER SIX

THE BALMACAAN COAT

Patterning concepts learned:
- **coat block**
- **2-piece raglan sleeve**
- **flared silhouette**
- **convertible collar (Prussian)**
- **hidden-button placket**
- **inseam pocket with welt**
- **sleeve tab**

6.1
Designed Balmacaan coat front.

6.2
Designed Balmacaan coat back.

**CHAPTER SIX:
THE BALMACAAN COAT**

THE HISTORY OF THE BALMACAAN COAT

Named after the Scottish estate near Inverness, the Balmacaan, or Bal for short, is the quintessential raincoat. This coat is often mistaken for a trench coat, but it differs in many respects owing to its clean lines, Prussian collar, raglan sleeves, and hidden-button plaque.

The story behind the cut of the coat harks back to a simpler time when it was often constructed in tweed and used as an overcoat for shooting and hunting due to its warmth and waterproof qualities. In the early part of the twentieth century, it also became popular as a motoring coat for both men and women in England and the United States for the very same reason.

The origin of the raglan sleeve can be credited to the misfortune of one Lord Raglan. In 1815, Lord Raglan lost his right arm as a result of complications from wounds obtained on the battlefield. His tailor, at the request of Raglan, ingeniously devised a new type of sleeve which extended the sleeve cap to the neck, omitting the traditional armhole. This design allowed for better ease of movement and kept the garment from slipping off his shoulder. It can be said that this new style literally helped him keep his shirt on. Originally called a pointed sleeve for obvious reasons, it wasn't officially referred to as a raglan sleeve until after the lord's death in 1855.

6.3
The American theater and film actress Katharine Hepburn poses in a red Balmacaan.

"I seem to always start a collection by designing outerwear and jackets."

Alexander Wang

| THE HISTORY OF THE BALMACAAN COAT | CONTEMPORARY BALMACAANS | THE PATTERN | MUSLIN OR TOILE FITTING | PRODUCTION PATTERN | TECHNICAL FLATS AND FINISHED PATTERN PIECES |

6.4
A young man in a Balmacaan overcoat, 1946.

6.5
Italian singer-songwriter and actress Marisa Sannia wears a pink Balmacaan coat, 1966.

6.6
A vintage photograph of two young women walking down the street in their Balmacaan coats.

While an English lord was the inspiration, it was an American industrialist who was responsible for the name Balmacaan. In 1905, Bradley Martin, as notoriously known for the lavish parties he threw as he was for making money, asked his London tailor to whip up a coat for him to wear while bird shooting at his country estate. The tailor drew inspiration from the hunting coats worn by the British aristocracy, who in turn had developed their version from sleeveless overcoats worn by the military decades earlier.

And what does this story have to do with a raincoat named after a place in Scotland, you may ask. It turns out that Martin leased the Balmacaan estate for many years, and when the coat quickly became all the rage among the movers and shakers he socialized with, his tailor requested permission to name the coat after the estate. It was even copyrighted to make it exclusive and, the rest is history.

The functional utility of the overcoat has remained popular throughout the twentieth century, and today the Balmacaan remains a true classic.

151

CONTEMPORARY BALMACAANS

6.7
Valentino: Runway, Paris Fashion Week
Womenswear Fall/Winter 2015/2016.

6.8
Christian Dior: Runway, Paris Fashion Week
Womenswear Fall/Winter 2015/2016.

| THE HISTORY OF THE BALMACAAN COAT | CONTEMPORARY BALMACAANS | THE PATTERN | MUSLIN OR TOILE FITTING | PRODUCTION PATTERN | TECHNICAL FLATS AND FINISHED PATTERN PIECES |

6.9
Prada: Runway RTW, Milan Fashion Week Fall 2014.

6.10
Saint Laurent: Runway, Paris Fashion Week Womenswear Fall/Winter 2015/2016.

CHAPTER SIX:
THE BALMACAAN COAT

THE PATTERN

Start with the coat front, back and sleeve blocks

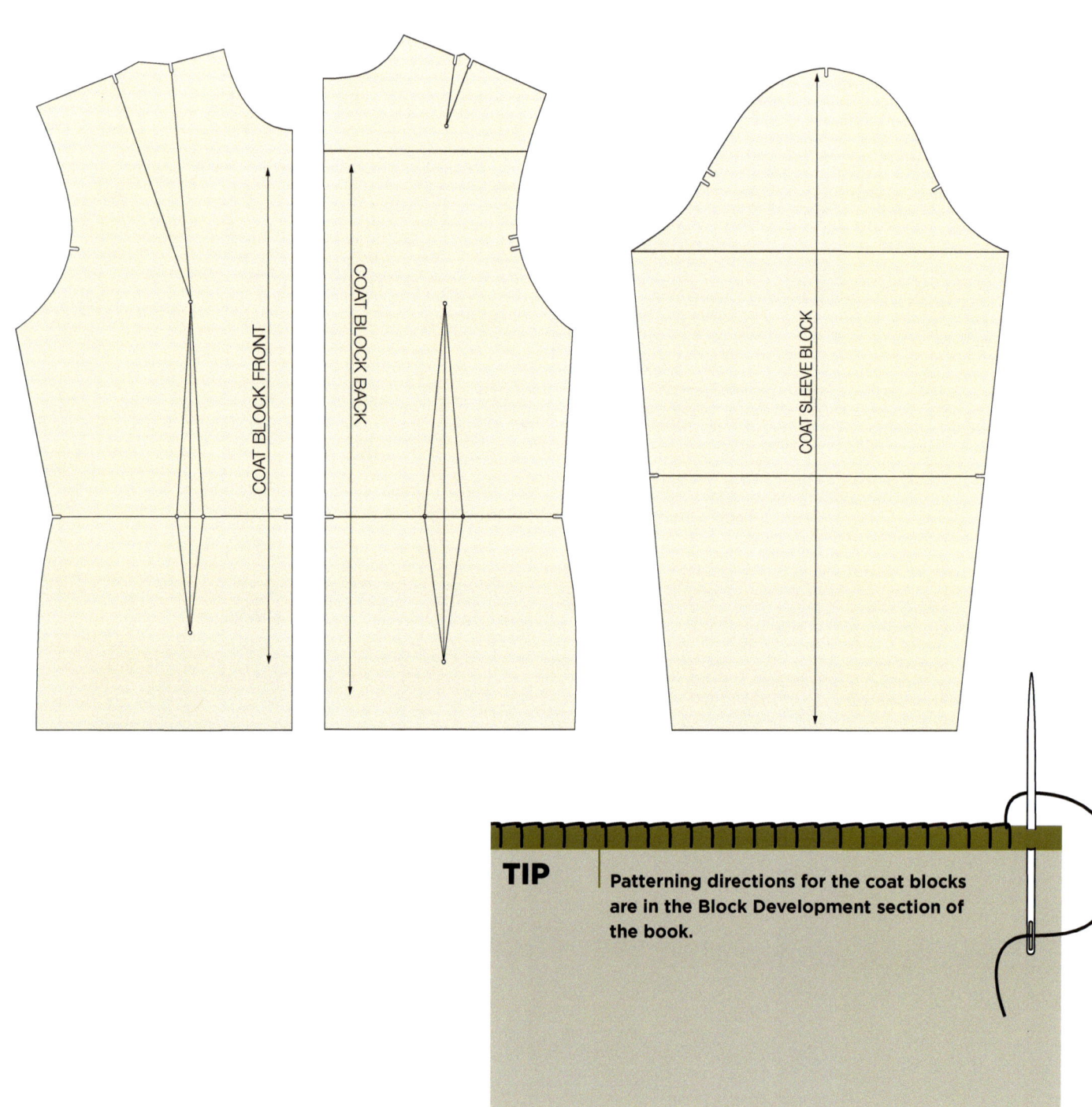

TIP Patterning directions for the coat blocks are in the Block Development section of the book.

Close shoulder darts

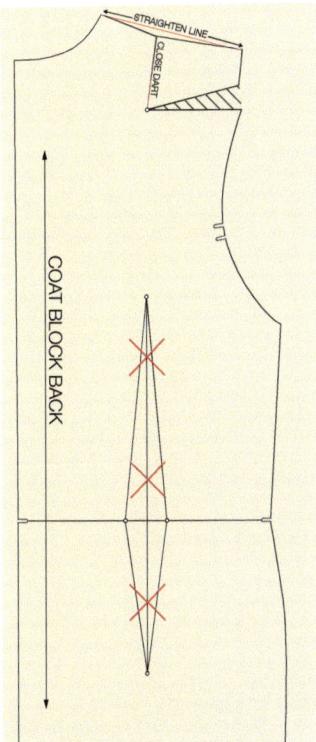

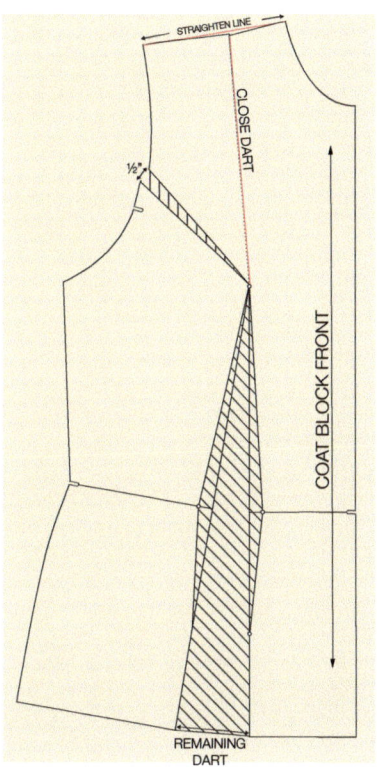

1. Trace back coat block.
2. Transfer shoulder dart to armhole by the slash and spread method.
3. Draw a line from the dart point to the armhole.
4. Cut slash line from this line to dart point.
5. Cut another slash line down dart leg on shoulder.
6. Close shoulder dart and tape shut.
7. Straighten shoulder line if not straight.
8. Release contour dart.
   Note: Releasing a dart simply means to ignore it.

9. Trace front coat block.
10. Transfer front shoulder dart to armhole and through contour dart by the slash and spread method.
11. Draw a line (red line) through the center of the contour dart to the bottom of the pattern.
12. Draw another line to the armhole above the notch.
13. Slash paper on these lines to bust point (apex).
14. Transfer ½ inch (1.2cm) of the shoulder dart to armhole.
15. Transfer the rest of the shoulder dart through the contour dart.
16. Straighten shoulder line if not straight.
    Note: Make sure to retain your waist notches on both patterns.

Lower neckline and clean up armscye

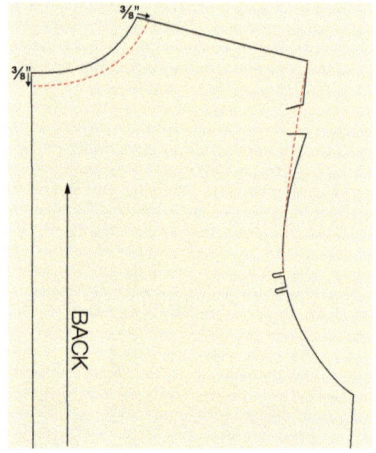
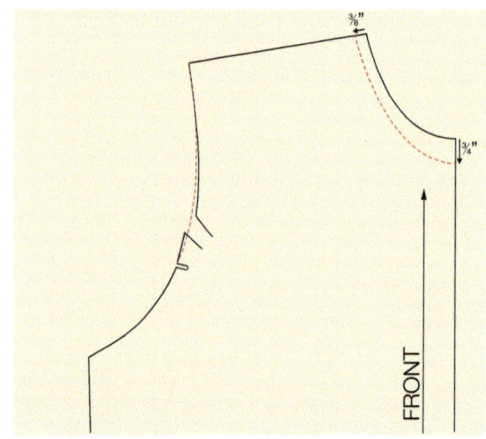

1. Lower center back neckline ⅜ inch (1cm).
2. Move shoulder in ⅜ inch (1cm) on both front and back patterns.
3. Lower center front neckline ¾ inch (1.75cm).
4. Redraw necklines (red dotted lines) using a French curve.
5. Measure front neckline, record_____.
6. Measure back neckline, record_____.
7. Clean up armscye to notches using a French curve (red dotted line).

Raglan sleeve development

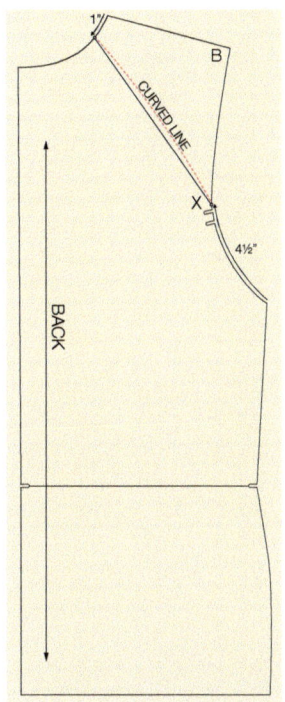
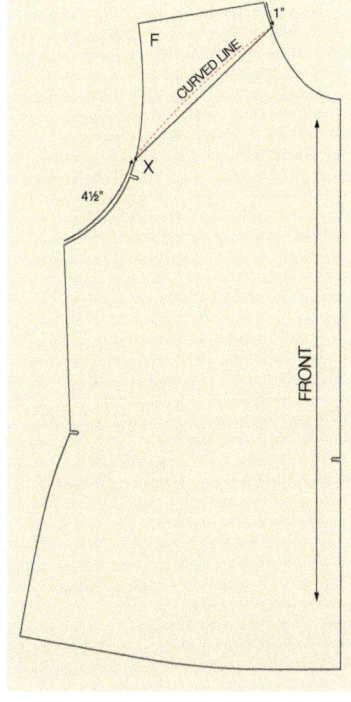
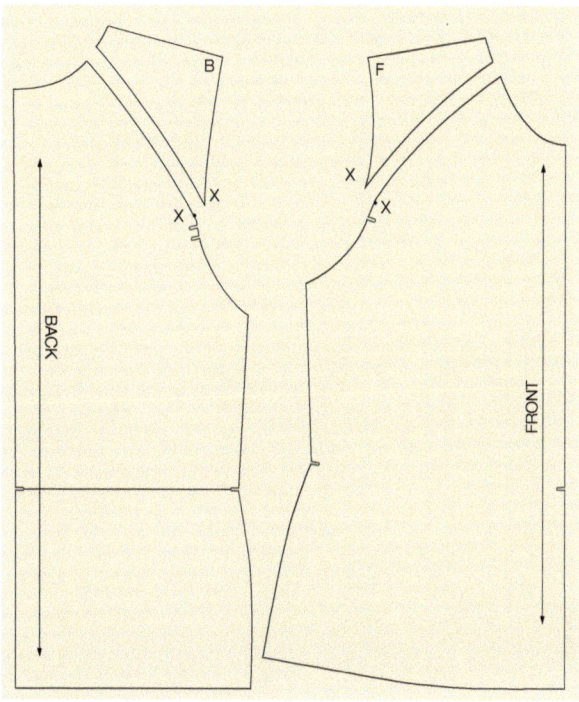

1. Mark X 4 ½ inches (11.2cm) up from armhole on both front and back patterns.
2. Mark B for back and F for front on shoulder tips as shown.
3. Mark 1 inch (2.5cm) down from high-point shoulder on neckline.
4. Draw a straight line from X to neckline mark.
5. Draw a curved line (red dotted line) extending approximately ¼ inch (6mm) above the midpoint of the straight line: this is your raglan style-line.
6. Cut out raglan yoke.
   Note: You can make this style-line any shape that you want for the raglan.

Adding raglan yoke to sleeve

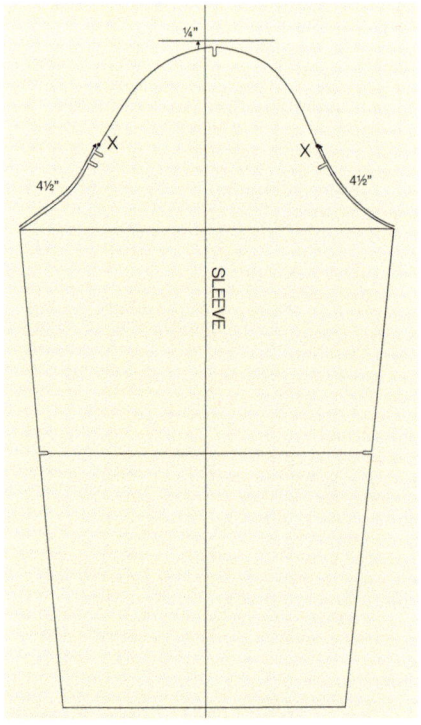
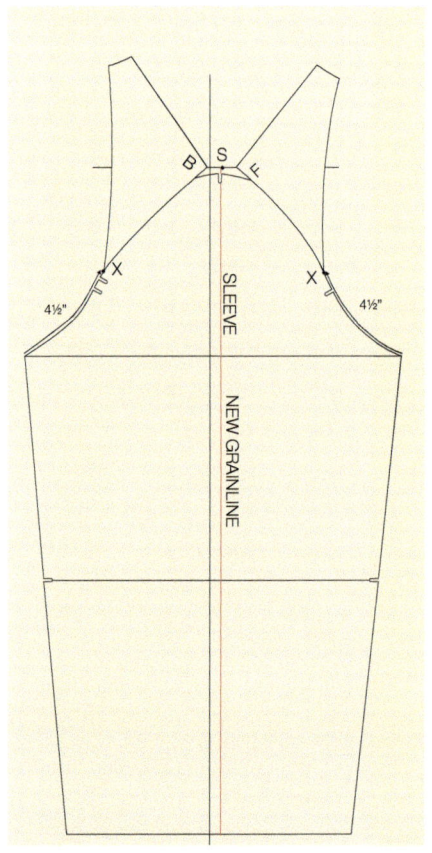

1. Trace coat sleeve block.
2. Square a guideline ¼ inch (6mm) up from sleeve cap.
3. Mark X 4 ½ inches (11.2cm) up from armhole on both front and back sleeve patterns.
4. Build your raglan by placing cut-out yokes on the sleeve cap matching Xs and pivoting yoke to touch guideline at shoulder tips.
5. Trace yokes and remove.
6. Mark S centered between shoulder tips B and F.
7. Reposition grainline (red line) to match S parallel to old grainline.

Completing raglan sleeve

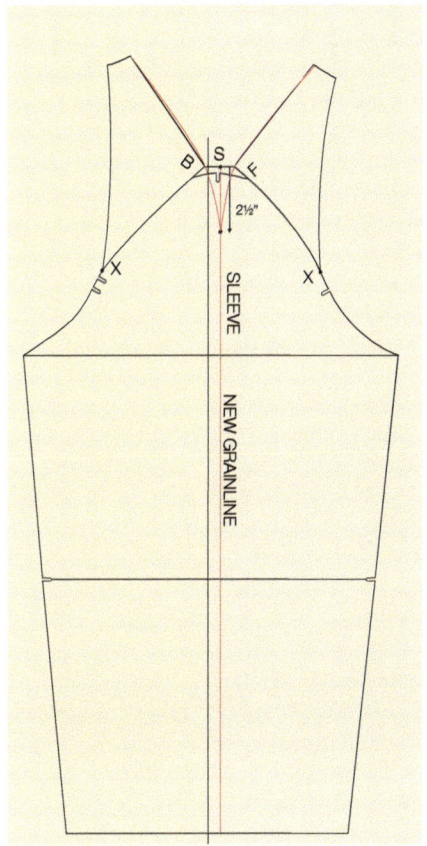

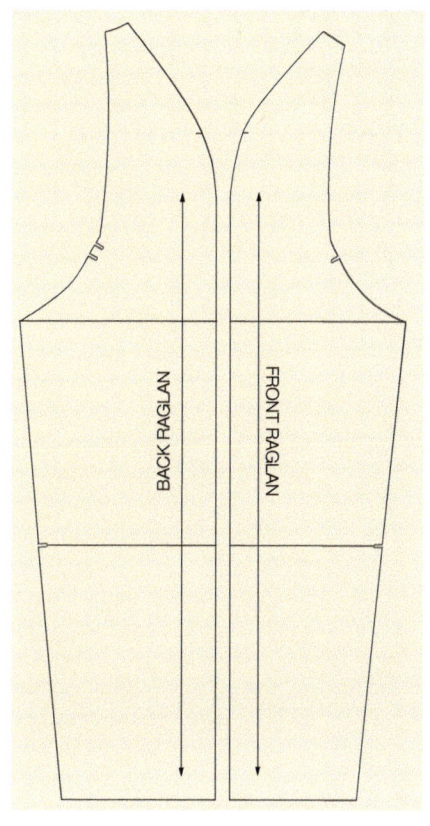

1. Measure 2 ½ inches (6.2cm) down from S and mark.
2. Draw a curved line (red curved line) touching shoulder tips and ending at point.
3. Cut out raglan front and back along new grainline, making sure to notch at shoulder tips B and F.
4. Draw new grainlines on front and back raglan sleeves parallel to old grainline.
5. Walk pattern from wrist up and equalize and blend front and back shoulder curves if necessary.

**CHAPTER SIX:
THE BALMACAAN COAT**

Adding length and extension to front pattern

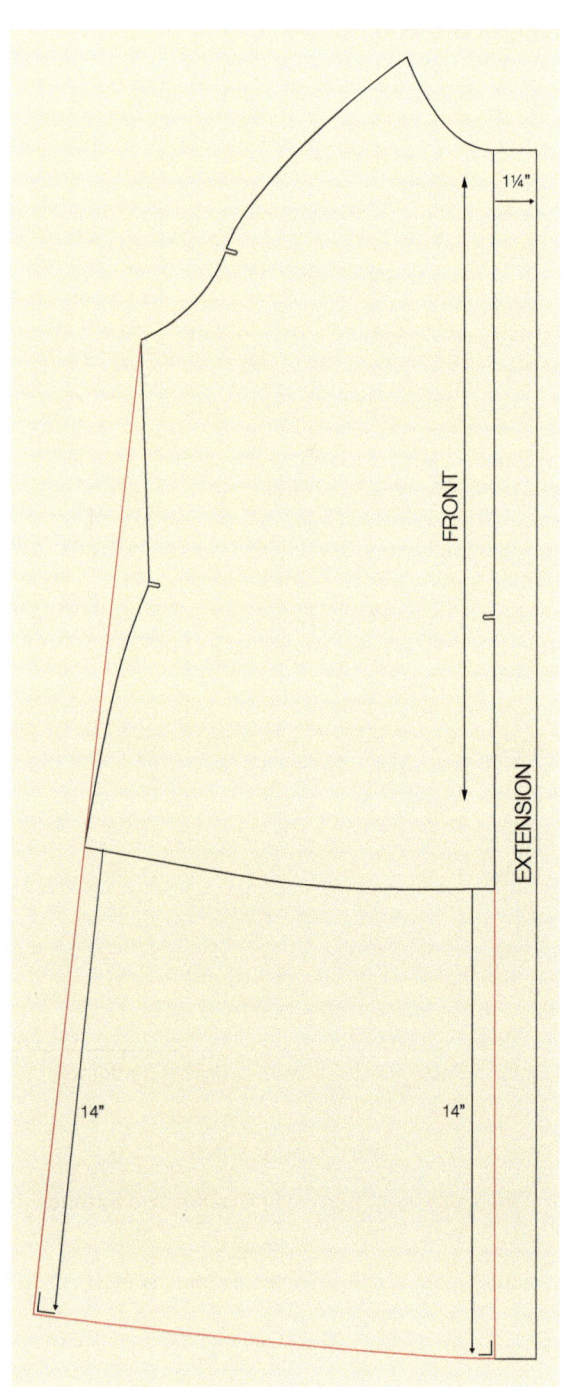

1. Trace front pattern.
2. Straighten side seam (red line) with ruler.
3. Extend side seam 14 inches (35cm) to lengthen coat.
   Note: This makes the coat above-the-knee in length.
4. Lengthen center front (CF) 14 inches (35cm) to match side seam measurement.
5. Draw the hemline (red line) making sure to square off at both front and side seams.
6. Add 1 ¼ inches (3cm) for button/hole extension parallel to center front.
   Note: Make sure that your extension matches the diameter of the buttons that you are using.

Adding length and flare to back pattern

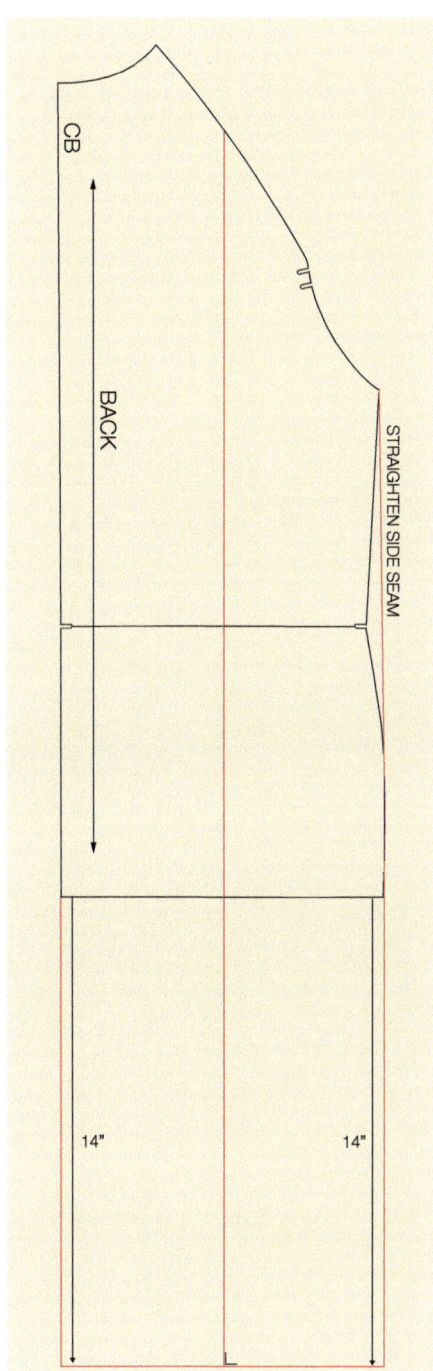

1. Trace back pattern.
2. Straighten side seam (red line) with ruler.
3. Extend side seam (red line) and back seam (red line) on pattern 14 inches (35cm) to lengthen coat.
4. Divide bottom of pattern in half and square a line (red line) up.
5. Slash and spread line 8 inches (20cm).
6. At center back (CB), measure 4 inches (10cm) down from neckline and mark.

CHAPTER SIX:
THE BALMACAAN COAT

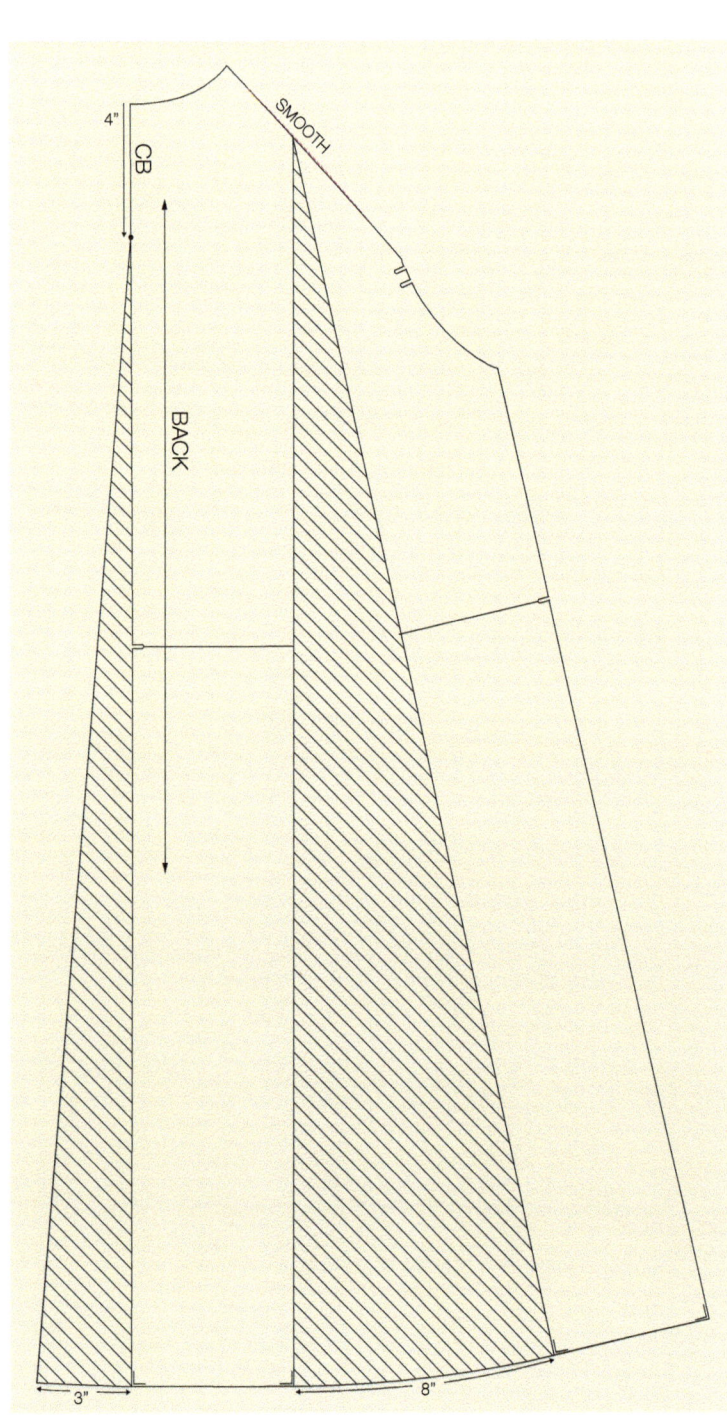

7. Extend hemline at CB of pattern 3 inches (7.5cm) and mark.

8. Draw a line connecting the points to flare.

9. Draw the hemline making sure to square off at both back and side seams.

10. Keep grainline parallel to original.

11. Smooth raglan line (red dotted line) if necessary. **Note: Back sweep of coat is intentionally greater than the front.**

Upper-collar development

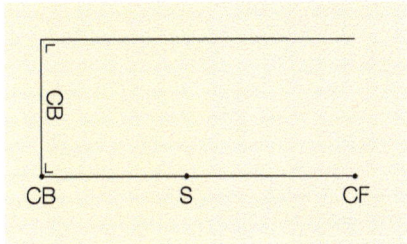
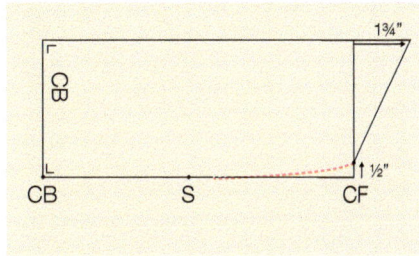
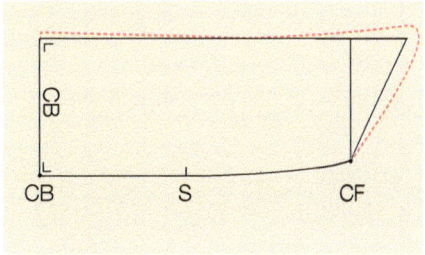

1. Draw a horizontal line equal to the front and back neckline measurement.
2. Mark center back (CB) and center front (CF).
3. Using back neckline measurement mark shoulder S.
4. Square a line 4 inches (10cm) up from CB.
5. Square another line at CB.
6. Square a line up from CF.
7. Mark a point ½ inch (1.2cm) up from CF.
8. Draw a curved line (red dotted line) from shoulder S to point.
9. Extend collar edge 1 ¾ inch (4.25cm) from CF line.
10. Connect CF to end of collar edge.
11. Adjust shape of collar as desired.
12. Notch shoulder.
    Note: I like to make a slight curve at the center back of the collar.

MUSLIN OR TOILE FITTING

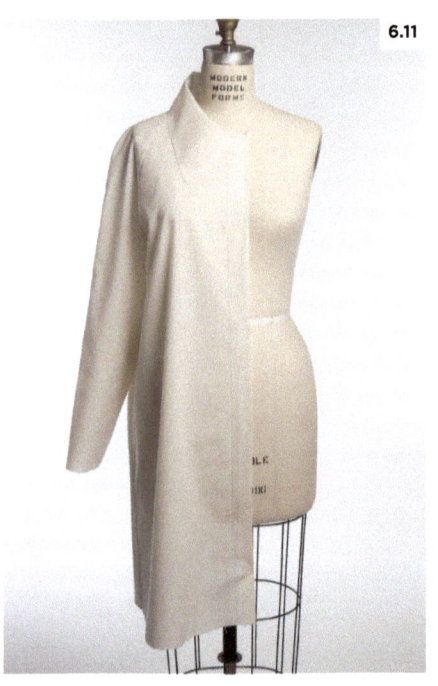

- Before you draft the facing, pocket, and lining patterns, prepare a muslin for fit.
- Do not add seam allowance (SA) to pattern as you will most likely be adjusting the muslin for fit.
- Draw the seam allowance (SA) directly onto the muslin after tracing the working pattern.
- Make any necessary fit corrections to pattern.
- Now you can move on to the facing, pocket, and lining patterns.

6.11 Checking muslin front fit.
6.12 Checking muslin back fit.
6.13 Collar detail.

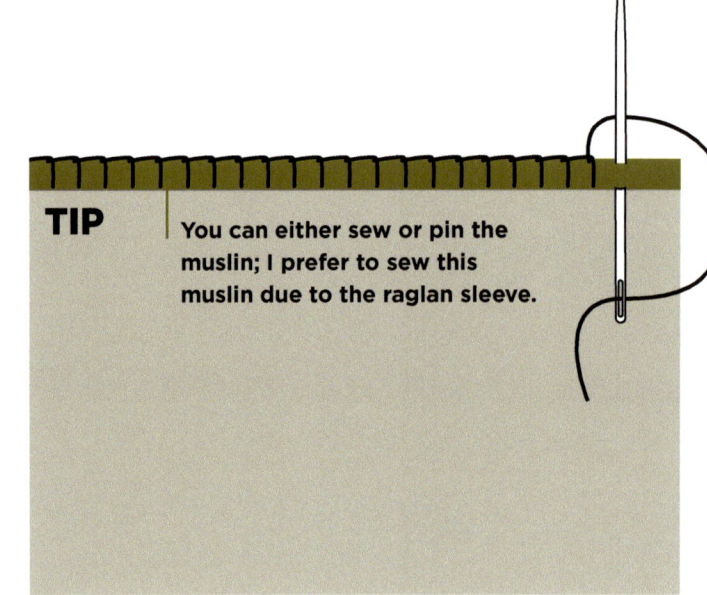

TIP You can either sew or pin the muslin; I prefer to sew this muslin due to the raglan sleeve.

Completing the upper- and under-collar

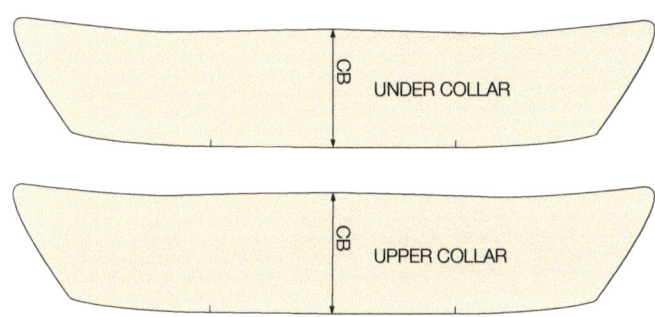

1. Fold paper in half and trace the collar twice: don't forget to mark your shoulder seam notch.
2. Mark the first pattern the upper-collar.
3. On the second pattern, draft under-collar by reducing the out-seam of the collar by ⅛ inch (3mm) at the CB and blending to zero at the collar point (red dotted line).
4. Mark grainlines parallel to CB.

Inseam pocket with welt

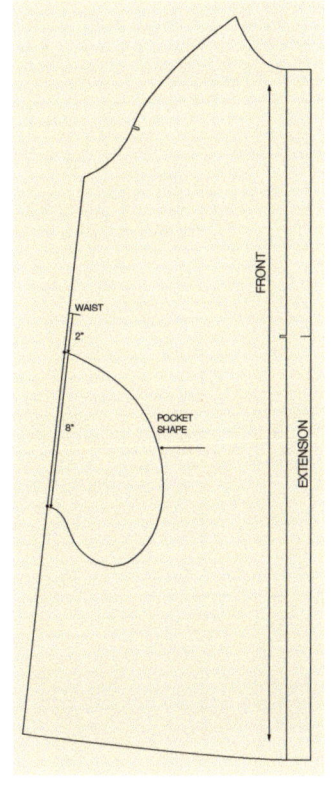
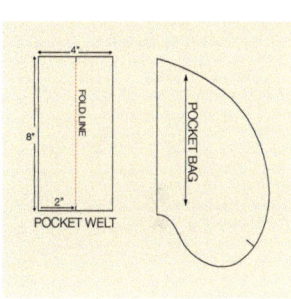

1. Mark pocket placement notch on both front and back patterns 2 inches (5cm) down from waist on side seams.
2. Mark pocket opening 8 inches (20cm) down and notch.
3. For a 2 inch (5cm) welt, square off a rectangle 4 inches (10cm) by 8 inches (20cm).
4. Mark a notch and dotted line (red dotted line) at 2 inches (5cm) for welt fold-line.
5. Draw desired shape of pocket bag on front pattern piece.
6. Using a tracing wheel, trace a copy for the pocket bag pattern.
   Note: I have ready-made stencils of basic pocket shapes to use when drafting them to save time and effort.

CHAPTER SIX:
THE BALMACAAN COAT

Sleeve tab

Front facing and front lining

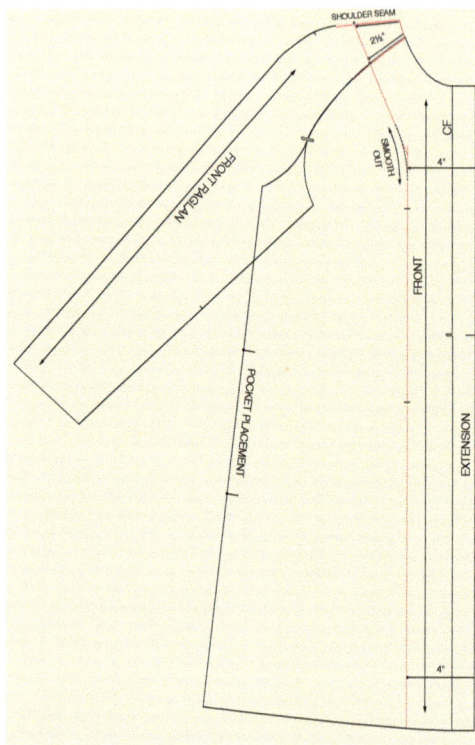
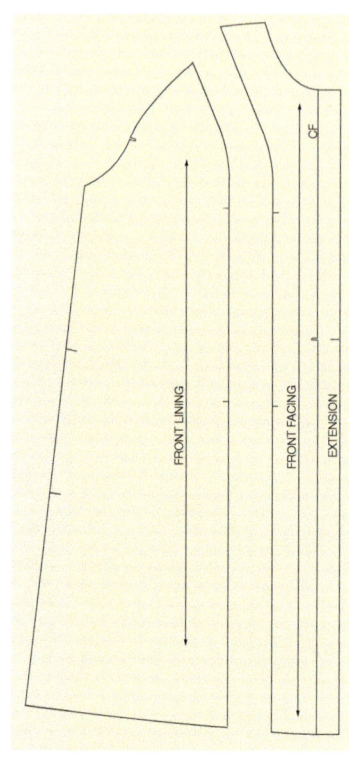

1. For a 1 ¼ inch (3cm) button, square off a rectangle 3 ½ inches (8.75cm) wide by 2 inches (5cm) long.
2. Mark a notch and dotted line (red dotted line) at 1 ¾ inches (4.25cm) for tab fold-line.

1. Trace front and front raglan sleeve pattern.
2. Lay front raglan sleeve pattern over front pattern, lining up raglan style-line.
3. Trace raglan sleeve neckline approximately 3 inches (7.5cm) down the shoulder seam.
4. With a tracing wheel, draw a line 2 ½ inches (6.2cm) from neckline on raglan sleeve (red dotted line) and extend that line into the front pattern.
5. Draw a parallel line (red dotted line) 4 inches (10cm) from center front extension (CF) until it intersects with the raglan line.
6. Remove front raglan sleeve pattern.
7. Smooth out where the two lines intersect.
8. Mark 2 control notches.
9. Cut out and mark front lining and front facing on new pattern pieces.

Back facing and back lining

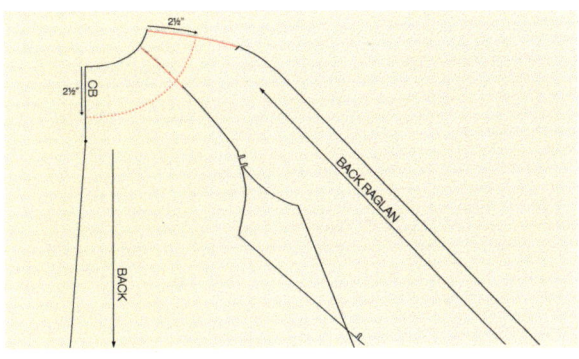

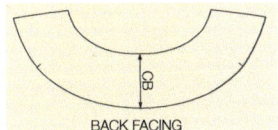

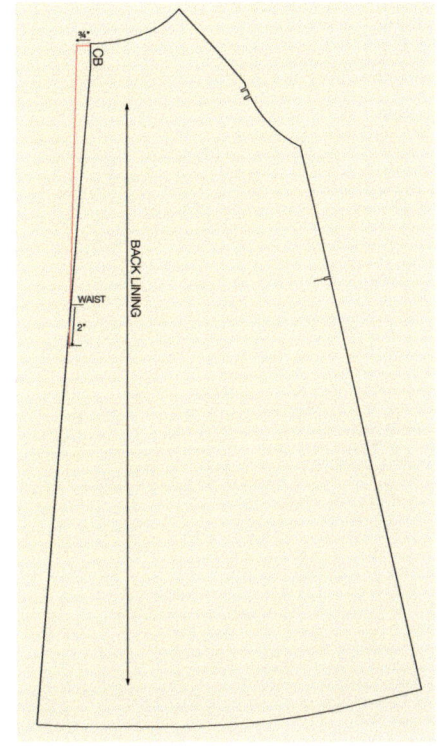

1. Trace back pattern.
2. Lay back raglan sleeve pattern over front pattern, lining up raglan style-line.
3. Trace raglan sleeve neckline and approximately 3 inches (7.5cm) down the shoulder seam (marked in red).
4. Remove back raglan sleeve pattern.
5. For back facing, draw a curved line 2 ½ inches (6.2cm) from neckline.
6. Cut out and open pattern up at center back line.
7. Notch shoulder and center back.
8. The remaining pattern is your back lining.
9. For back lining action pleat, mark 2 inches (5cm) down from waist and ¾ inch (1.75cm) out from center back and draw a straight line (red line).

CHAPTER SIX:
THE BALMACAAN COAT

Raglan sleeve lining

Button and buttonhole placement

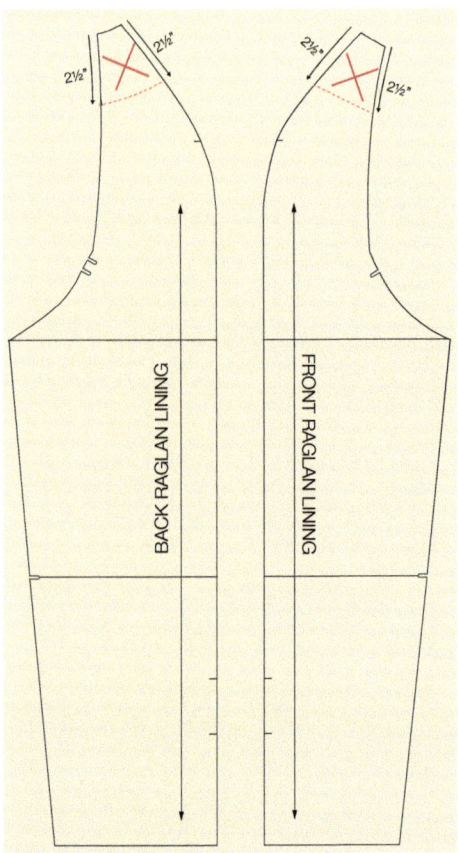

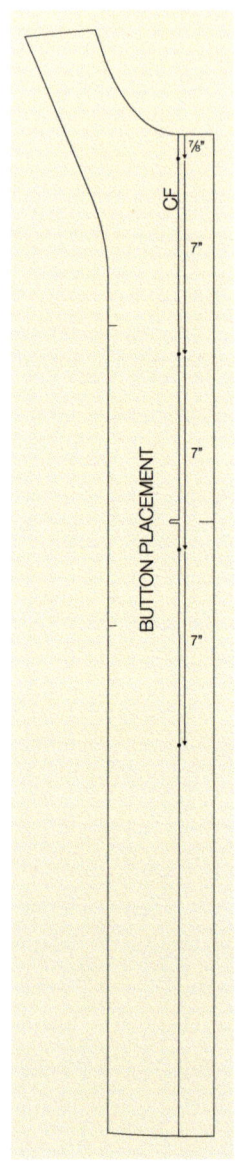

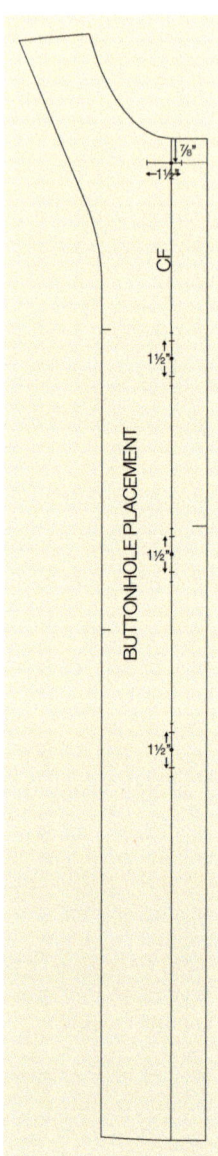

1. Trace front and back raglan sleeve patterns.
2. Draw new seam-lines (red dotted lines) 2 ½ inches (6.2cm) down from neckline.
3. Cut out and discard top pieces as these have already been incorporated into the front and back facings.

Hidden button placket

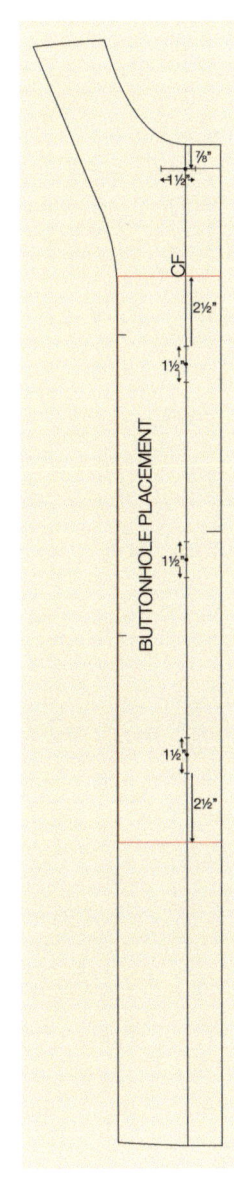

1. Trace front facing pattern.
2. You must first determine button/hole placement and spacing before you draft your hidden-button placket.
3. For this design, there are 4 buttons spaced 7 inches (17.5cm) apart.
4. To determine the first button placement, add ½ of the diameter of the button you are using plus ¼ inch (6mm).
   Note: For a 1 ¼ inch (3cm) button, ½ the diameter = ⅝ inch (1.5cm) + ¼ inch (6mm) = ⅞ inch (2cm).
5. Mark a drill point ⅞ inch (2cm) down from the neckline on the center front line.
6. Mark and drill the placement for the remaining 3 buttons, spacing them 7 inches (17.5cm) apart.
7. The top buttonhole will show and therefore be placed horizontally; the remaining hidden buttonholes will be placed vertically on the placket.
8. To determine the size of the buttonhole, add the diameter of the button plus the depth of the button to ensure that the button will slide through the buttonhole smoothly.
   Note: For the buttons used on this coat the buttonhole measurement is 1 ½ inch (3.75cm).
9. To determine the placement of the horizontal buttonhole, add ½ the diameter of the button plus ¼ inch (6mm) and mark this distance away from the center front.
   Note: For a 1 ¼ inch (3cm) button, ½ the diameter = ⅝ inch (1.5cm) + ¼ inch (6mm) = ⅞ inch (2cm).
10. Mark top buttonhole placement with a 1 ½ inch (3.75cm) line and two slashes as shown.
11. For the vertical buttonholes, the buttons are centered; mark the buttonhole placement ¾ inch (1.75cm) up and down from the button drill point with a line and two slashes as shown.

1. Trace the button/buttonhole placement pattern.
2. Transfer the button/buttonhole markings.
3. Square a line (red line) 2 ½ inches (6.2cm) up from the second buttonhole measurement.
4. Square a line (red line) 2 ½ inches (6.2cm) down from the last buttonhole measurement.
5. The outlined red on the paper is your placket pattern: you will need to cut two of them.
6. Retain all notches.
   Note: The placket can be made out of lining or lighter weight wool and will only be placed on the right side of the garment.

PRODUCTION PATTERN

Seam allowances and hems

TIP Before adding SAs and hems, make sure to walk your patterns and make any necessary corrections if seams or control notches do not match.

Front pattern seam allowance and hem

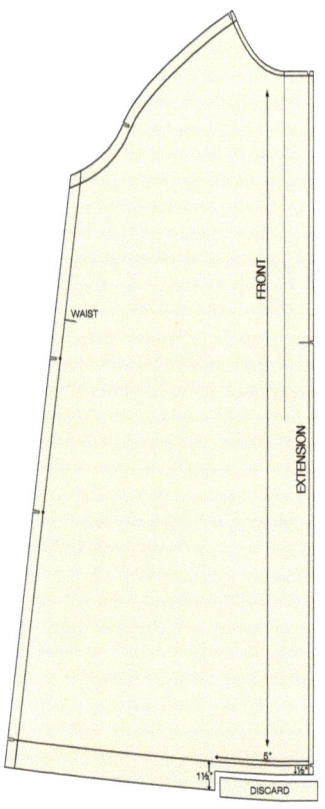

1. Trace front pattern.
2. Add ½ inch (1.2cm) SA to all seams with the exception of the front, neckline, and hem.
3. Add ¼ inch (6mm) SA to the front and neckline.
4. Add 1 ½ inches (3.75cm) for hem.
5. Measure 3 inches (7.5cm) in from original front hemline and square down to hem.
6. Measure ½ inch (1.2cm) SA down from original hemline and notch.
7. Discard the "wedge" when cutting out the pattern.
   Note: The hem when folded will match the sewing line of your front facing.

Back pattern seam allowance and hem

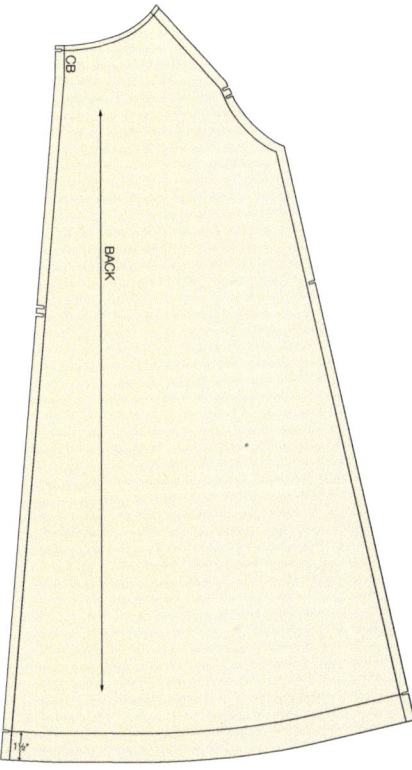

1. Add ½ inch (1.2cm) SA to all seams with the exception of the back neckline and hems.
2. Add ¼ inch (6mm) SA to back neckline.
3. Add 1 ½ inches (3.75cm) for hem.

Upper-collar seam allowance

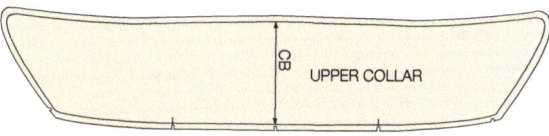

1. Add ¼ inch (6mm) SA to all seams for upper-collar.
2. Notch at CB, shoulder, and the SA.

Under-collar seam allowance

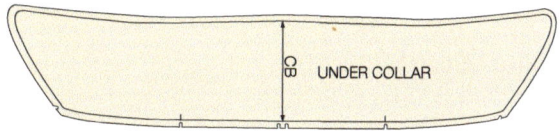

1. Add ¼ inch (6mm) SA to all seams for the under-collar.
2. Make a double-notch at back (one on each side of the CB).
3. Notch shoulder and the SA.
   Note: Mark SAs and cut out pattern while paper is still folded.

CHAPTER SIX:
THE BALMACAAN COAT

Front facing seam allowance and hem

Hidden-button placket seam allowance

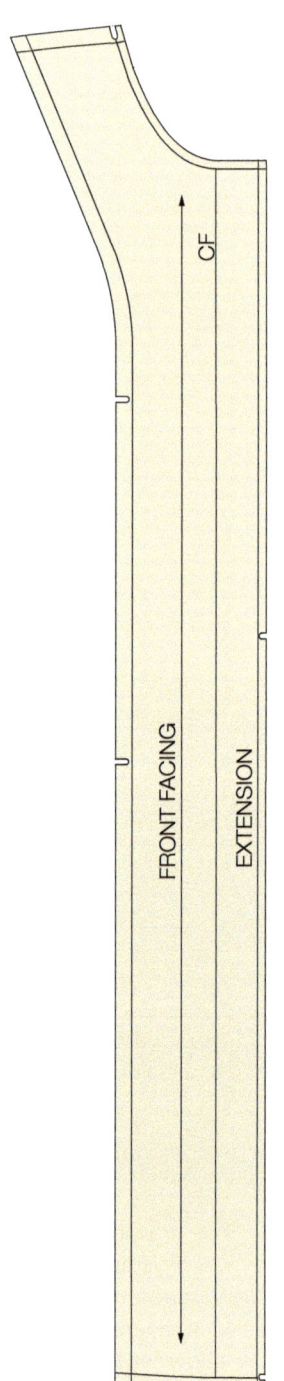

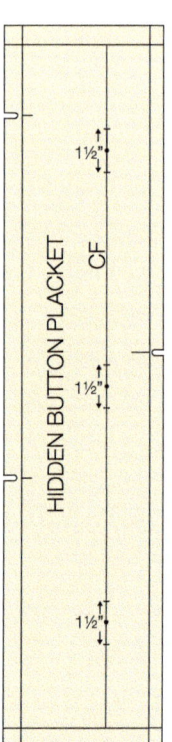

1. Add ¼ inch (6mm) SA to front neckline and down CF.
2. Add ½ inch (1.2cm) SA to all other seams.

1. Add ¼ inch (6mm) to CF.
2. Add ½ inch (1.2cm) to remaining seams.

Back facing seam allowance

Raglan sleeve seam allowance and hem

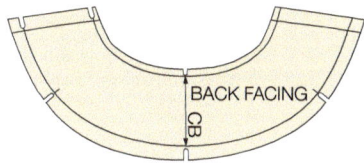
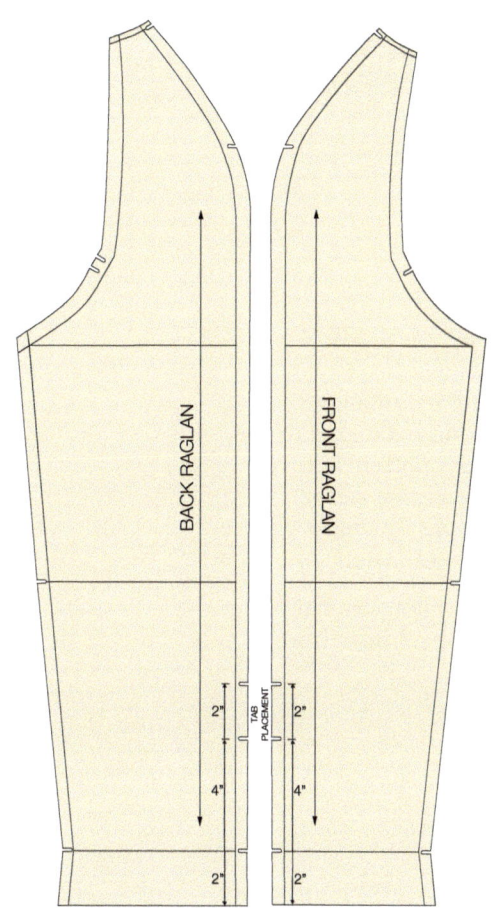

1. Add ¼ inch (6mm) to neckline.
2. Add ½ inch (1.2cm) SA to shoulder and outer curve.

1. Add ½ inch (1.2cm) SA to all seams with the exception of the hem.
2. For tab placement, notch sleeve 4 inches (10cm) up from hemline.
3. Mark another notch 2 inches (5cm) up.
4. Mark hems 2 inches (5cm).
   Note: Make sure to fold paper back at hemline when cutting out to ensure the hem lies correctly on garment.

CHAPTER SIX:
THE BALMACAAN COAT

Front, back, and raglan sleeve linings seam allowance and hems

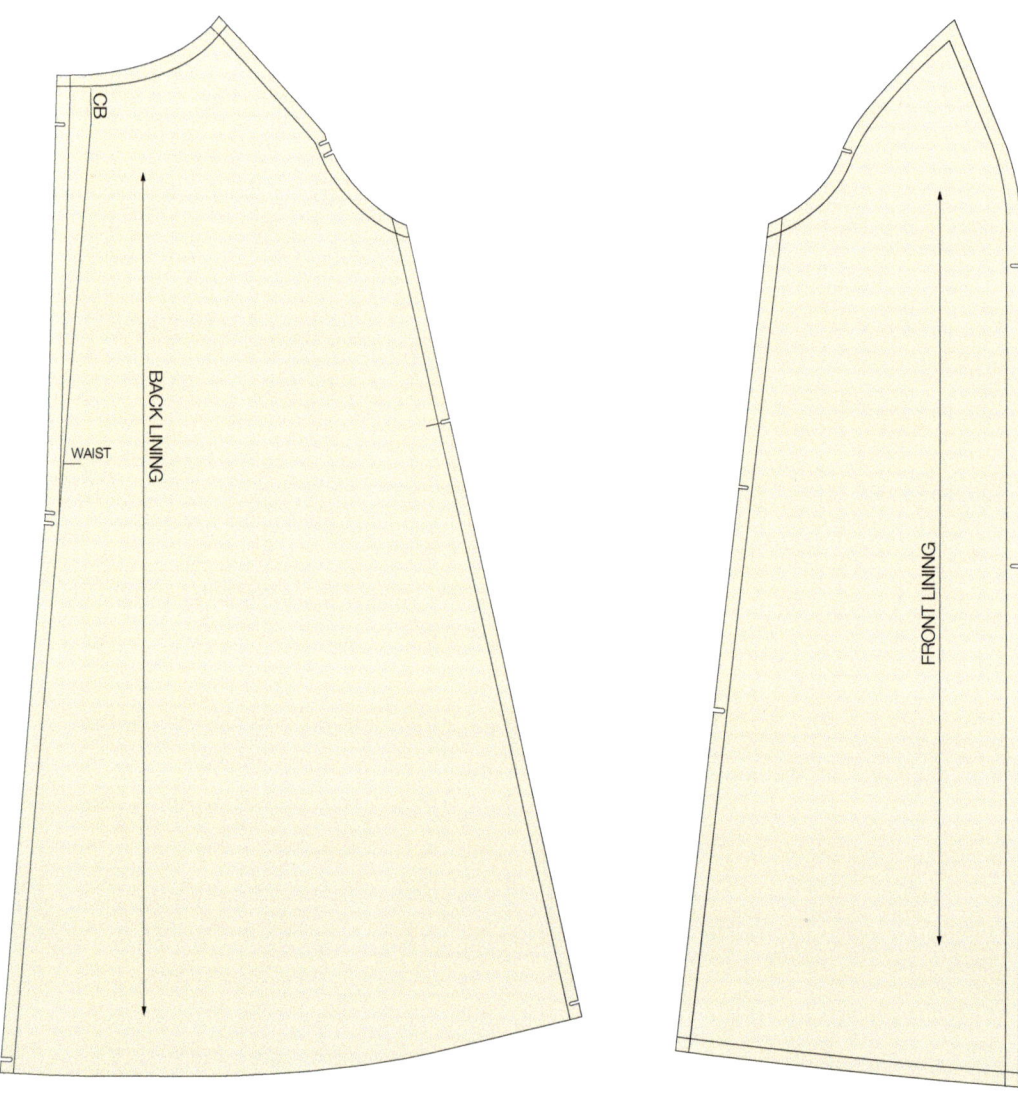

1. Add ½ inch (1.2cm) SA to all seams with the exception of the hem.
2. You do not add a SA to the hem as it is already "built in"; mark ½ inch (1.2cm) up and notch.

| THE HISTORY OF THE BALMACAAN COAT | CONTEMPORARY BALMACAANS | THE PATTERN | MUSLIN OR TOILE FITTING | **PRODUCTION PATTERN** | TECHNICAL FLATS AND FINISHED PATTERN PIECES |

Inseam pocket, welt and sleeve tab seam allowance

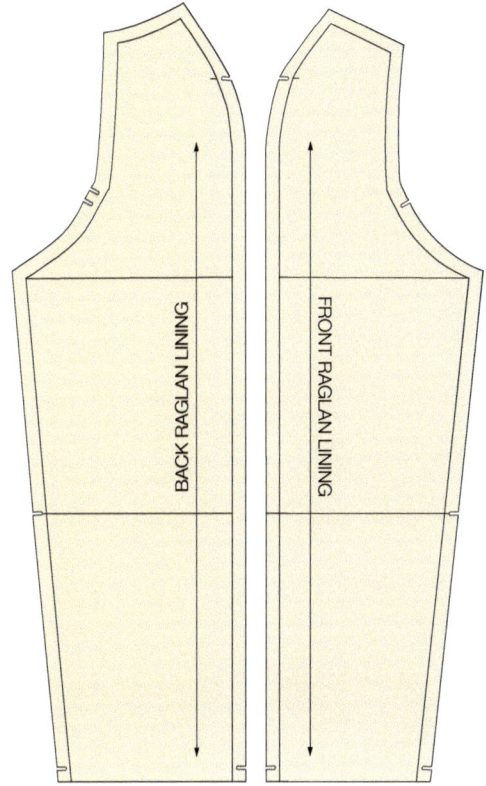

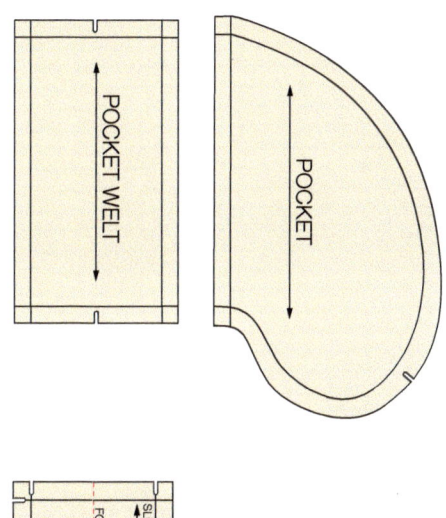

1. Add ½ inch (1.2cm) SA to all seams.

CHAPTER SIX:
THE BALMACAAN COAT

TECHNICAL FLATS AND FINISHED PATTERN PIECES

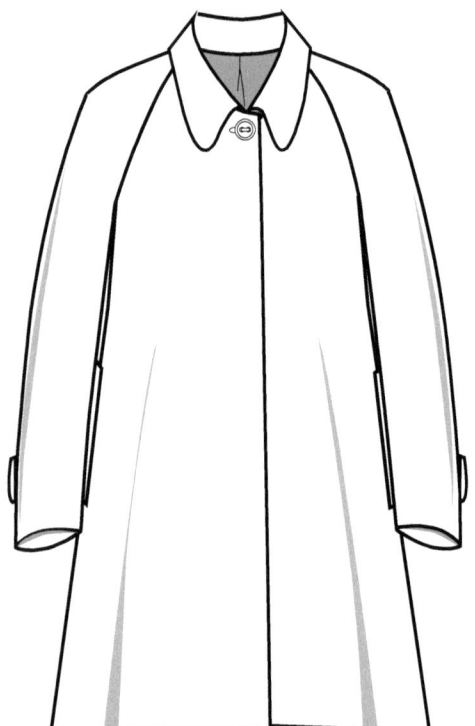
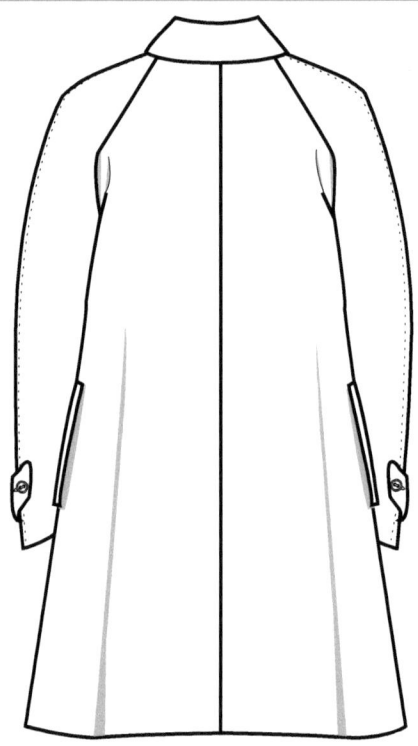

Self:

1. Front (cut 2).
2. Back (cut 2).
3. Front raglan sleeve (cut 2).
4. Back raglan sleeve (cut 2).
5. Sleeve tab (cut 2).
6. Upper-collar (cut 1).
7. Under-collar (cut 1).
8. Front facing (cut 2).
9. Back facing (cut 1).
10. Pocket welt (cut 2).

Lining:

1. Front (cut 2).
2. Back (cut 2).
3. Front raglan sleeve (cut 2).
4. Back raglan sleeve (cut 2).
5. Pocket bag (cut 4).
6. Hidden-button placket (cut 2).

> "Fashion is the armor to survive the reality of everyday life."
>
> Bill Cunningham

| THE HISTORY OF THE BALMACAAN COAT | CONTEMPORARY BALMACAANS | THE PATTERN | MUSLIN OR TOILE FITTING | PRODUCTION PATTERN | **TECHNICAL FLATS AND FINISHED PATTERN PIECES** |

6.14
Side detail of Balmacaan coat.

CHAPTER SEVEN

THE FROCK COAT

Patterning concepts learned:
- **peak lapel**
- **armhole princess style-line**
- **waistline seam**
- **flared sleeve**
- **flared skirt**
- **inverted back pleat**

7.1
Frock coat front.

7.2
Frock coat back.

7.1

7.2

THE HISTORY OF THE FROCK COAT

The frock coat is actually not a coat at all but a long fitted jacket distinguishable by its waistline seam and flared skirt.

It was worn most notably by author and playwright Oscar Wilde in the mid-nineteenth century. Quite the "dandy", Wilde took his appearance and leisurely activities very seriously. Not to be outdone, the French had their own version of the "idle man about town", known as a "faneur".

During this time, few women sported the frock coat, with the notable exception of French authoress George Sand. Sand had a penchant for donning men's clothes and was as famous for having illustrious affairs with other prominent artists of the day, including musician Frédéric Chopin, as she was for her writing.

The double-breasted version of the frock is also known as the Prince Albert, named after Queen Victoria's husband. Strict dress codes were enforced in the Victorian era and the Albert version, with its satin and peak lapels, was worn strictly as formal attire.

7.3
Illustration of frock coat, 1855.

"The dandy should aspire to be uninterruptedly sublime. He should live and sleep in front of a mirror."

Charles Baudelaire

7.4
Oscar Wilde, 1889, wearing a frock coat.

7.5
Authoress George Sand dressed in a frock coat walking with Henri de Latouche in Paris.

7.6
Teddy Boys in south London, 1955; the movement revived the frock coat during the 1950s.

In the 1950s the frock coat was revived by a youth movement in Britain known as the Teddy Boys, who acquired the name from their wearing of Edwardian-inspired clothing. Primarily working-class Londoners, Teddy Boys helped to popularize rock and roll in Europe. Their dandyism added much-needed color and excitement to post-war Britain. The original Teds called their custom-made frocks "drapes" and paired them with high-waist, sixteen-inch trousers. The heyday of the Teddy Boy era was relatively short and ended in the early 1960s. Yet, sixty years later, there still exists a vibrant and global Teddy Boy subculture with music festivals the "Ted Do" and the "Wildest Cats in Town" helping to keep the movement alive.

Contemporary interpretations of the frock appear almost every season in both men's and women's fashion, keeping the spirit of the dandy alive and well.

CONTEMPORARY FROCKS

7.7
Vivienne Westwood Red Label: Runway, London Fashion Week Fall/Winter 2013.

7.8
Thom Browne: Runway, Mercedes-Benz Fashion Week Fall 2013.

| THE HISTORY OF THE FROCK COAT | CONTEMPORARY FROCKS | THE PATTERN | MUSLIN OR TOILE FITTING | PRODUCTION PATTERN | TECHNICAL FLATS AND FINISHED PATTERN PIECES |

7.9
Moncler Gamme Rouge: Runway,
Paris Fashion Week Fall 2015.

7.10
Givenchy: Runway, Paris Fashion Week
Fall/Winter 2015/2016.

THE PATTERN

Start with basic bodice and sleeve blocks

Adjust blocks for shoulder pads

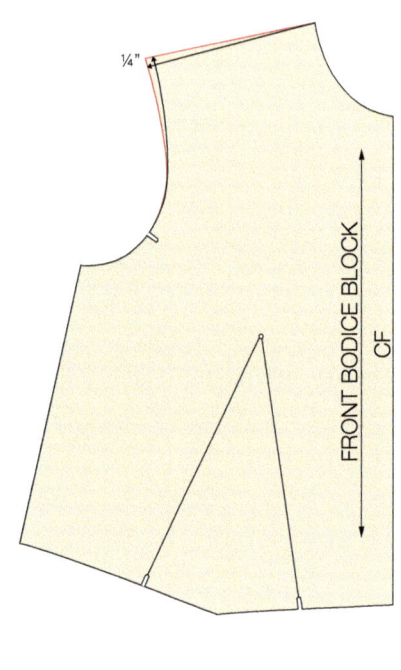

1. For ½ inch (1.2cm) shoulder pad, raise shoulder up and out ¼ inch (6mm) on both front and back blocks.
2. Record front shoulder measurement_____.
3. True up armhole curve with a French curve.

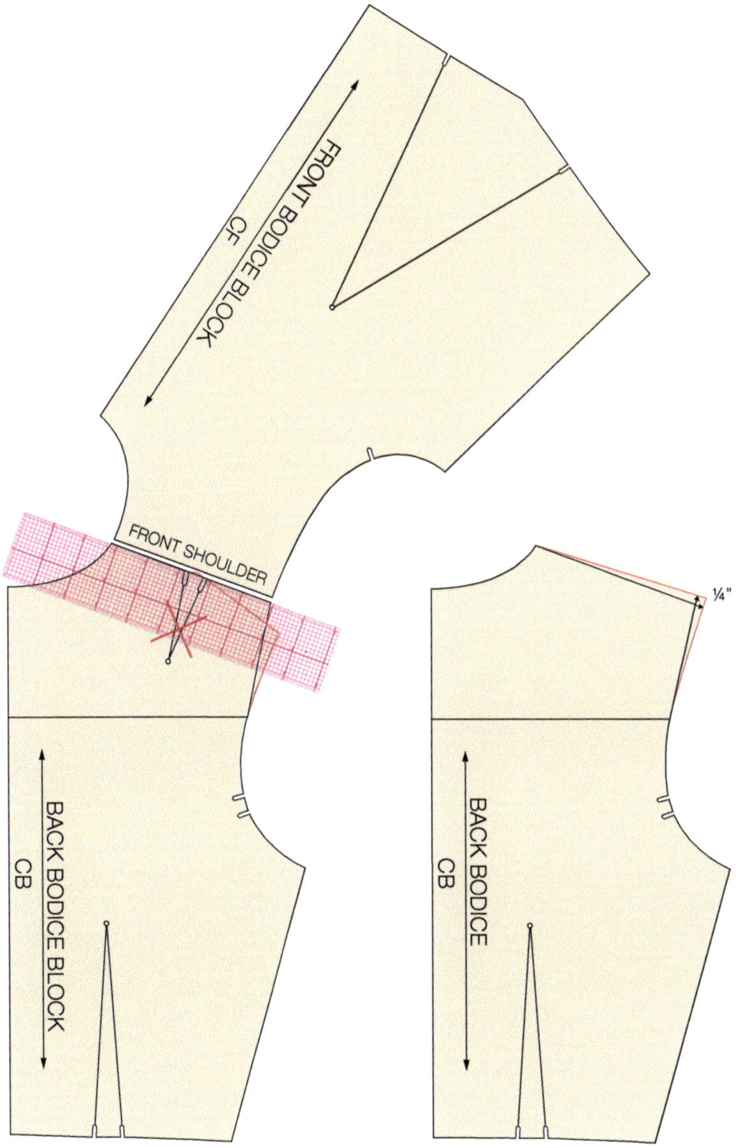

4. For the back block, you must first eliminate the shoulder dart.
5. Place ruler even with shoulder line at the neckline and draw a straight line.
6. Use the front shoulder measurement and mark the back shoulder to match.
7. True up armhole curve with French curve.
8. Now you can adjust for the shoulder pad using the same measurements as you did for the front.

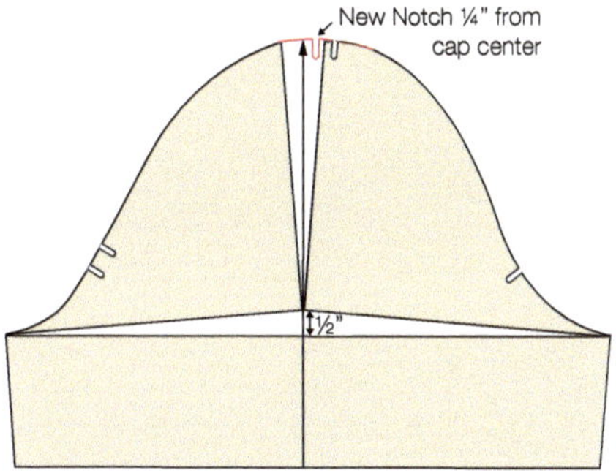

9. Slash sleeve pattern at center of cap and through biceps line.
10. Lift the pattern up ½ inch (1.2cm) (the size of your shoulder pad) and tape down.
11. True up cap with French curve and re-mark center of cap.
12 Move shoulder notch so it is ¼ inch (6mm) from cap center.
    Note: Make sure you are happy with the fit of the blocks before you begin drafting the pattern.

Drafting the peak lapel

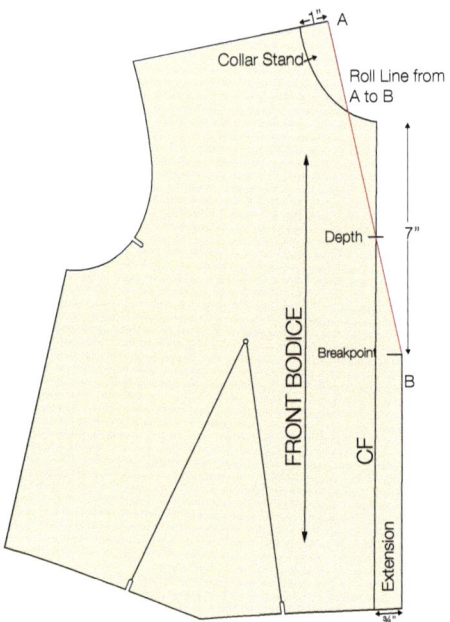 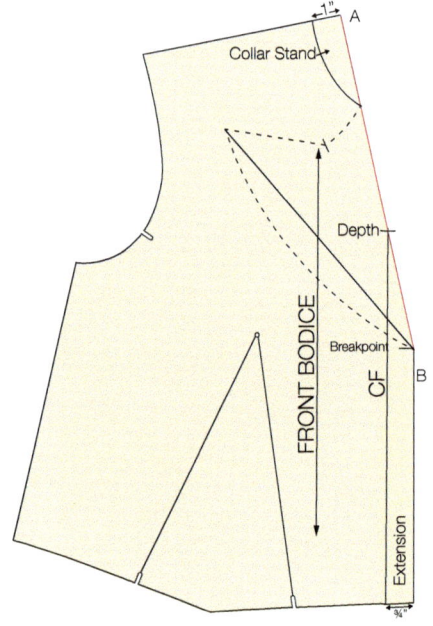

1. Extend neckline 1 inch (2.5cm), mark A.
2. Draw extension for buttonholes out ¾ inch (1.75cm).
3. Measure down from neckline 7 inches (17.5cm) and mark measurement on extension line; this is your breakpoint, mark B.
4. Draw a line from A to B; this is your roll-line.
5. Fold back paper on roll-line and trace neckline curve.
6. Continue the curve 1 ¾ inches (4.25cm) onto the bodice front and notch.
   Note: This is where your collar will end on the jacket.
7. Determine the size and shape of the lapel; start with a straight line from breakpoint B and shape as you wish.
8. Transfer lapel-line to folded paper using a tracing wheel.
   Note: To be a peak lapel, the line from notch must angle up.

Collar development

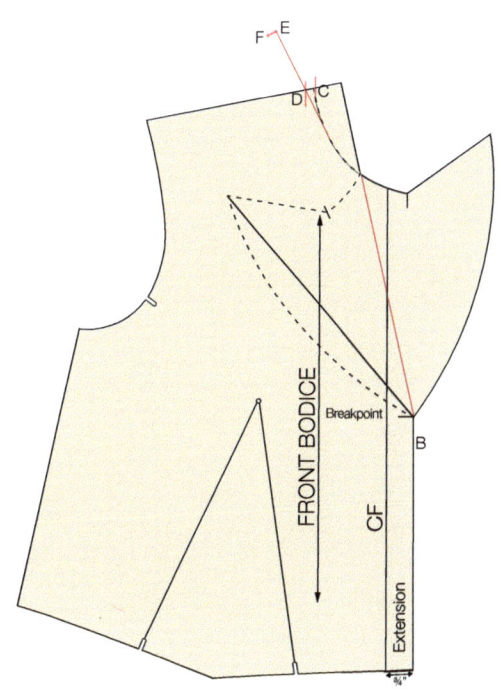

9. Unfold paper and draw lapel.
10. Now you are ready to draft the collar.
    Note: Drafting the lapel-line onto the bodice front allows you to see how the lapel will look on the finished garment.

1. Measure ¼ inch (6mm) in from C (original neckline), mark D.
2. Take back neckline measurement, record_____.
3. Place ruler at midpoint of neckline curve and extend line to make the D to E line.
4. D to E = back neckline measurement plus ⅛ inch (3mm).
5. Square off ½ inch (1.2cm) to the left for F.

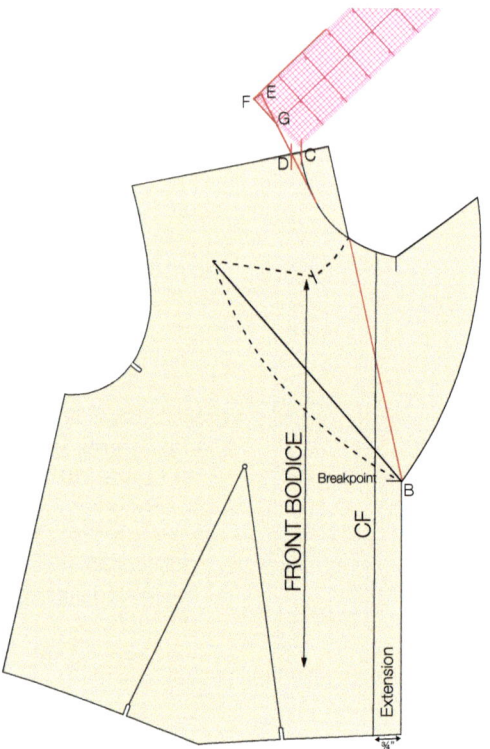 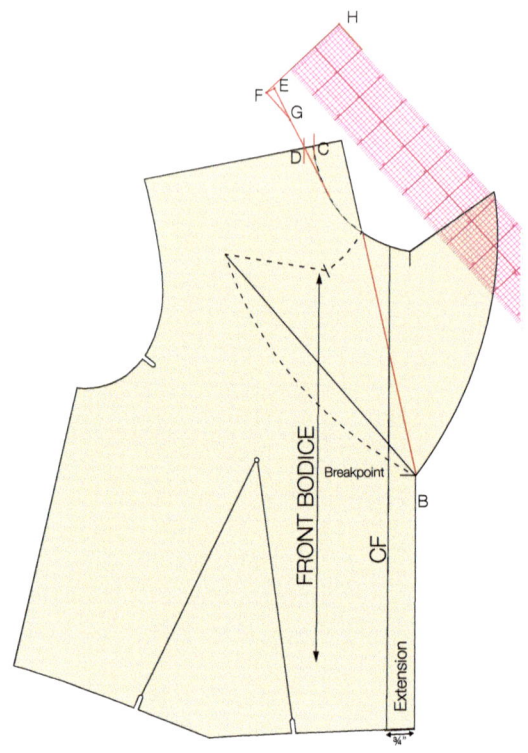

6. D to G = ½ of the D to E measurement.

7. Draw a line from G to F.

8. Placing your ruler on the G to F line, square off a line 3 inches (7.5cm) long, mark H (this is the CB of the collar).

9. Square down from H.

| THE HISTORY OF THE FROCK COAT | CONTEMPORARY FROCKS | THE PATTERN | MUSLIN OR TOILE FITTING | PRODUCTION PATTERN | TECHNICAL FLATS AND FINISHED PATTERN PIECES |

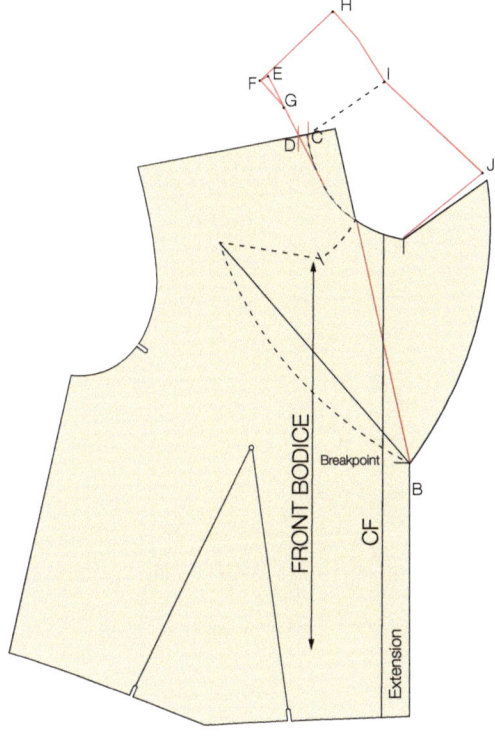

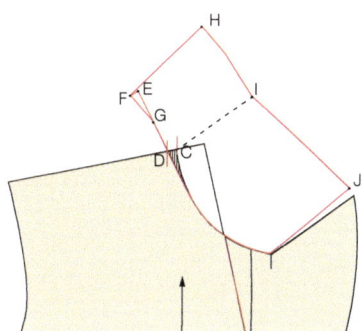

10. Using the F to H measurement, draw a line parallel with F, G, and D line until you get to I (this is where the collar will hit the shoulder on the jacket).

11. Draw a line from lapel notch to J (this line will determine the spacing between the collar and lapel).

12. Complete collar by drawing a line from I to J.

13. Trace the upper-collar and cut out.

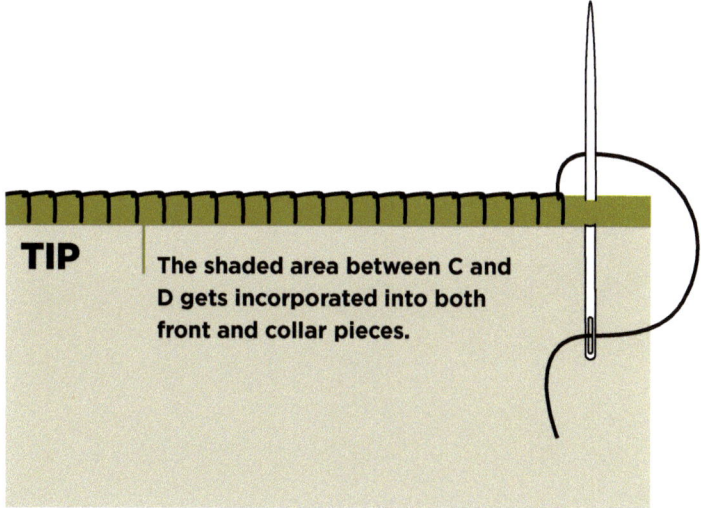

TIP The shaded area between C and D gets incorporated into both front and collar pieces.

Armhole princess front

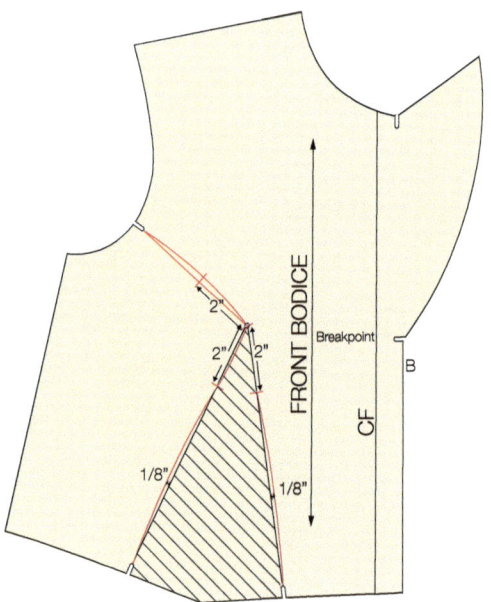 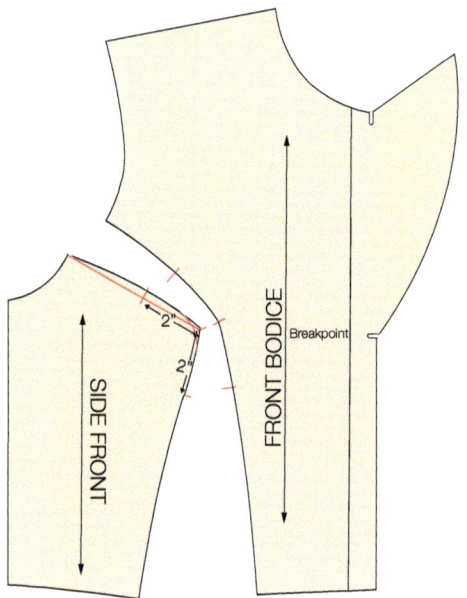

1. Draw dart legs to apex—notch.
2. Draw a straight line from apex to armhole; draw a slight curve above.
3. Mark control notches 2 inches (5cm) from apex on all lines.
4. Draw a ⅛ inch (3mm) curve down both dart legs starting at notches.
   Note: This will add shape to the bodice under bust.
5. Cut front and side front pieces apart making sure to cut out the dart.
6. Smooth out the bust-line if it looks too pointy or uneven.
7. Walk the pattern using an awl starting at the waist; adjust pattern as needed to balance style-line at armhole.

| THE HISTORY OF THE FROCK COAT | CONTEMPORARY FROCKS | **THE PATTERN** | MUSLIN OR TOILE FITTING | PRODUCTION PATTERN | TECHNICAL FLATS AND FINISHED PATTERN PIECES |

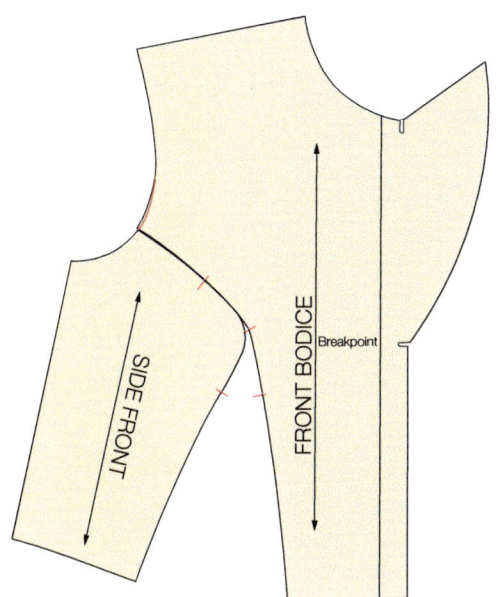
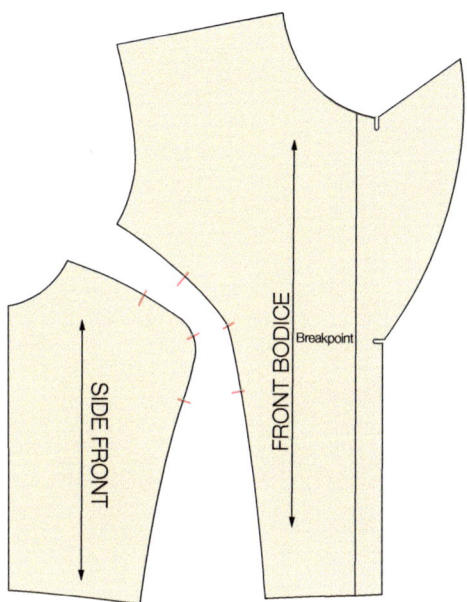

Armhole princess back

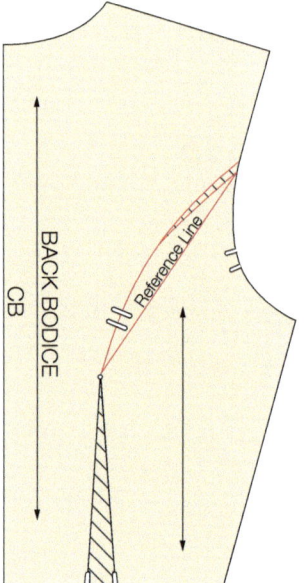
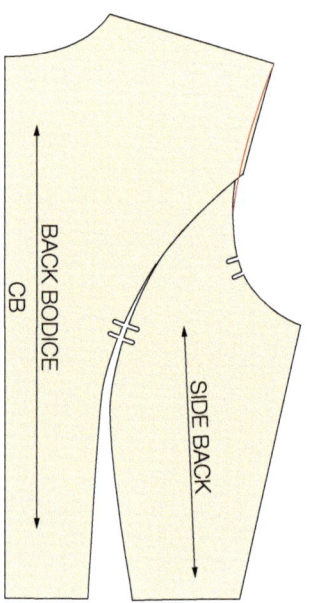

1. Mark grainline for side back pattern piece parallel to CB.
2. Draw a straight line from dart point to armhole (this gives you a reference point for princess line).
   Note: You can mark this point wherever you like, but remember, the closer to the under-arm, the more curved the princess line will be.
3. Draw a curved line from armhole to dart point—double-notch for back.
4. Draw another curved line ¼ inch (6mm) down from princess line connecting with the original curve 3 ½ inches (8.75cm) down (the length of the shoulder dart).
5. Cut out back and side back patterns making sure to eliminate the darts (shaded area).
6. Walk the pattern using an awl starting at the waist; adjust pattern as needed to balance style-line at armhole.

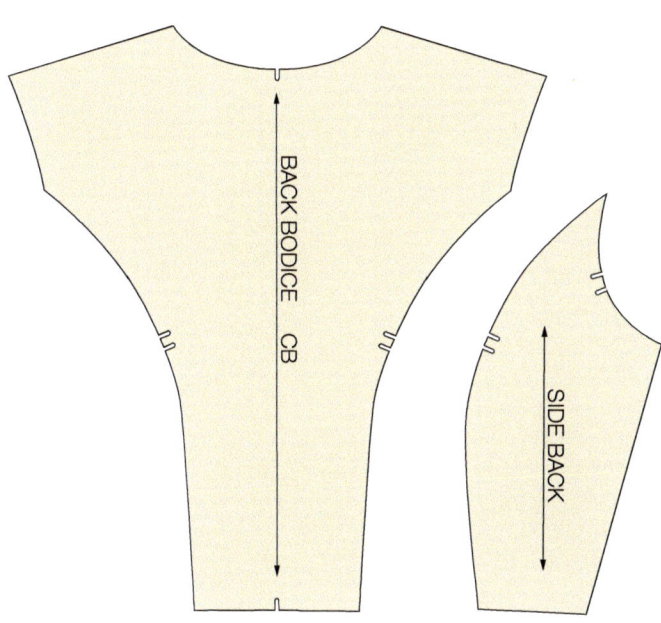

7. Open up back pattern to eliminate CB seam.

Flared sleeve

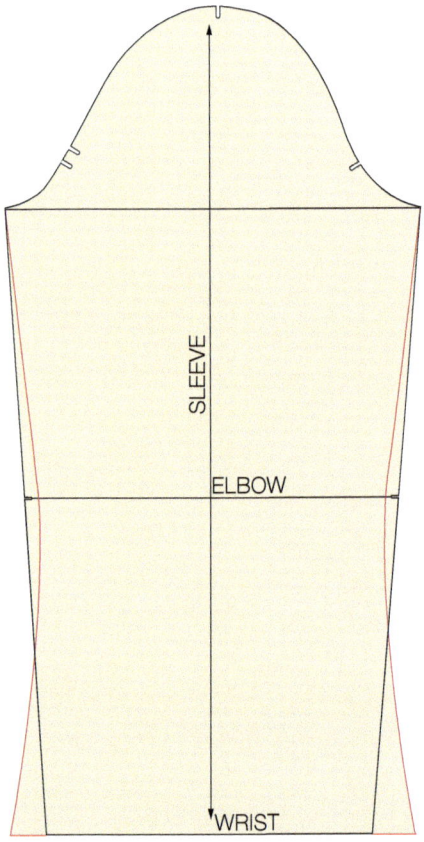

Flared skirt

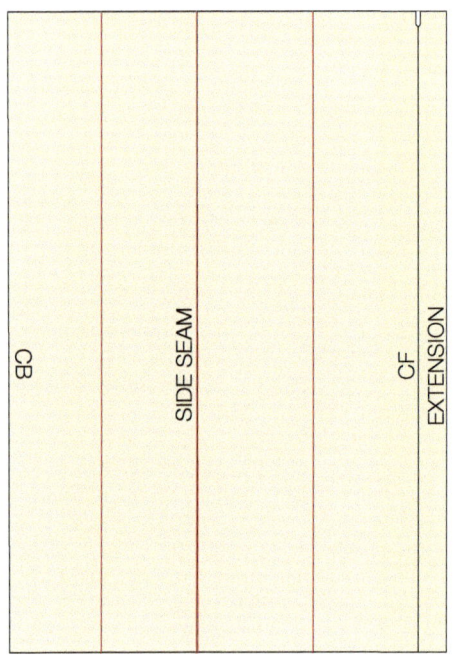

1. Mark in ½ inch (1.2cm) at elbow and 1 inch (2.5cm) out at wrist.
2. Draw a straight line from under-arm to elbow.
3. Draw a curved line from elbow to wrist using a hip-curve making sure both sides are balanced.

1. Measure front waist arc_____.
2. Measure back waist arc_____.
3. Add together along with ¾ inch (1.75cm) for extension _____.
4. Draw a rectangle using this measurement for the width, marking the CF, CB, extension, and side seam.
5. Measure the desired length of the skirt to complete the rectangle.
6. Mark slash-lines on the side seam, and divide the front and back in half to create three slash-lines total (marked in red).

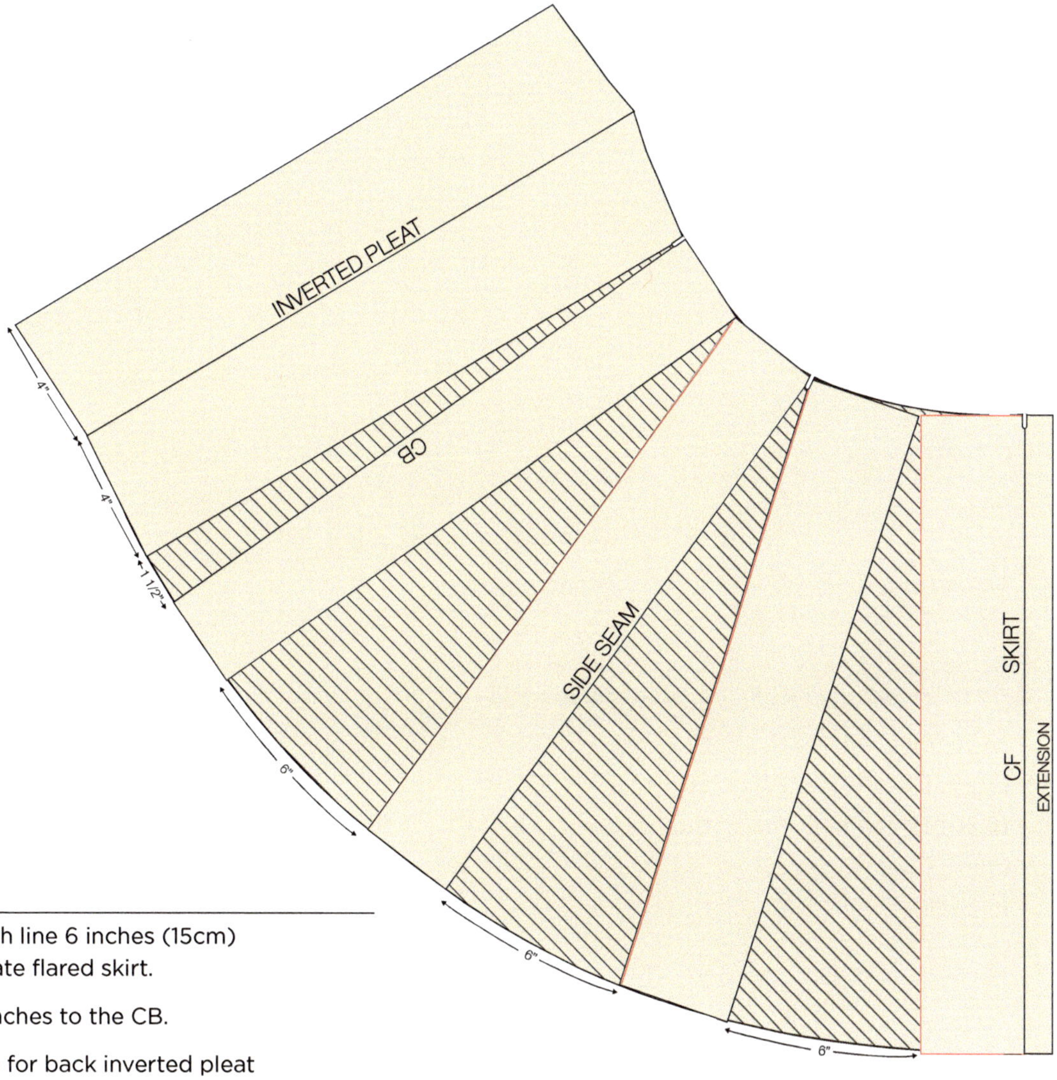

7. Slash and spread each line 6 inches (15cm) (shaded area) to create flared skirt.

8. Spread 1 ½ (3.7cm) inches to the CB.

9. Add 8 inches (20cm) for back inverted pleat (this will give you two 4 inch (10cm) pleats at CB).

10. True up curves of pattern.
    Note: Make sure to fold the inverted pleat back as if you were sewing it when truing up the pattern to accommodate the curved waistline.

CHAPTER SEVEN:
THE FROCK COAT

MUSLIN OR TOILE FITTING

7.11 Checking muslin front for fit.
7.12 Checking muslin back for fit.
7.13 Pinning detail.

- Before you draft the facings and lining patterns, prepare a muslin for fit.
- Do not add SAs to pattern as you will most likely be adjusting the muslin for fit—draw the SAs directly onto the muslin.
- Make any necessary fit corrections to pattern.
- Now you can move on to the facings and lining patterns.

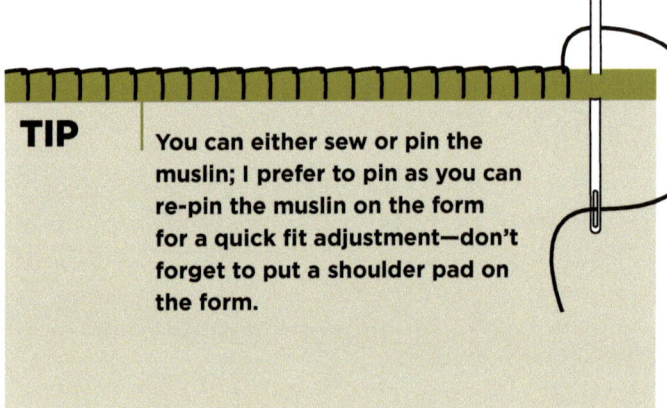

TIP You can either sew or pin the muslin; I prefer to pin as you can re-pin the muslin on the form for a quick fit adjustment—don't forget to put a shoulder pad on the form.

Completing the upper- and under-collar

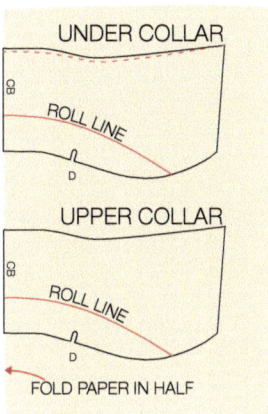 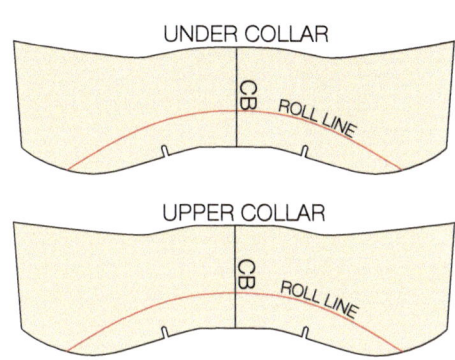

1. Fold pattern paper in half and trace the collar twice, making sure to notch D, which is your shoulder seam.

2. Draft under-collar by reducing the outer seam of the collar by ⅛ inch (3mm) at CB and blending to zero at collar point (red dotted line).

3. Mark the roll-line by marking up 1 inch (2.5cm) at CB and blending with roll-line from the front pattern.

Front facing

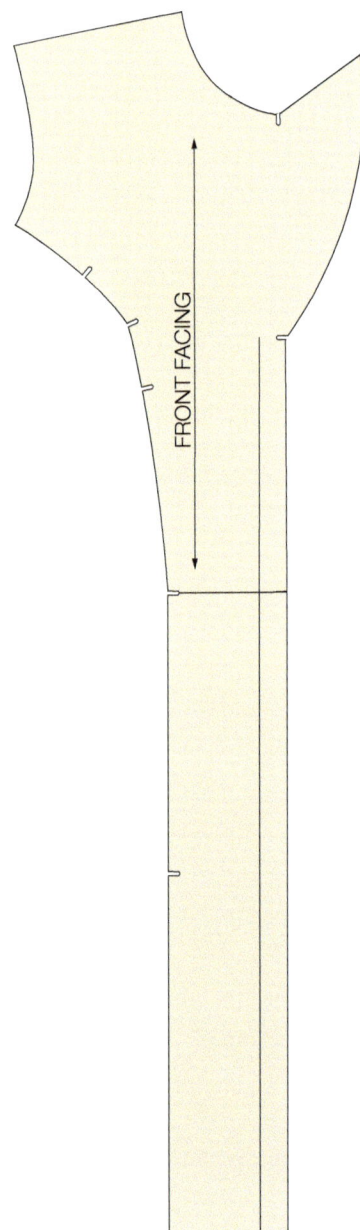

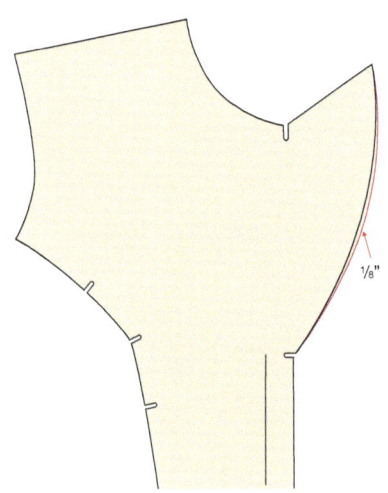

1. Measure the front pattern waistline including extension, record_____.
2. Retrace front pattern extending length to equal skirt measurement from waistline.
3. Notch waist and another control notch for sewing reference.
4. Add ⅛ inch (3mm) blending from breakpoint to edge of lapel.
   Note: This is so lapel can be pressed under the ⅛ inch (3mm) so the stitching line does not show on the garment.

Back facing and lining

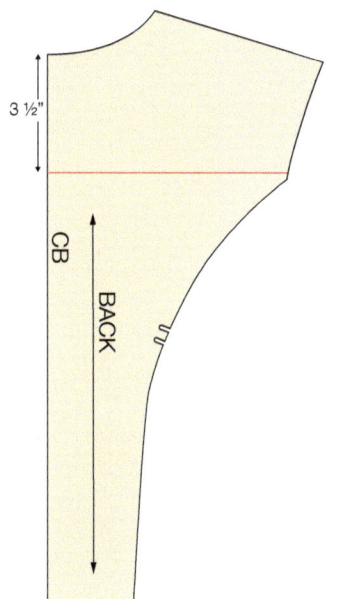
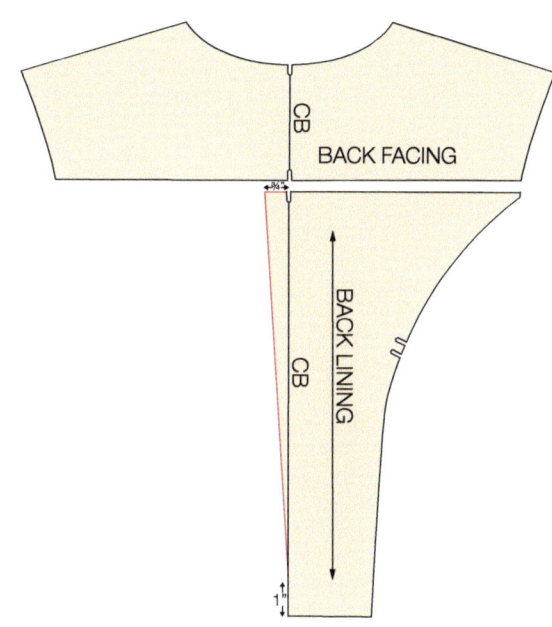

1. Using your original back pattern piece, square a 3 ½ inch (8.75cm) line down from CB neckline and cut apart.

2. The top pattern is your back facing—open pattern up and redraw.

3. Create an action pleat down the CB by drawing a straight line 1 inch (2.5cm) up from CB waistline and ¾ inch (1.75cm) out from top of lining piece, notch. **Note: Grainline does not change which means you must cut two back patterns to allow for the action pleat.**

Front skirt lining

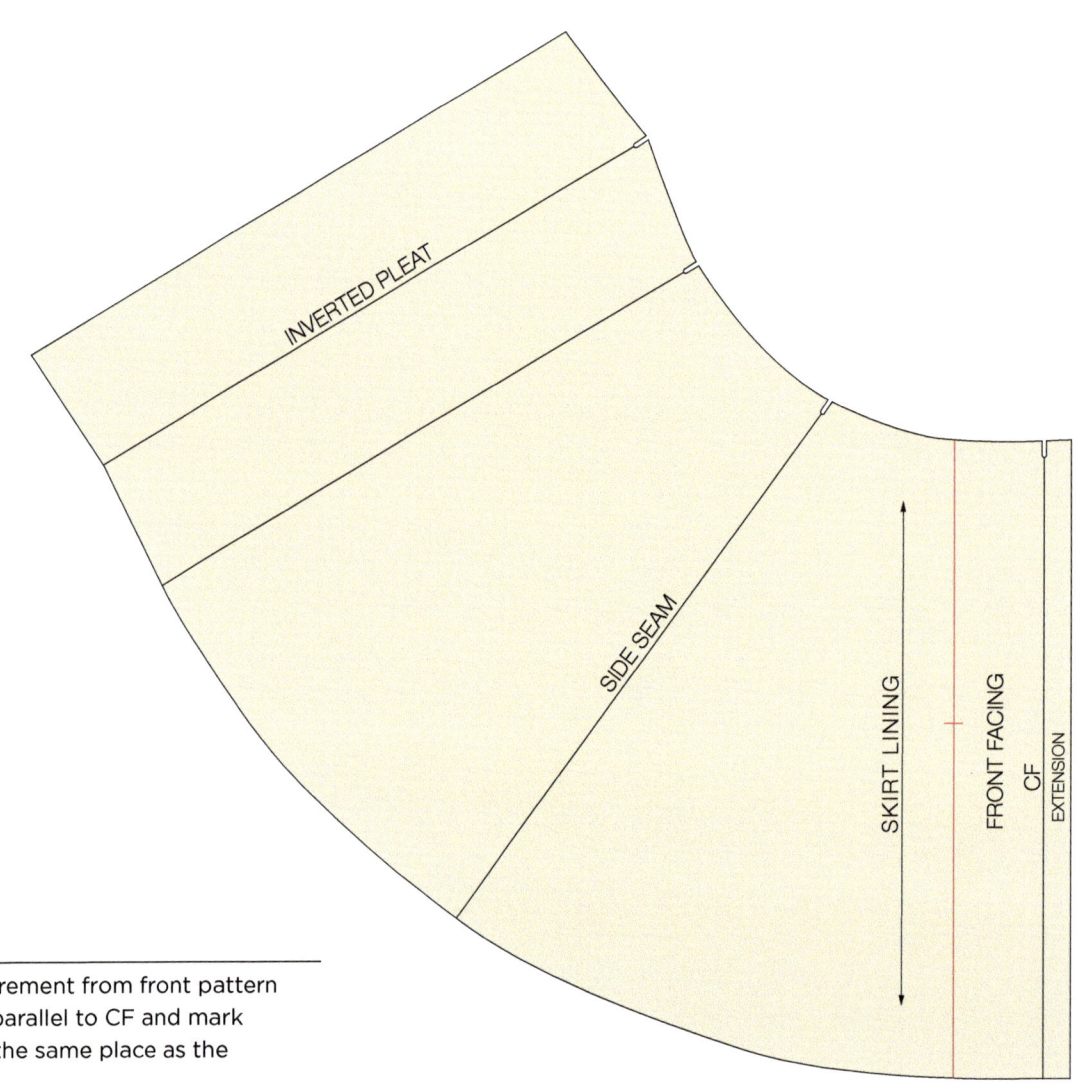

1. Using waist measurement from front pattern piece, draw a line parallel to CF and mark a control notch in the same place as the front facing.

2. Cut out at line and discard front piece (this is the bottom part of your front facing that you have already developed).

3. The remaining piece is your front skirt lining.

Side front and side back lining

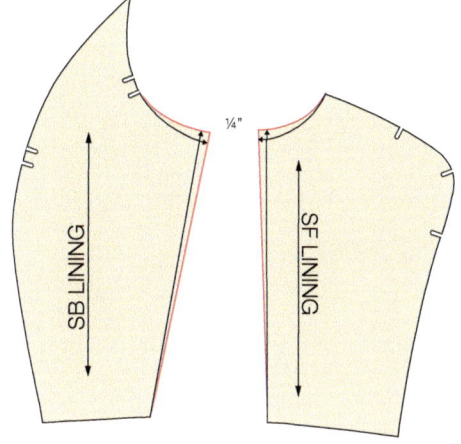

Sleeve lining

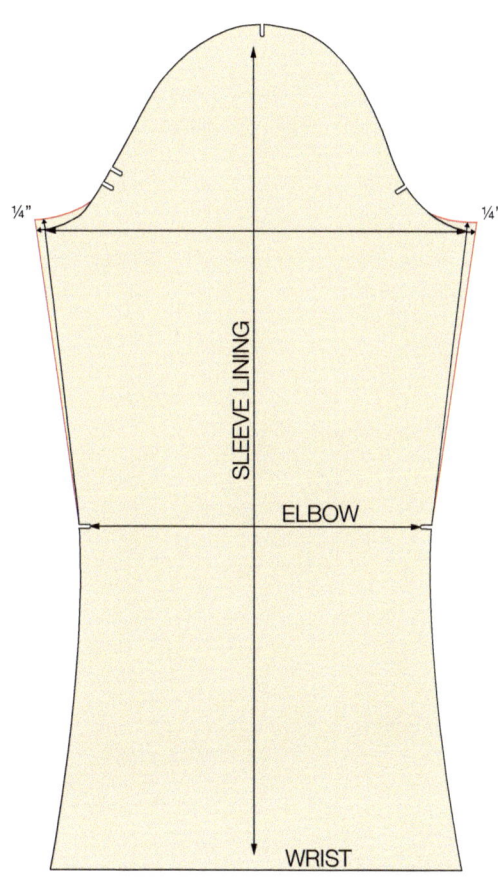

1. Starting at waistline draw out and up ¼ inch (6mm) to allow for ease in the lining pieces.

2. Blend to front princess line and CB notches.

1. Starting at elbow draw out and up ¼ inch (6mm) to allow for ease in the lining pieces.

2. Blend armhole curves to notches.

PRODUCTION PATTERN

Seam allowances and hems

> **TIP**
> - Before adding SAs and hems make sure to walk your pattern and make any necessary corrections if seams or control notches do not match.
> - Now you can make your production pattern.

Upper-collar seam allowance

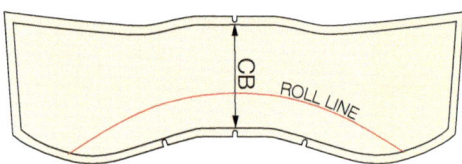

1. Add ¼ inch (6mm) SA to all seams for upper-collar.
2. Notch at CB, shoulder, and the SA.

Under-collar seam allowance

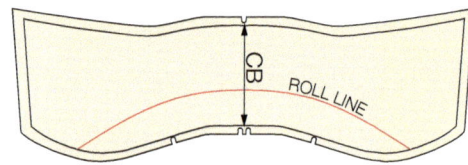

1. Add ¼ inch (6mm) SA to all seams for under-collar.
2. Make a double-notch at back (one on each side of the CB).
3. Notch shoulder and the SA.
   Note: Mark SAs and cut out pattern while paper is still folded!

| THE HISTORY OF THE FROCK COAT | CONTEMPORARY FROCKS | THE PATTERN | MUSLIN OR TOILE FITTING | **PRODUCTION PATTERN** | TECHNICAL FLATS AND FINISHED PATTERN PIECES |

Back, side back, and side front seam allowance

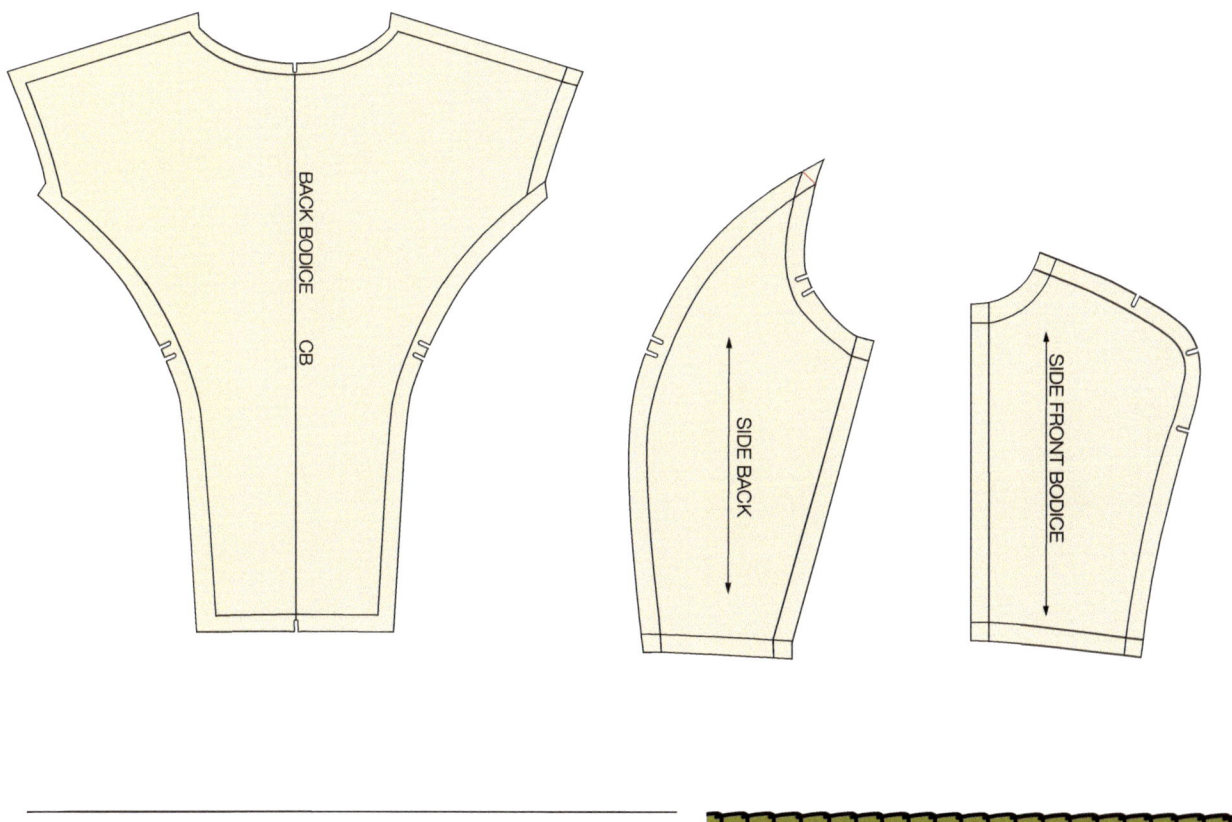

1. Trace the back pattern piece.
2. Add ½ inch (1.2cm) SA to all seams with the exception of the back neckline.
3. Add ¼ inch (6mm) SA to the back neckline.
4. Add ½ inch (1.2cm) SA to all seams for the side front and side back.

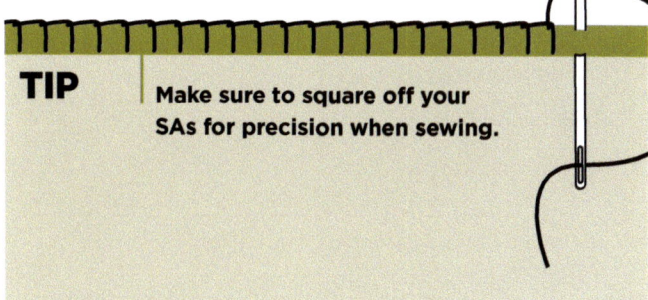

TIP | Make sure to square off your SAs for precision when sewing.

CHAPTER SEVEN:
THE FROCK COAT

Sleeve seam allowance and hem

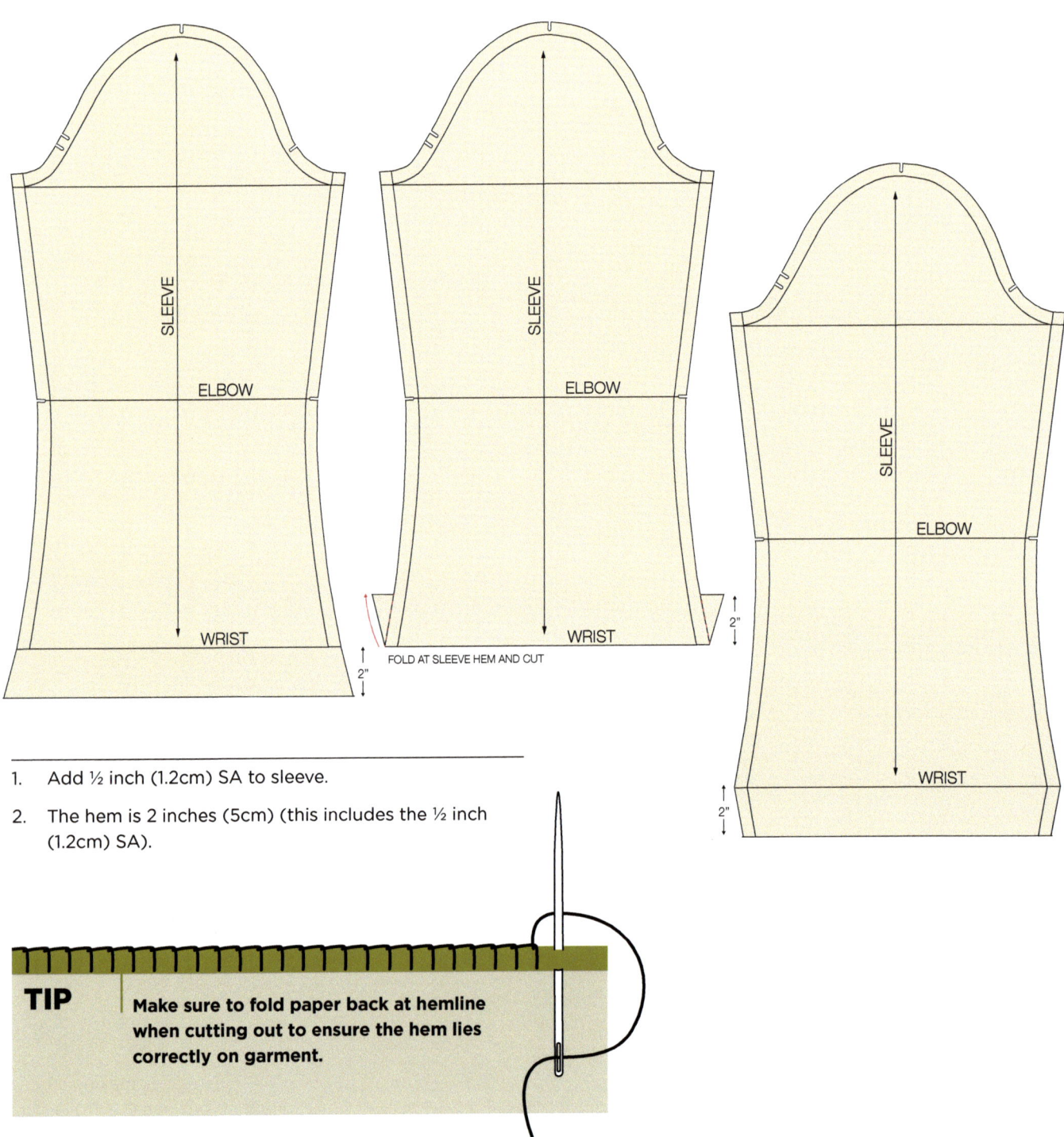

1. Add ½ inch (1.2cm) SA to sleeve.
2. The hem is 2 inches (5cm) (this includes the ½ inch (1.2cm) SA).

TIP Make sure to fold paper back at hemline when cutting out to ensure the hem lies correctly on garment.

Skirt seam allowance and hem

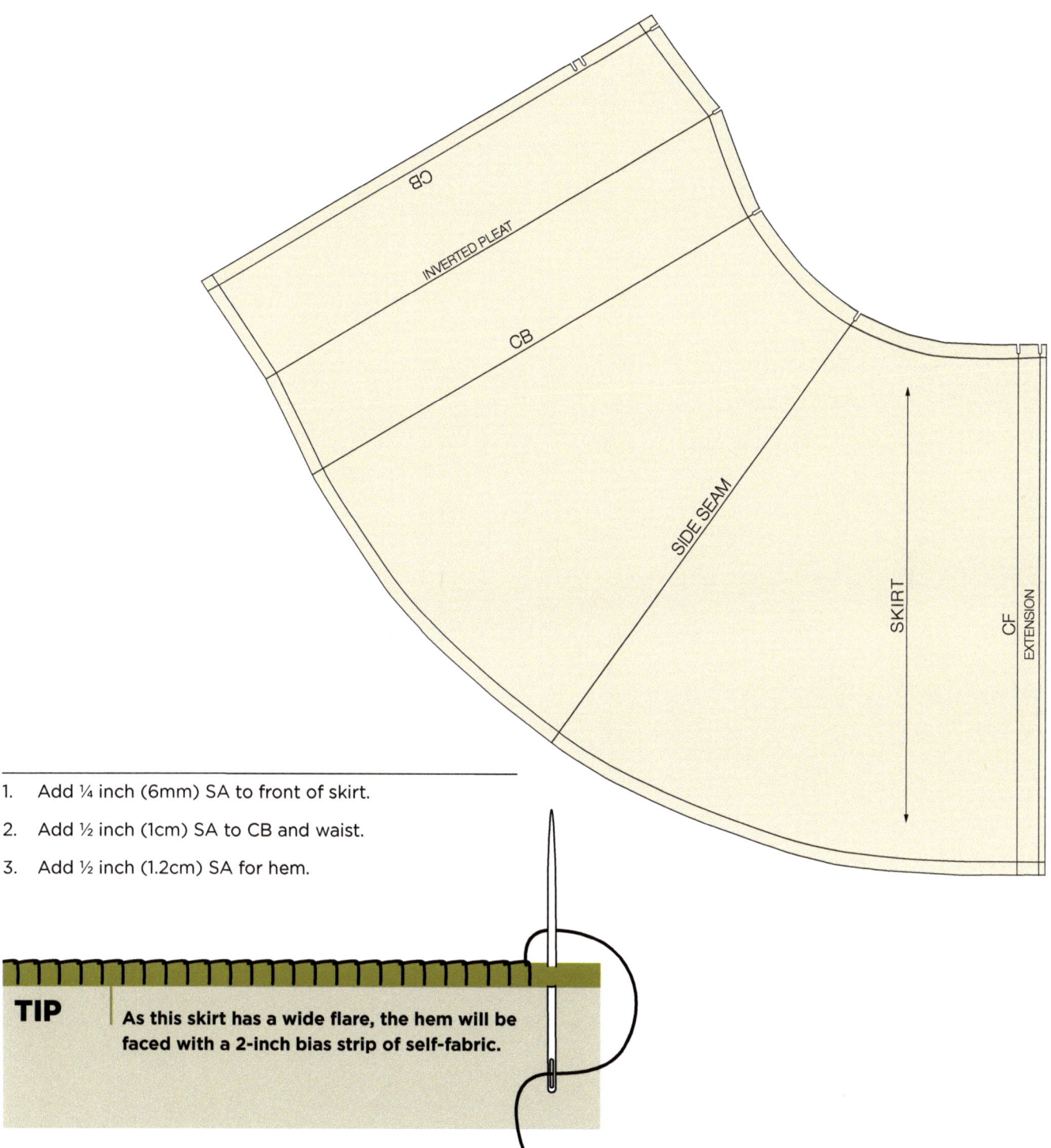

1. Add ¼ inch (6mm) SA to front of skirt.
2. Add ½ inch (1cm) SA to CB and waist.
3. Add ½ inch (1.2cm) SA for hem.

TIP As this skirt has a wide flare, the hem will be faced with a 2-inch bias strip of self-fabric.

Front, front facing, and back facing seam allowance

Back, side back, and side front lining seam allowance

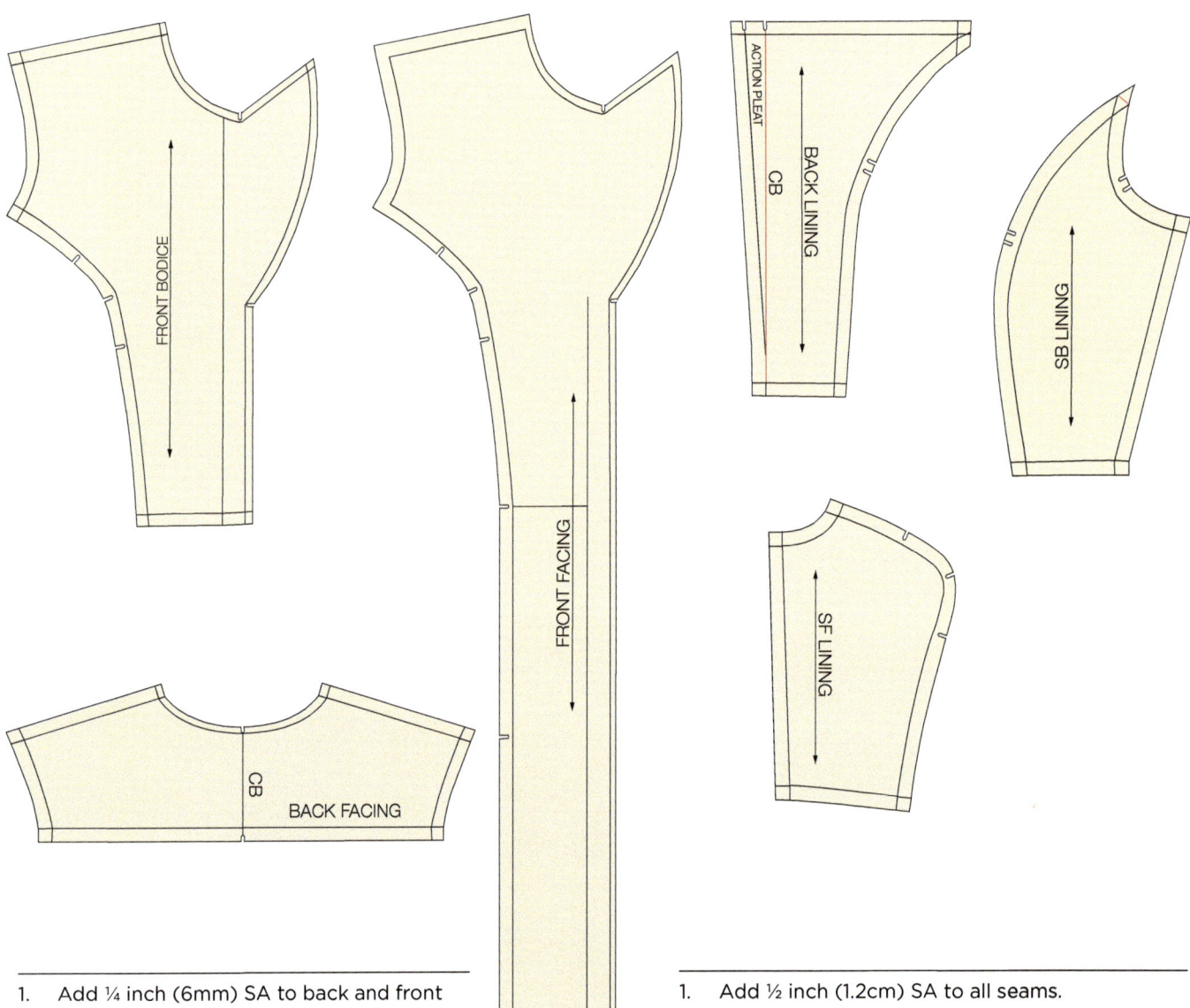

1. Add ¼ inch (6mm) SA to back and front necklines and down CF.
2. Add ½ inch (1.2cm) SA to all other seams.
   Note: Don't forget control notches!

1. Add ½ inch (1.2cm) SA to all seams.
   Note: Make sure to square off your SAs.

Sleeve and skirt lining seam allowance and hems

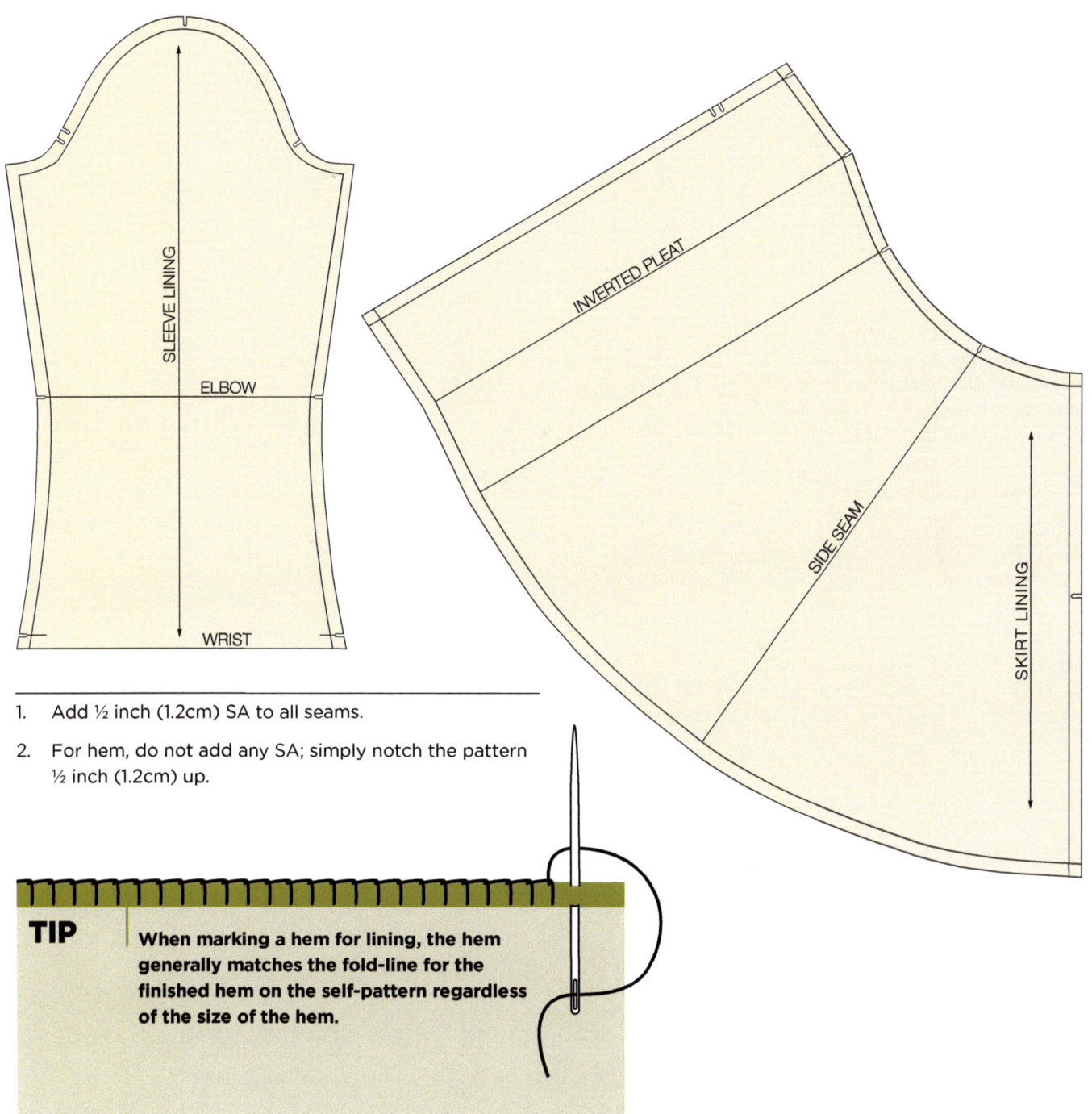

1. Add ½ inch (1.2cm) SA to all seams.
2. For hem, do not add any SA; simply notch the pattern ½ inch (1.2cm) up.

TIP When marking a hem for lining, the hem generally matches the fold-line for the finished hem on the self-pattern regardless of the size of the hem.

CHAPTER SEVEN: THE FROCK COAT

TECHNICAL FLATS AND FINISHED PATTERN PIECES

Self:

1. Front (cut 2).
2. Side front (cut 2).
3. Back (cut 1).
4. Side back (cut 2).
5. Sleeve (cut 2).
6. Skirt (cut 2).
7. Front facing (cut 2).
8. Back facing (cut 1).
9. Upper-collar (cut 1).
10. Under-collar (cut 1).

Lining:

1. Side front (cut 2).
2. Back (cut 2).
3. Side back (cut 2).
4. Sleeve (cut 2).
5. Skirt (cut 2).

> **"One should either be a work of art, or wear a work of art."**
>
> Oscar Wilde

7.14
Front detail of frock coat.

APPENDIX

GLOSSARY

Action pleat—Pleat located at the center back of the lining in a jacket that allows for ease of movement

Apex—The bust point

Armhole princess style-line—A dart equivalent seam that starts in the armhole of a garment

Armscye—The armhole

Bias—A diagonal line 45 degrees to the straight and cross-grain of a fabric

Block—A basic pattern (also called a sloper) representing the shape of the body from which other patterns are derived

Breakpoint—The location at the front of the jacket where the lapel folds back; this is the start of the roll-line

Classic princess style-line—A dart equivalent seam that starts at the shoulder of a garment

Collar—The part of a garment that finishes off the neckline

Collar stand—The section of the collar that raises the collar off the neck

Control notch—Notches indicate where seams match in a garment; they are the "road map" to reading a pattern

Dart—A shape, usually triangular, on a pattern used to take away excess fabric in order to fit the contour of the body

Depth—The location on the lapel of a garment where the fabric overlaps

Drill point/hole—The reference point used in patternmaking for dart, pocket, buttonhole, tuck, and vent placement. In industry the drill hole is always marked inside the finished seam in order to cover the markings on the finished garment

Ease—Extra measure at key points (sleeve, back, shoulder, and bust) added for comfort and movement

Face—The correct side of fabric

Face-up—In patternmaking, you will write "face-up" on the pattern to indicate placing the fabric with the correct side facing up when you cut it out

Front extension—The added width on the front of a pattern needed for the addition of buttons and buttonholes

Gorge line—Seam-line where the collar and the lapel join

Grainline—The line which indicates the direction of the grain on a pattern. Patterns are usually placed on the straight grain (warp)

High-point shoulder—The location where the shoulder meets the neckline

Interfacing—A support fabric either sewn in or fused on used for stabilizing an area of a garment

Lining—A lightweight fabric constructed in the shape of the garment, which is used to finish and protect the inside of the garment

Muslin—a cotton fabric used to make a mock-up of the garment for fit purposes; the actual sample is called either a "muslin" or a "toile"

Notch—See Control notch

Placket—Finishing for an opening; can be cut on the bias or straight grain

Production pattern—The final, corrected pattern. This is the only pattern which has seam allowance and hem drawn on it

Roll-line—The line where the lapel or collar turns and folds back towards the body

Seam allowance (SA)—The area between the seam-line and the cutting line of the fabric

Self—In patternmaking, "self" indicates fashion fabric

Slash and spread—Technique in patternmaking where you cut and spread the pattern to create fullness

Sleeve cap—The top part of the sleeve

Style-line—A seam-line on a garment used to create a visual effect

Sweep—The width of the garment's hemline

Technical flat—The technical drawing used in the fashion industry to show the design details of a garment

Toile—See Muslin

Tuck—A fold or pleat that has been stitched down

Truing-up a seam—The process of checking and correcting seam-lines in a pattern to ensure they match up

Vent—An opening used in the hem of jackets and skirts to allow for ease of movement

Walking a pattern and/or seam—Used to true up a seam by placing the seam-lines of two patterns together and matching them lengthwise to ensure they are equal

BIBLIOGRAPHY AND RECOMMENDED READING

Aldrich, W. *Pattern Cutting for Women's Tailored Jackets: Classic and Contemporary*. Oxford: Blackwell Publishing, 2002.

Birnbach, L. *The Official Preppy Handbook*. New York: Workman Publishing, 1980.

Burnham, D. K. *Cut My Cote*. Ontario: Royal Ontario Museum, 1997.

Carlson, J. *Rowing Blazers*. New York: Vendome Press, 2014.

Carman, S. *British Military Uniforms From Contemporary Pictures*. New York: Arco Publishing Company, 1957.

Carr, R. *Couture: The Art of Fine Sewing*. Portland: Palmer/Pletsch Publishing, 1993.

Chenoune, F. *A History of Men's Fashion*. Paris: Flammarion, 1993.

Craik, J. 2005. *Uniforms Exposed: From Conformity to Transgression*. New York: Berg, 2005.

Duburg, A. and van der Tol, R. *Draping: Art and Craftsmanship in Fashion Design*. Netherlands: De Jonge Hond, 2009.

Ferris, R. and Lord, J. *Teddy Boys: A Concise History*. Reading: Milo Books Ltd, 2012.

Hayashida, T. *Take Ivy*. Brooklyn: Powerhouse Books, 2010.

Henry Poole & Co. (2015). [online]. Available online: https://henrypoole.com/history-of-henry-poole-tailor-of-savile-row/the-tuxedo/ (accessed 19 July 2015).

Hopkins, J. *Basics Fashion Design 07: Menswear*. London: AVA Publishing, 2011.

Johnson, J. (2011), "Off with their Coattails", *The Wall Street Journal*. [online] 30 April. Available online: http://www.wsj.com/articles/SB10001424052748704132204576285250103874450 (accessed 22 May 2013).

Joseph-Armstrong, H. *Patternmaking for Fashion Design*, New York: Prentice Hall, 2009.

Kim, M. and Kim, I. *Patternmaking for Menswear: Classic to Contemporary*, New York: Fairchild Books, 2014.

McBee, R. *Born to be Wild: The Rise of the American Motorcyclist*. Chapel Hill: University of North Carolina Press, 2015.

M. Müller and Sohn. *Metric Patternmaking for Jackets and Coats with Sleeve/Bodice Combinations*, Munich: Deutsche Bekleidungs-Akademie, 2008.

Motor Age, "What Fashion Dictates for Spring and Summer Motoring: Coming Season's Styles for Men and Women at the Wheel". 1915. [online]. XXVII (27), p. 8. Available online: https://books.google.com/books?id=x-EkfAQAAMAAJ&pg=RA2-PA8&lpg=RA2-PA8&dq=balmacaan+coat+history&source=bl&ots=guqFMOash-K&sig=KwrVV9r-i34PijPU7ZgBTX_y4j0&hl=en&sa=X&ved=0CFEQ6AEwC2oVChMI592Jrr_gxwIVRFg-Ch3oAAPz#v=onepage&q=balmacaan%20coat%20history&f=false (accessed 8 March 2015).

Nakamichi, T. *Pattern Magic*. London: Laurence King, 2010.

Powell, P. *Tailored Fashion Design*. New York: Fairchild Books, 2011.

Rawlings, T. *Mod: A Very British Phenomenon*. London: Omnibus Press, 2001.

Rissanen, T. and McQuillan, H. *Zero Waste Fashion Design*. New York: Fairchild Books, 2016.

Rosen, S. *Patternmaking: A Comprehensive Reference for Fashion Design*. New York: Prentice Hall, 2004.

Sato, S. *Transformational Reconstruction*. St. Helena: Center for Pattern Design, 2011.

Schott NYC. (2015). [online]. Available online: https://www.schottnyc.com/about.cfm (accessed 5 January 2015).

Shaeffer, C. *Couture Sewing Techniques*. Newtown: Taunton Press, 2001.

Shaeffer, C. *Fabric Sewing Guide*. Cincinnati: Krause Publications, 2008.

Sherwood, J. *Bespoke: the Men's Style of Savile Row*. New York: Rizzoli International Publications, 2010.

Tanaka, R. *Motorcycle Jackets: A Century of Leather Design*. Atglen: Schiffer, 2006.

Taylor, M. J. "Looking for Mr. Benson: The Black Leather Motorcycle Jacket and Narratives of Masculinities". In *Fashion in Popular Culture: Literature, Media and Contemporary Studies*, edited by J. Hancock II, T. Johnson-Woods, and V. Karaminas. Chicago: Intellect Ltd, 2013.

Victoria and Albert Museum. 2015. [online]. Available online: http://www.vam.ac.uk/content/articles/i/robert-orbach/ (accessed 7 July 2015).

Von Nordheim, T. *Vintage Couture Tailoring*. Wiltshire: Crowood Press, 2012.

Wu, J. *Chinese Fashion: From Mao to Now*. London: Bloomsbury Academic, 2009.

APPENDIX

PICTURE CREDITS

All reasonable attempts have been made to trace, clear, and credit the copyright holders of the images reproduced in this book. However, if any credits have been inadvertently omitted, the publisher will endeavor to incorporate amendments in future editions.

Cover: Photograph by Scott Shigley

Jacket/coat photography: Scott Shigley

Technical drawings and flats: Alisa Caron

P3 and P7: Photographs by Scott Shigley

P9: Illustration by Alisa Caron

Chapter 1
P26: Photo by Bob Thomas/Popperfoto/Getty Images

P26: Photo by Nina Leen/The LIFE Picture Collection/Getty Images

P27: Photo by Paul Wright/Getty Images

P27: Photo by Hill Street Studios/Eric Raptosh/Getty Images

P28: Photo by Catwalking/Getty Images

P28: Photo by Danny Martindale/WireImage

P29: Photo by Arun Nevader/Getty Images

P29: Photo by Gamma-Rapho/Getty Images

Chapter 2
P50: Photo by Transcendental Graphics/Getty Images

P51: Photo by Eugene Robert Richee/Getty Images

P51: Photo by John D. Kisch/Separate Cinema Archive/Getty Images

P51: Photo by Bill Ray/The LIFE Picture Collection/Getty Images

P52: Photo by Victor VIRGILE/Getty Images

P52: Photo by Victor VIRGILE/Getty Images

P53: Photo by Pascal Le Segretain/Getty Images

P53: Photo by Victor VIRGILE/Getty Images

Chapter 3
P72: Photo by Ann Ronan Pictures/Print Collector/Getty Images/ Artist: Nathaniel Dance-Holland

P73: Photo by Universal History Archive/Getty Images

P73: Photo by William James Warren/Getty Images

P73: Photo by George Pimentel/WireImage

P74: Photo by Victor VIRGILE/Gamma-Rapho via Getty Images

P74: Photo by Kristy Sparow/WireImage

P75: Photo by Victor VIRGILE/Gamma-Rapho via Getty Images

P75: Photo by Victor VIRGILE/Gamma-Rapho via Getty Images

Chapter 4
P98: Photo by Michael Ochs Archives/Getty Images

P99: Photo by Popperfoto/Getty Images

P99: Photo by Michael Ochs Archives/Getty Images

P99: Photo by PYMCA/UIG via Getty Images

P100: Photo by Victor VIRGILE/Gamma-Rapho via Getty Images

P100: Photo by Antonio de Moraes Barros Filho/Getty Images

P101: Photo by Thierry Chesnot/Getty Images

P101: Photo by Kristy Sparow/Getty Images

Chapter 5
P124: Photo by LEON NEAL/AFP/Getty Images

P125: Photo by Hulton Archive/Getty Images

P125: Universal History Archive/Getty Images

P125: Photo by Jack Hollingsworth/Getty Images

P126: Photo by Victor VIRGILE/Gamma-Rapho via Getty Images

P126: Photo by MARTIN BUREAU/AFP/Getty Images

P127: Photo by Victor VIRGILE/Gamma-Rapho via Getty Images

P127: Photo by Randy Brooke/WireImage

Chapter 6
P150: Photo by Mondadori Portfolio via Getty Images

P151: Photo by Planet News Archive/SSPL/Getty Images

P151: Photo by Mondadori Portfolio via Getty Images

P151: Photo by SuperStock/Getty Images

P152: Photo by Pascal Le Segretain/Getty Images

P152: Photo by Victor VIRGILE/Gamma-Rapho via Getty Images

P153: Photo by Victor VIRGILE/Getty Images

P153: Photo by Michel Dufour/WireImage

Chapter 7
P180: Photo by Hulton Archive/Getty Images

P181: Photo by W. & D. Downey/Hulton Archive/Getty Images

P181: Engraving by Paul Gavarni/ Photo by DEA/G. Dagli Orti/Getty Images

P181: Photo by Popperfoto/Getty Images

P182: Photo by Ian Gavan/Getty Images

P182: Photo by Anna Webber/Getty Images

P183: Photo by Victor Boyko/Getty Images

P183: Photo by Pascal Le Segretain/Getty Images

INDEX

Page numbers in *italic* denote figures and in **bold** denote glossary terms.

action pleats 38, 62, 88, 112, 138, 167, 199, **210**
AF Vandevorst *126*
Albert, Prince of Wales 50
anti-establishmentism 98-9
apex **210**
armhole princess style-line 80-1, 104, 106, *121*, 190-3, *209*, **210**
armscye **210**
asymmetrical exposed front zipper closure *97*, 107-8, 115

back vents 58, 62, 65
Baker, Josephine 51
balmacaan coats 148-76, *149*, *177*
  collar *149*, 163, 165, 171
  contemporary *152*, *153*
  facings and linings 166-8, 172, 173, 174-5
  flared silhouette *149*, 161-2
  hidden-button placket *149*, 160, 168-9, 172
  history 150-1, *150*, *151*
  muslin fitting 164, *164*
  pattern development 154-63, 165-9
  pockets 165, 175
  production pattern 170-5
  seam allowances and hems 170-5
  sleeves *149*, 157-9, 168, 173, 175
  sleeve tabs 166, 175, *177*
  technical flats 176
basic blocks 10, 12
Beatles 73
bias **210**
bias strips 205
Birnbach, Lisa 27
blazers 24-46, *25*, *47*
  collar 33, 37, 43, *47*
  contemporary 28, 29
  facings and linings 37-9, 41, 44, 45
  history 26-7, *26*, *27*
  lapels 32, *47*
  muslin fitting 36, *36*
  pattern development 30-5, 37-9
  pockets 35, 45
  production pattern 40-5
  seam allowances and hems 40-5
  sleeves 30, 36, 39, 42, 44
  technical flats 46
  3-panel style-line *25*, 31
block development 8-24
  basic blocks 10, 12
  coat block 11, 15
  jacket block 11, 13
  mannish block 11, 14
  1-piece sleeve 16-17
  2-piece contoured sleeve 18-22
blocks **210**
  basic 10, 12
  bodice 10, 12, 184
  coat 11, 15, 154
  jacket 11, 13, 14, 15, 54, 128
  mannish 11, 14, 30
  1-piece sleeve 16-17
  torso 10, 11, 12, 13, 76, 102
  2-piece contoured sleeve 18-22
bodice block 10, 12, 184
Brando, Marlon 98, *98*
breakpoints *9*, **210**
breast pockets *123*, 133, 134-5, 144-5
Browne, Thom *182*
button extensions *see* front extensions

Chanel 75
China 124-5, *125*
classic princess style-line *49*, 57-9, **210**
coat block 11, 15, 154
collars **210**
  balmacaan coats *149*, 163, 165, 171
  blazers 33, 37, 43, *47*
  convertible *97*, 108, 111, 114, *149*, 163, 165, 171
  frock coats 187-9, 197, 202, *209*
  mandarin 84, 90, *95*
  mao jackets 132-3, 142, *147*
  military jackets 84, 90, *95*
  motorcycle jackets *97*, 108, 111, 114
  shawl *9*, *49*, 55-6
  tuxedos *49*, 55-6
collar stands *9*, 132, 142, *147*, **210**
control notches *9*, **210**
convertible collars
  balmacaan coats *149*, 163, 165, 171
  motorcycle jackets *97*, 108, 111, 114
Cook, James 72
Creatures Of The Wind 29
cuffs, flared *71*, 85, 89, 93
cutaway style-line *71*, 82-4

dandyism 72, 180, 181
darts **210**
depth *9*, **210**
Dietrich, Marlene 51, *51*
dinner jackets *see* Tuxedos
Dior, Christian 152
draping 10
drill point/hole **210**

ease **210**
exposed zippers
  asymmetrical front zipper closure *97*, 107-8, 115
  sleeve vent with godet 109, 113, 117, 119
  welt pockets 105, 119, *121*
extensions *see* front extensions

face **210**
faced hems 88-9, 91, 92
face-up **210**
facings and linings
  balmacaan coats 166-8, 172, 173, 174-5
  blazers 37-9, 41, 44, 45
  frock coats 198-201, 206-7
  mao jackets 137-9, 142, 143-5
  military jackets 87-9, 91, 92, 93
  motorcycle jackets 111-13, 115, 118-19
  tuxedos 61-3, 66, 67
flared cuffs *71*, 85, 89, 93
flared silhouette *149*, 161-2
flared skirts *179*, 194-5, 200, 205, 207
flared sleeves 194, 201, 204, 207
flat patterning 10
frock coats 178-208, *179*, **209**
  armhole princess style-line 190-3, *209*
  collar 187-9, 197, 202, *209*
  contemporary *182*, *183*
  facings and linings 198-201, 206-7
  flared skirt *179*, 194-5, 200, 205, 207
  history 180-1, *180*, *181*
  inverted back pleats *179*, 195, 200
  lapels 186-7, *209*
  muslin fitting 196, *196*
  pattern development 184-95, 197-201
  production pattern 202-7
  seam allowances and hems 202-7
  sleeves 194, 201, 204, 207
  technical flats 208
front extensions **210**
  balmacaan coats 160, 166
  blazers 32
  frock coats 186, 194
  mao jackets 131, 137
  tuxedos 55

APPENDIX

INDEX

Gaultier, Jean Paul 53
gay culture 98
Givenchy *183*
godets 109, 113, 117, 119
gorge line *9*, **210**
grainline **210**
Gucci 74, *75*

hems
  faced 88-9, 91, 92
  see also production patterns
Hendrix, Jimmy 73, *73*
Hepburn, Katharine *150*
hidden-button plackets *149*, 160, 168-9, *172*
high-point shoulder **210**
hip pockets *123*, 134-5, 144-5
Hollister, California 98

inseam pockets 165, *175*
interfacing **210**
  see also facings and linings
inverted back pleats, frock coats *179*, 195, 200
Ivy style 26-7, *26*

jacket block 11, 13, 14, 15, 54, 128
Jacobs, Marc *127*
Jagger, Mick 73
Jarrar, Bouchra *101*
Jones, Grace 51, *51*

lapels
  blazers 32, *47*
  frock coats 186-7, *209*
  motorcycle jackets 107-8, *121*
  peak 186-7, *209*
  semi-notched 32, *47*
Lauren, Ralph *52*

"Le Smoking" 51, *51*
linings **210**
  action pleats 38, 62, 88, 112, 138, 167, 199, **210**
  see also facings and linings
Louis Vuitton *100*

mandarin collar 84, 90, *95*
mannish block 11, 14, 30
mao jackets 122-46, *123*, *147*
  collar 132-3, 142, *147*
  contemporary *126*, *127*
  facings and linings 137-9, 142, 143-5
  history 124-5, *124*, *125*
  muslin fitting 136, *136*
  pattern development 128-35, 137-9
  pockets *123*, 133-5, 144-5
  production pattern 140-5
  seam allowances and hems 140-5
  sleeves 128, 135, 139, 143, 144
  technical flats 146
  tunic style *123*, 129-31
Mao Zedong 124, *124*, *125*
Martin, Bradley *151*
Martin, Chris 73
military jackets 70-94, *71*, *95*
  armhole princess style-line 80-1
  collar 84, 90, *95*
  contemporary 74, *75*
  cutaway style-line *71*, 82-4
  facings and linings 87-9, 91, 92, 93

flared cuffs *71*, 85, 89, 93
history 72-3, *72*, *73*
muslin fitting 86, *86*
pattern development 76-85, 87-9
production pattern 90-3
seam allowances and hems 90-3
shoulders 77-9
sleeves 76, 79, 85, 89, 93
technical flats 94
Mods 27, *27*, 99
Moncler Gamme Bleu *28*
Moncler Gamme Rouge *183*
motorcycle jackets 96-120, *97*, *121*
  armhole princess style-line 104, *106*, *121*
  asymmetrical exposed front zipper closure *97*, 107-8, 115
  collar *97*, 108, 111, 114
  contemporary *100*, *101*
  exposed zipper sleeve vent with godet 109, 113, 117, 119
  facings and linings 111-13, 115, 118-19
  history 98-9, *98*, *99*
  lapels 107-8, *121*
  muslin fitting 110, *110*
  pattern development 102-9, 111-13
  production pattern 114-19
  seam allowances and hems 114-19
  sleeves 102, 109, 113, 117, 118, 119
  technical flats 120

welt pockets with exposed zippers 105, 119, *121*
muslin **210**
muslin fittings
  balmacaan coats 164, *164*
  blazers 36, *36*
  frock coats 196, *196*
  mao jackets 136, *136*
  military jackets 86, *86*
  motorcycle jackets 110, *110*
  tuxedos 60, *60*

notches *see* control notches

pattern drafting 10
peak lapels 186-7, *209*
plackets **210**
  hidden-button *149*, 160, 168-9, *172*
pleats
  action 38, 62, 88, 112, 138, 167, 199, **210**
  inverted back *179*, 195, 200
pockets
  balmacaan coats 165, *175*
  blazers 35, 45
  breast *123*, 133, 134-5, 144-5
  with exposed zippers 105, 119, *121*
  with flap 59, 67, *69*, *123*, 133-5, 144-5
  hip *123*, 134-5, 144-5
  inseam with welt 165, *175*
  mao jackets *123*, 133-5, 144-5
  motorcycle jackets 105, 119, *121*
  tuxedos 59, 67, *69*
  welt 35, 45, 59, 67, *69*

Poole, Henry 50, 51
Portobello Road 73
Potter, James Brown 50-1
Prada *153*
preppy style 27, *27*
Prince Albert coat 180
production patterns **210**
  balmacaan coats 170-5
  blazers 40-5
  frock coats 202-7
  mao jackets 140-5
  military jackets 90-3
  motorcycle jackets 114-19
  tuxedos 64-7
punk rock 99, *99*

Raglan, Lord *150*
raglan sleeves 150
  balmacaan coats *149*, 157-9, 168, 173, 175
Ramones 99, *99*
Rockers 99, *99*
Rolling Stones 73
roll-line *9*, **210**
Royal Hussars 72, *73*

SA *see* seam allowances (SA)
Saint Laurent, Yves 51, *51*, *52*, *101*
Sand, George 180, *181*
Sannia, Marisa *151*
Sauvajeon, Danielle *51*
Schott Perfecto 98, *98*
seam allowances (SA) **210**
  balmacaan coats 170-5
  blazers 40-5
  frock coats 202-7
  general guidelines 23
  mao jackets 140-5
  military jackets 90-3
  motorcycle jackets 114-19

214

INDEX

tuxedos 64–7
self **210**
semi-notched lapels 32, *47*
Sergeenko, Ulyana *74*
shawl collars *9*, *49*, 55–6
shoulder darts 34
shoulder pads 16, 78, 79, 184–5
silk organza 119
slash and spread **210**
sleeve blocks
  basic 10, 12
  1-piece 16–17
  2-piece contoured 18–22
sleeve caps 16–17, 19, 79, 185, **210**
sleeves
  1-piece
    block development 16–17
    frock coats 194, 201, 204, 207
    military jackets 76, 79, 85, 89, 93

raglan 150
balmacaan coats *149*, 157–9, 168, 173, 175
2-piece contoured blazers 30, 36, 39, 42, 44
block development 18–22
mao jackets 128, 135, 139, 143, 144
motorcycle jackets 102, 109, 113, 117, 118, 119
tuxedos 54, 60, 63, 65, 66
sleeve tabs 166, 175, *177*
sleeve vents 135, 139, 143, 144
with exposed zipper and godet 109, 113, 117, 119
slopers *see* blocks
style-lines **210**

armhole princess 80–1, 104, 106, *121*, 190–3, *209*, **210**
classic princess *49*, 57–9, **210**
cutaway *71*, 82–4
3-panel *25*, 31
Sun Yat-sen 124, *125*
sweep **210**

technical flats **210**
  balmacaan coats 176
  blazers 46
  frock coats 208
  mao jackets 146
  military jackets 94
  motorcycle jackets 120
  tuxedos 68
Teddy Boys 181, *181*
3-panel style-line *25*, 31
toile *see* muslin
Tom of Finland 98
torso block 10, 11, 12, 13, 76, 102
truing-up seams **210**

tucks **210**
tunic style *123*, 129–31
tuxedos 48–68, *49*, *69*
  back vent 58, 62, 65
  classic princess style-line *49*, 57–9
  collar *49*, 55–6
  contemporary *52*, *53*
  facings and linings 61–3, 66, 67
  history 50–1, *50*, *51*
  muslin fitting 60, *60*
  pattern development 54–9, 61–3
  pockets 59, 67, *69*
  production pattern 64–7
  seam allowances and hems 64–7
  sleeves 54, 60, 63, 65, 66
  technical flats 68

uniforms, military 72, *72*, *73*

Valentino *152*, *153*
vents **210**
  back 58, 62, 65
  see also sleeve vents
Vivienne Westwood Red Label *28*, *182*

waistline seams *179*
walking patterns and/or seams **210**
Wang, Alexander *53*
Warhol, Andy *124*
welt pockets 35, 45
  with exposed zippers 105, 119, *121*
  with flap 59, 67, *69*
  inseam 165, 175
Wilde, Oscar 180, *181*

Yamamoto, Yohji *29*, *100*, *126*, *127*

Zhongshan suits 124
zippers *see* exposed zippers

APPENDIX

ACKNOWLEDGMENTS

After years of complaining about the lack of good patternmaking books that covered jacket designs in an interesting format, I decided to write one myself. The impetus to get the work published was made possible with the support and help of my graduate school advisor, Michelle Navarre Cleary, PhD. I was also fortunate to have a great friend and colleague, Sharon Shoji, who offered vital feedback and graciously edited my copy throughout all phases of the manuscript.

Special thanks also go to:

Alisa Caron for taking on the numerous patterning illustrations and making them look so amazing.

Photographer Scott Shigley, who through the years has always made my designs look incredible.

My Bloomsbury editor Colette Meacher, who answered my numerous questions and made this book a reality.

This book is dedicated to my mother, Nancy Vanderlinde, who has continually supported my dreams, never doubted my talent, and has always been my biggest fan.

The publishers would like to thank: Laura Green, Programme Leader for Creative Pattern Cutting University Centre Doncaster College; Jayne Littlehales, Award Leader for FdA in Fashion Studies Stafford College; Judy Huyck, Lecturer in Fashion Design and Merchandising Southern Illinois University; Anne Hand, School of Engineering and Textiles Philadelphia University; Bruce Montgomery, Professor in Design Craftsmanship Northumbria University; Pat Parish, Senior Fashion Lecturer West Kent College; Sally Folkes, Lecturer in Creative Pattern Cutting Birmingham City University; Dr. Virginia Wimberley, Assistant Professor in Clothing and Textiles University of Alabama; and Nora McDonald, Professor of Fashion Design and Merchandising West Virginia University.